CECIL SHARP

CECIL SHARP

HIS LIFE AND WORK

by

MAUD KARPELES

faber and faber

This edition first published in 2008
by Faber and Faber Ltd
3 Queen Square, London WC1N 3AU

Printed by CPI Antony Rowe, Eastbourne

A CIP record for this book is available from the British Library

ISBN 978–0–571–24324–2

Contents

Contents

Contents

Illustrations

Illustrations

Preface

THE ORIGINAL BIOGRAPHY of Cecil Sharp written by A. H. Fox Strangways in collaboration with Maud Karpeles was published in 1933. A second edition[1] with a few revisions and additions including an introduction appeared in 1955, ten years after the death of Mr. Fox Strangways. Now that the second edition of the book, like the first, is out of print, I have taken the opportunity of partly rewriting it. After some deliberation I reluctantly decided to ascribe myself as the sole author, since I could not with fairness attribute to Mr. Fox Strangways a work for which he was not ultimately responsible and one which, in the event, contains but a small proportion of his writing.

A. H. Fox Strangways had known Cecil Sharp for twenty-two years and was one of his best friends. He had always taken an interest in Cecil Sharp's work and, as music critic to *The Times* and editor of *Music and Letters*, he had frequently given evidence of his interest in the sympathetic and discerning articles on folk song and folk dance which he contributed to these periodicals.

As Cecil Sharp's Literary Executor it was incumbent on me to arrange for the writing and publication of his life and, doubting my own literary ability to perform the task, it was natural that I should turn to Fox Strangways. I had originally intended that my share in the preparation of the biography should be limited to clerical work, to handing over the material in my possession and to the communication of my personal recollections. However, as time went on, it appeared that the book was not progressing, because, owing to his other commitments, Mr. Fox Strangways had been unable to give as much attention to it as he had hoped. It was therefore agreed between us that my verbal communications should be supplemented by a written account of Cecil Sharp's life and this ultimately formed the basis of the biography. Except for the two complete chapters on the Appalachian Mountains and some portions of other chapters, my contributions were

[1]Both the first and second editions were published by the Oxford University Press.

intended to serve as raw material, but Mr. Fox Strangways instead of extracting from them what he required for his own story was for the most part content to patch and modify instead of rewriting. The result was naturally not entirely satisfactory.

In the present volume I have rewritten many passages in order to give a better balanced and more connected account of Cecil Sharp's life. I have also re-examined all the correspondence and other papers and have included some additional material which seemed to me to be of interest. An epilogue replaces and amplifies my introduction to the second edition. Fox Strangways'beautiful summary, for which he alone was responsible, has been left intact and appears in the Appendix.

In the first and second editions, thanks are given to the many who have helped by sending letters from Cecil Sharp and communicating their recollections of him. For reading the draft of the book and making many helpful criticisms the authors acknowledge their gratitude to 'Mr. A. P. Oppé, who collaborated with Sharp in *The Dance* (1924), and Dr. Vaughan Williams, who more than anyone else has in word and deed made Sharp's cause his own'.

In renewing my thanks to all who have previously given help, I would acknowledge my gratitude to Fox Strangways himself without whom this biography might never have been written. Fox Strangways has commented thus on our collaboration: 'A pervasive sense of humour was included in it; pertinent criticism and obstinate argument were not excluded.' He could with truth have added that our task was throughout inspired and lightened by the love and affection which we had in common for Cecil Sharp.

To Miss Margaret Dean-Smith, Sir Gilmour Jenkins, Mr. Douglas Kennedy, Mr. Michael Kennedy and Miss Joan Sharp, who have read the draft of this present volume in whole or in part, I would express my deep gratitude and thanks for the many valuable suggestions and criticisms they have made; and additional thanks are due to Mr. Michael Kennedy for having read and checked the proofs. Finally, I would acknowledge my indebtedness to Mrs. John Noyes, Librarian of the Vaughan Williams Library at Cecil Sharp House, for her help in supplying information and placing books and documents at my disposal.

MAUD KARPELES

London, 1967

I

Boyhood and Early Manhood
1859 — 91

> I made no vows, but vows
> Were then made for me; bond unknown to me
> Was given, that I should be, else sinning greatly,
> A dedicated spirit.
>
> WILLIAM WORDSWOLRTH, *The Prelude*

CECIL JAMESSHARP was born on St. Cecilia's Day, 22nd November 1859, at Denmark Hill,[1] and died on Midsummer Eve, 23rd June 1924, at 4 Maresfield Gardens, Hampstead.

His father, James, who was born in 1827, was a slate-merchant in Tooley Street, London. He had entered the business unexpectedly at the age of sixteen owing to the death of an elder brother; and at fifty he retired. The reason he gave for retiring at this early age was that slates had come to be replaced by tiles, but one has a suspicion that he wished to get more out of life than commerce could offer and that in particular he wanted to acquire in later life the education that had been denied him in his youth. He loved music, particularly Handel and Mozart; he had a taste for old furniture, glass and coins; and he was interested in archaeology and architecture. He was never happier than when visiting cathedrals. Cecil, whom he often took with him, kept up the practice with friends after his father's death. He was good company and had a quiet sense of humour. Cecil loved and admired him and spoke of him affectionately as 'the General' in later years.

[1]In 1870 his parents moved to Cornwall Gardens, South Kensington.

James Sharp married Jane Bloyd, the youngest daughter of Joseph Bloyd, a lead-merchant in the City. Joseph Bloyd was a Welshman and his wife, Elizabeth Angell, was thought to be of Italian extraction. Jane, Cecil's mother, was tall, of fine carriage, with Italian features. She seems to have had the secret of youth up till her death at ninety. She, too, had a love of music which she shared with her husband throughout a happy married life. She was a graceful hostess and fond of society. Cecil was never as close to her as he was to his father, possibly because some of the younger children claimed more of her attention. After her death in February 1915, he wrote of her: 'She was a child's mother rather than a man's – not perhaps being very capable of sympathizing with a man's work in the world. But . . . no one could have looked after and loved her children more than she.'

Cecil was the third child and eldest son. He had four brothers and four sisters and there were two boys who died as babies. Llewellyn (Lewen), the brother who came next to him, was an architect in good practice. In this large family, the father's pride, there was an elder and a younger group, and between them Lewen was a kind of liaison officer. To the elder group belonged Mabel, who helped her mother with the younger ones, and Ethel (Mrs. Malcolm McCall), who, with Cecil, was often at the pianoforte. When they played at 'church', Mabel said prayers, Ethel played the 'organ', and Cecil wrote and preached the sermon for the junior congregation. His youngest sister, Evelyn (Mrs. H. W. Nevinson), was a writer of distinction. A friend of the ugly duckling, she was a fighter both in words and deeds against social injustices and was a leading member of the women's militant suffrage movement. Her writing, be it in the form of children's stories or books on more serious subjects, is imbued with wit and imagination. A fascinating account of the family life in her younger days is given in her reminiscences, *Unfinished Adventure* (1955).

Cecil went to school when he was 'rising eight' at Miss Bennett's Lansdowne Road, Brighton. Two of his letters are given below exactly as he wrote them. One may perhaps see in them a fore-shadowing of the generosity and sociability which in adult life were such marked characteristics of his nature.

October 4th 1867

My dear Mama,
I felt rather lonely the first day but now I am very happy indeed. I had a piece of my cake for my luncheon and I gave a piece to each of the boys and they said they had never tasted such a nice one. All my things they like much better than theirs send my best love to believe me your affectionate son

CECIL JAMES SHARP

(Undated and unsigned; probably
enclosed with the preceding letter.)

My dear Ethel,
I wish you many happy returns of the day. Tell Mamma I am very happy. A boy has just come for some string I must go and give him some all the boys come and crowd round me for string and they say Sharp or new fellow give me some of your nice useful string will you and I say yes of course. I recognised Goss directly I saw him I do like him so and I like Authur Pitman I am so fond of him I send you this little Mother of pearl knife. I thank you very much for your kind letter

Believe me

Thus to his mother and sister at eight years old; and thus to his son, at fifty-eight:

I am glad you are going to Brighton, which at this time of year [April] ought to be very jolly – though ordinarily I hate the place. I have pleasant memories because my parents, being then in the fashion, usually spent Oct.–Dec. there, and took me out 3 or 4 times a week from the dame's school where I suffered an ignoble existence for two years – 108 Lansdowne Place, by the way, was its beastly address. Look it up, and throw a stone through the window if it is still a school!

Cecil was a nervous boy. He had a constant fear of spilling ink, because the penalty was to take a dirty rag out of a dark cupboard to wipe it up. One day the penalty was incurred and his terror was doubled by his finding a beetle in the rag. And he was a sensitive boy. An early and vivid recollection was the sound of a brass band in the street when he was in bed; in his ecstasy he wept. He had throughout life a physical dread of noises.

Cecil's love of music, inherited from his mother, fostered by his sister Ethel and encouraged by his father, showed itself at an early age. This and the fact that he was not very strong may have determined his parents to send him to Uppingham, which Edward Thring had developed from insignificance into one of the healthiest and best equipped schools in England and it was at that time the only Public School in which music, under Paul David, was taken seriously. Cecil entered the lower school in 1869 and the upper in 1872. He left, probably on account of weak health, in 1874. Nothing is now known of his school career except that he studied the pianoforte and joined in the singing class. Some thirty years later he writes[1] that his interest in school songs was first awakened at Uppingham where Mr. Paul David, encouraged by its famous headmaster, the Rev. E. Thring, showed how im-important a place the choir may hold in the life of a Public School'. One of the pleasantest recollections of his school life was listening to quartets played by members of the music staff. A tablet in the school chapel commemorates 'the Writer and Musican. Collector of English Folk Songs'.

On 18th May 1874 Cecil was sent to Mr. George Heppel of Highfield, Weston-super-Mare, who had a coaching establishment for the University and the army. He passed the Cambridge local and was then prepared for the University. Mr. Heppel thought well of his mathematics.

Cecil became intimate with the family during one holiday when he was laid up with a broken collar-bone and this led to a good deal of concerted music-making and private theatricals. To the music-making came Constance Birch, who later became Cecil's wife. She was a tall and beautiful girl with brown wavy hair and brown eyes. She sketched well, sang and played the violin. A member of Mr. Heppel's large family, who was a small child at the time, has remarked on Cecil's wonderful understand-ing of children. She writes after an interval of nearly sixty years:

My chief impression was his versatility . . . One of the outstanding interests when he was at Highfield was the yearly play. The pupils took the production entirely on themselves. Cecil Sharp was always in it heart and soul . . . I was too young to remember much about The Merchant of Venice in which he was Antonio, but next year when A Midsummer Night's Dream was undertaken it was decided to requisition us children for the fairies. I played Titania to his Nick Bottom at the age of six or seven; and my smaller sisters and their friends, aged between

[1]Preface to *A Book of British Song.*

4

Cecil Sharp. From a portrait by Sir William Rothenstein

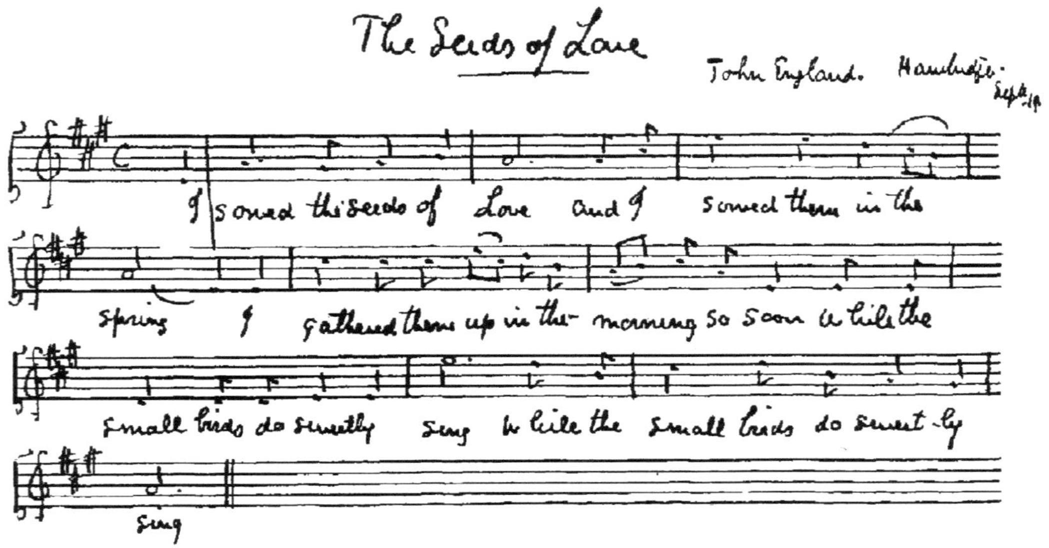

II Facsimile of the first folksong noted by Cecil Sharp

three and five, were carried from the nursery, clad in green and yellow, to flit about and lisp 'and I' at preconcerted moments. I believe such another Nick Bottom has never been seen. No actor has ever surpassed him in his singing of the 'Ousel Cock'.

Already at Weston Cecil suffered from hay-fever, the precursor of the asthma that plagued him to the end.

After a few years at Weston-super-Mare he went to the Rev. J. T. Sanderson to be coached for Cambridge. He entered at Clare College in October 1879 where he took his degree in Mathematics.

His bent for music declared itself while at College and he took the first examination for the Mus. Bac.

He was secretary of the debating society, and although he did not find speaking easy he used to propose annually 'that the House of Lords be abolished', a proposal which gained no support. He rowed in the second and first Clare boat. The record is given below.[1] Looking back on those days, he said: 'Rowing was a great pleasure to me at Cambridge, though I did not get further than my first College eight, then eighth on the river.' Part of his enjoyment was expressed in Limericks. He wrote one on each member of the crew; to which T. R. Wardale, afterwards Tutor, replied on their behalf with one quite as opprobrious and honours were even. Cecil gave up doggerel verse during a serious illness and did not again acquire the knack.

His life at Cambridge is described in a communication to A. H. Fox Strangways from Henry J. Ford, the painter:

We got to know each other at Clare as freshmen of the same standing. Sharp at once became a leader of the musical men: I was *not* musical, though I liked to listen well enough. We had three good musicians in that year: Cecil, Fred T. MacDonnell – a really fine dramatic baritone and *musical* (horrid word!) to the core, as anyone could see – and Fred Bagnall who possessed a very sweet high tenor voice and sang like a bird. Sharp could sing a little, and could play the pianoforte well enough to accompany adequately. I don't think he was at all a real

---

[1] December 1880. Stroked one of the College trial eights to victory. From the Captain's book: Sharp (stroke). Capital worker, 2nd year man. Rowed in last year's 2nd. About the best man in trials: very keen.

Lent 1881. 2nd boat. Sharp (11st. 10) started at No. 5, raced as No. 7. They made a bump. Captain's comment: Works hard, but a bad seven; fair at five or three; better on stroke side.

May 1881. 1st boat. Sharp No. 3. They were bumped twice. Comment: No. 3 was useless after Grassy.

pianist, though very useful: but his enthusiasm and high idealism and knowledge of music were, I fancy, unquestioned by those who knew[1].

He at once became an important figure in our College society. His good humour was unfailing, also his high spirits and love of good company. He seemed a bit older in mind than those of us who were fresh from school. He had left Uppingham for a year or so[2] before coming up, and had had more opportunities of seeing life. He was almost as enthusiastic about his mathematics as about Wagner, the new and enormous star on the heavens of music. Much did he discourse on these subjects, of which I lay in wondering and somewhat contemptuous ignorance.

He worked harder at his music than at his mathematics. He got up concerts with MacDonnel, W. H. Wing, Bagnall, and Oliver Puckridge – people's concerts, I think they were – and he gave, among other things, a performance on the ocarina; and another on a row of bits of glass which you hit with a hammer (an instrument which, as far as I am concerned, has no name, neither does it deserve one). He got tremendous encores for a spirited if barbaric performance.

We differed somewhat in religion and politics; he, a Freethinker in the early days and a Radical; I, a wavering Christian and uncertain Conservative, much shaken up, I remember, by *Alton Locke* in politics, and by *Religion and Dogma* when it came to religion. In after years he returned to the bosom of the Church. Talking our oldVtalk over, I asked how it was that he had so changed, and he had the effrontery to say that it was such Christians, professing ones, as I that drove him into the hostile camp. Of course that was nonsense and only an attempt to score off me. The thing that brought him back to Christianity (though in fact he was, of course, always the best of Christians in the broad and human sense) was, he told me, seeing a young parson in Australia sitting on a fence telling fairy stories to a lot of children.

The fact is, Sharp was a happy, emotional creature, and he was never afraid of obeying the call of his emotions. He was excitable and warm-hearted, and a strong, full-blooded man, full of kind thoughts about others, and eager to enjoy, and help others to enjoy, everything in life that is enjoyable.

Sharp went all out for everything that interested him, was eager, argumentative, a fighter, but always a jovial good fellow. He used to sing a comic song – 'The Emu': words by Bret Harte:

> Where's that specimen pin
> Which I gaily did win

[1] He had rooms out of College, in Tennis Court Road, so as to be able to make as much music as he liked.

[2] Five years.

In raffle, and gave unto you –
Not a word said the guilty Emu.

to a tune of his own.

He had, as you know, a handsomely Roman nose, somewhat ruddy in tone, and it became a commonplace to speak of him – 'Punch' was his nickname – as 'rubescing', when he grew warm in argument – which happened often. A very vital personality in our little world; a foretaste of what he became afterwards in everybody's big world.

But his views seemed to me to be founded not on the deeps, but on the shallows – netted with sun and shade, and showing bright fish darting about and lovely weeds and flashing dragon-flies – of passion and human sympathies and antipathies. However I doubt whether this is worth remarking, as it is the same with us all, at least all of us who are at all nice to be with.

After Henry Ford, one of his best friends was W. H. Wing, the possessor of a pleasing baritone voice, who in after years used to sing in illustration of Cecil Sharp's lectures. The circle of his friends also included Sir Owen Seaman of *Punch* and Edward D. Rendall. The latter conducted the 'Concordia' (men's voices) at Trinity, to which Stanford lent his help: Cecil was among the first tenors. Rendall was the composer of a setting of 'The Compleat Angler' and other attractive and sincere music; he had charge of the music at Dulwich College and subsequently at Charterhouse. There was also a deaf friend for whose sake Cecil learned finger-language, in which he conversed with rapidity, and even devised improvements on the usual form. Another friend at this period was Dr. James Kingston Barton; Cecil, together with George Bernard Shaw, Charles Hayden Coffin and others, was a constant visitor at his musical 'At Homes' in South Kensington.

When Cecil came down from Cambridge in 1882, his father, believing that a young man should find his own way in the world, told him that he should seek his own fortune and that the colonies (as they then were), preferably Australia, might offer the best prospects. Cecil's own account is given by Henry Ford:

He said he knew nothing at the time of his departure about the geography of Australia, so he took a map and saw the name of Ade-laide. That set him thinking of his adored Beethoven song, 'Adelaïde', and this was ample reason to our 'Punch' to decide on his future habi-tat. Such his merry, happy-go-lucky nature!

He sailed in October 1882 with £10 or £20 in his pocket which his father had provided in addition to paying his fare. During the voyage he beguiled the time by playing chess and by music-making, including conducting the music for the Sunday church service. He made many friends, but apparently none who might be of use to him after arrival in Australia. However, he fell in with a wise man who advised him to take any job that came his way and tell his employer he knew how to do it. Following this advice, the first job he took after landing was washing hansom cabs in a mews in Adelaide. He had watched a man washing the wheels and spinning them, and apparently the important thing to do was to hiss loudly. There was no difficulty about that, he thought, for an experienced player of the ocarina, so he answered an advertisement and took the post.

Cecil Sharp reached Adelaide in November 1882 and early in 1883 he found an occupation as a clerk in the Commercial Bank of South Australia. It is said that he was not very good at the job and he himself used to boast that he lost the bank £100 during his first week – possibly an exaggeration.

After leaving the bank he read with C. C. Kingston and assimilated enough legal knowledge to become, in April 1884, Associate to Sir Samuel James Way, Bart., Chief Justice of South Australia (1876–1916) and Clerk of Arraigns. This position of Associate offers a special opportunity to those who wish to rise at the Bar; they hear not only the cases and decisions, but day-to-day comments on the pleadings and criticisms of the pleaders. Cecil Sharp became intensely interested in the work and there was a brief period when he thought of entering the South Australian Bar. Sir Samuel, a brilliant lawyer and a hard worker, had an exceptionally large circle of acquaintances and, as Chief Justice, was called on to do a great deal of entertaining. Cecil Sharp, whose duties were in part those of social secretary, thoroughly enjoyed arranging the various social functions and sorting out tricky problems of precedence. But his official duties left him little free time and often necessitated throwing up personal engagements at short notice, thus making it difficult for him to carry on the various musical activities on which he had embarked. He therefore resigned his position in February 1889 and devoted himself entirely to music.

Cecil Sharp had in his pocket when he landed an introduction to

Arthur Boult, organist of St. Peter's Cathedral, Adelaide. He set to work to practise and before long was installed as assistant organist. He found congenial company among the music-loving members of the German colony, and in 1883 he was acting as Honorary Director of the Adelaide String Quartet Club, to which he appointed Herr Immanuel Gottfried Reimann as pianist. He early became known to all the musical people in Adelaide, including the Governors, first Sir W. C. F. Robinson (1883–9) and afterwards the Earl of Kintore. He conducted the Government House Choral Society; and an operetta, *Dimple's Lovers*, for which he had written the music to a libretto by Guy Boothby, was performed at Government House (1890). He also conducted the Cathedral Choral Society, for whom he wrote some Nursery Rhymes that have been described as 'remarkably melodious'. Later on he took charge of the Adelaide Philharmonic Choir, who, when he left in 1891, gave him, in remembrance of them, 'a watch to keep time and a stick with which to beat it.'

He secured many private pupils for pianoforte, singing, theory, and composition; and in January 1889 he entered into partnership with Herr Reimann as joint Director of the Adelaide College of Music, Herr Reimann contributing the capital and Cecil Sharp the connexion. He is described as 'a born leader in music'; within ten months of his joining the College the attendance was doubled, and his lectures and lessons are spoken of enthusiastically. An old pupil writes:

> In a short time he had sixty pupils. We all adored him; we were usually spoken of as 'the sixty love-sick maidens'. . . . I learned a great deal more from him than singing . . . The change from a certain silly old German who made love to all his pupils was refreshing.

Cecil Sharp's stay in Australia was interrupted by two visits to England. The first was in 1886 after a serious attack of typhoid which left him paralysed in both legs. He found his parents in their new home, an old manor-house at Weston Turville, Buckingham-shire. The doctors were not encouraging; but by sheer force of will he managed to walk a few paces daily, gradually increasing them until he could cover the full length of the drive; and finally he cured himself. During his stay at Weston Turville he used to help his sister Ethel with her 'Penny Readings' by playing the piano, the ocarina and the xylophone. Cecil was inordinately proud of his accomplishment in performing this last instrument, which he had made himself from the trees in his parents' garden. This same instrument made its appearance again much later when it was used for the music of the 'tongs and bones' in Granville Barker's production of *A Midsummer Night's Dream* (1914). During his convalescence Cecil taught himself to play the banjo.

He wanted to stay in England and educate himself seriously in music, but he could find no employment, so he returned with reluctance to Australia. The second visit to England was from January to March 1891; and during that short time, as before, he tried in vain to get his musical compositions published.

To Mrs. Walter Howard,   29. 2. 1891
I have opened my campaign and have begun storming London although as yet with no success. The annoying part of it all is that London scarcely seems to be aware of my fierce onslaught and does not even raise a drawbridge to protect herself.

Soon after his return to Adelaide (March 1891) the partnership between him and Herr Reimann was dissolved. The leading members of the staff, Herr Vollmar and Herr Heinicke, threw in their lot with Herr Reimann, under whose sole direction the College was continued, becoming the Elder Conservatoire in 1898. Cecil Sharp was urged to stay on in the city and continue his musical profession; and an address containing over three hundred signatures, headed by that of the Bishop, expressed this desire of his friends, but he decided to return to England. He had no doubt that he could have made a career for himself in Adelaide, but he had 'not the heart to set to work and begin all over again'.

His great friends in Australia were the Duffields, Walter the father and Geoffrey the son (who organized the Solar Observatory), the Howards, and Guy Boothby. Others were E. B. Grundy, a lawyer with whom he at one time shared rooms in Carrington Street, and Charles Marson, a clergyman, of whom we shall hear more. The letters which follow preserve the memory of the Adelaide days.

W. Geoffrey Duffield to the
   Rt. Hon. H. A. L. Fisher,   17. 8. 1925
[enclosing a donation to the Cecil Sharp House Fund]
Cecil Sharp was one of our oldest friends; we first knew him in Adelaide when he was a gay, debonair Judge's Associate – a role which

those who knew him in later life in England will find it hard to realize that he had ever played. With Guy Boothby he wrote a comic opera[1] which as a boy I remember hearing. A few years ago I played over one of the airs from it and asked him to name the composer; he had forgotten his own child and ascribed it to Schumann . . . He and I used to subscribe ourselves 'Brother Musico' – I forget how it originated; I have never earned the title, unless playing wrong notes on the double-bass is a sufficient qualification.

The picture is filled in for us by a letter of Charles Marson's about 1890:

We had such a delightful evening at the Duffields: Sharp, Otto Fischer, and the D's, and the talk was of the merriest and the music of the best. A fierce argument about Carlyle and 'abstraction' carried us into metaphysics. Not a word of scandal all the evening. Fischer sang Schumann's 'Ich grolle nicht' and Sharp played one of his sonatas admirably; but he would not play 'anything great' as the piano was not good enough, he told our hostess, with such merry geniality that she could not be offended . . . Cecil Sharp abhors Girton and Newnham and the 'mental loudness' they produce in girls . . . He is a really good and enthusiastic man who is married to music and serves her with a knightly and unending service.

The experience which Cecil Sharp gained in Australia stood him in good stead in later years. He had had particularly favourable opportunities for developing his social talents; his legal training had quickened his sense of logic, and through his own persistent efforts he had turned himself from an amateur into a professional musician. It is of interest that even in those early days he stressed the importance of melody in educating the public to appreciate good music.

---

[1] This operetta, *Sylvia*, was performed at the Theatre Royal, Adelaide. It is perhaps prophetic that one of the numbers is entitled a 'Morris Dance'.

II

Music as a Profession
1892–1905

Such sweet compulsion doth in musick ly
JOHN MILTON, *Arcades*

IN JANUARY 1892, at the age of thirty-three, Cecil Sharp was back in England with no resources to speak of, but with plenty of enthusiasm and high hopes of establishing himself as a professional musician. These hopes were not immediately fulfilled and he had a hard struggle. He was handicapped by the fact that he had not had an orthodox musical training, being almost entirely self-taught. He was an omnivorous reader and an industrious and enterprising worker who knew how to turn his practical experience to good account. In the event, he may have acquired more knowledge and ability than many who had undergone a conventional musical training; but several of his fellow-musicians thought otherwise and regarded him as an outsider.

For a few months after his arrival in London he lived with his brother Lewen in Duke Street, Adelphi. In April he took rooms at 5 Langham Chambers, Langham Street, with a large ground-floor studio which housed a grand pianoforte. The landlady was a woman after his own heart. As he was about to sign the agreement he noticed that the rent was £10 less than had been verbally arranged, but when he pointed out the mistake she said it was of no consequence since they both knew what it really ought to be.

Cecil Sharp delighted in entertaining. He writes:

My tea-party went off very well. It was delightfully informal and friendly. I always introduce everybody to everybody else, and my muffins are *sans reproche*, which only happens in bachelor establishments.

His large room was the scene of the many lectures on music which he gave at that time. As with most young musicians of his day, Wagner was his god. He preached him in and out of season and his voluble enthusiasm brought him many willing listeners. In addition to lecturing he took what work he could find. He played the pianoforte at musical 'At Homes' and small concerts and often accompanied his friend, Duloup, a Dutch violinist. But he was anxious about his prospects.

To Mrs. Walter Howard,   17. 3. 1892
I am still wandering round in search of work and building plans ceaselessly as I am more than ever disposed to remain in England if I can make a living . . . but I am beginning to realize that it means a struggle. One wants time, and life is so short there is the constant danger that opportunity will come too late, and then it arrives only to tantalize.

He found his greatest satisfaction in musical composition. He struggled to get his works known and he received some encouragement. He confides in his friend Mrs. Howard:

6. 4. 1892
The Musical went off very well on Saturday. Bispham sang my song *beautifully* and Shakespeare accompanied it . . . before a critical audience [including Fanny Davies and Leonard Borwick]

and some months later:

I think I may fairly claim a great success with Schott yesterday. He commended the sonata very highly, saying it was scholarly yet full of melody.

On his visits to his parents at Weston Turville, he spent much time in playing the organ and he wrote anthems for the church service and one for a friend's wedding.

In addition to the opera and operetta already referred to, Cecil Sharp wrote, in all, as far as can be discovered, about twenty songs and thirty instrumental pieces.[1] Some part-song arrange-

[1] The manuscripts are in the Vaughan Williams library at Cecil Sharp House, London.

ments of nursery-rhymes, two pianoforte pieces and two songs were published (see p. 207). His writing which is to some extent modelled on Schumann has charm; it is simple, straightforward and melodious. But it is doubtful whether by this means he would ever have fully revealed the artist that was in him.

He had intended to take lessons in composition on his return to England, but need forced him instead to give them in elementary harmony; and Mrs. Walter Howard shepherded pupils to him, beginning with herself and her sisterin-law. He writes in January 1893:

> I am greedy for employment. Private pupils are so uncertain and they treat me so unceremoniously that I am anxious to get as much lecturing, etc., in schools as I possibly can. This is the only certain thing that I can see.

In addition to his lecturing and teaching he succeeded in getting the conductorship of various small choral societies. He writes (18. 1. 1893) to Constance Birch:

> I took my first practice of my Society at Bedford Park last night. It was fairly successful, but I shall soon get tired of these small Societies. I want something bigger. Everlasting glees become tiresome – they are so finicking.

And (26. 1. 1893):

> I am itching to get work which I know I am qualified to do, but people are so afraid of giving an unknown man a trial, and I am not a good hand at advertising myself.

Mr. C. J. Dale (father of Benjamin Dale, the composer), Chairman of the Finsbury Choral Association, recognised Cecil Sharp's qualities, and after he had taken several practices and gone through protracted negotiations he was, in June 1893, appointed conductor. In his own words:

> He the [Secretary] handed me a letter, an official announcement of my appointment, but they only offer me twenty guineas for the season, whereas the Secretary before told me £25. However, I expect they are anxious about finances – at any rate I said nothing.

In addition, he was appointed at Mr. Dale's invitation to the Staff of the Metropolitan College, Holloway, where he conducted the orchestra, lectured, and had private pupils. He made his choir work hard and it seems that they liked him for it. It was said that there was no uncertainty in his beat and that his rhythm was his strong point. He held the appointment for four years; and the incident which led to his resignation in July 1897 is as follows.

Miss Muriel Foster wished to be released at two days' notice from her engagement to sing in *The Redemption* in order to accept another engagement which was held to be of importance to her career. Dr. (later Sir) Hubert Parry of the Royal College of Music, where Miss Foster was studying, held Cecil Sharp responsible for the refusal of her request and before hearing the facts wrote him a violent letter, to which Cecil Sharp, who was always ready to take up a challenge, sent an indignant reply. In fact, it had been the Committee of the Association that had made the decision and accepted the responsibility. This was duly pointed out to Dr. Parry, but he refused to withdraw his letter. The Committee, reflecting that Dr. Parry and two of his friends were vice-presidents of the Association, decided that nothing was to be gained by incurring his displeasure and Cecil Sharp was asked to let the matter drop. He refused and, feeling that the Committee had failed in its obligations to him, he resigned on 25th May. At the same time he had the correspondence printed and circulated to the members of the chorus and it also reached the public Press. To Cecil Sharp an engagement was sacrosanct, whether his own or another's, but in this particular instance, contrary to Dr. Parry's supposition, the responsibility, as we have seen, had not rested with him. One can only join in the eulogies of Miss Foster's behaviour in trying circumstances and believe that the incident probably helped rather than hindered a distinguished career. A few years later the Association broke up.

At the beginning of 1893, Cecil Sharp was appointed music-master at Ludgrove, a preparatory school mainly for Eton. He held the appointment until 1910. He started with Mrs. Dunn (wife of Arthur Dunn,[1] the headmaster) and fourteen boys as pupils, but the number soon increased. During the greater part of the eighteen years he taught either three or four days a week at the school, spending two or three nights away from home. Later on, when he lived at Hampstead, he used to cycle to New Barnet in all weathers,

---

[1] After Mr. Dunn's death in 1902 the school was taken over by G. O. Smith in partnership with Mr. W. J. Oakley and Mr. A. K. Brown.

starting at 7 a.m., and it was a matter of self-pride that throughout the eighteen years he was never once late. He never lost his interest in the work, or his temper with the boys, who were devoted to him. The Masters' Common Room liked him too: one says 'Life together was such a jolly one'; another speaks of 'a breadth of outlook', which reminds us of Charles Marson's 'not a word of scandal' on an earlier page. He liked to air his Radical views and 'pull the legs of the Tories', and his wild flights of rhetoric were (except once, when he voiced pro-Boer doctrines) taken in good part.

His teaching at Ludgrove was of direct consequence to his life work; it brought home to him the need to lay a foundation of musical taste among young people by providing them with good songs which would make an immediate appeal.

Early in January 1893 Cecil became engaged to Constance Dorothea Birch whom he had known when he was a schoolboy at Weston-super-Mare. The engagement brought him the greatest happiness. Something of what it meant to him is expressed in a letter to Constance in which he quotes his beloved Wagner:

'The love of the strong for the strong is *Love*, for it is the free surrender to one who cannot compel us.' This expresses something of my meaning when I tell you I want you and myself each to preserve our individualities ; for then is our love the true and voluntary surrender to each other without compulsion. Love which exacts is no love worth the naming.

For a moment it looked as though Constance was unable to breathe the air on these heights of idealism, and we find Cecil holding out a hand to support her:

You are always 'wanting a sign', which is not a good thing . . . If you are continually cross-examining yourself . . . and are sifting and analysing your many feelings and thoughts . . . which of their very nature must of necessity be variable, you will for a certainty sooner or later muddle yourself to such an extent that one moment you can say 'Yes', and the next 'No', to your oft-repeated questions. Remember how by much thinking you can forget the face of your dearest friend. It is just the same with feelings. Take their average; don't analyse every passing phase . . . Life must be taken *broadly*, not minutely. The general trend of things is infinitely more important than their direction at any particular moment.

In matters of religion he and Constance were not in complete agreement and his letters of that period show that he uncompromisingly faced the issue without either sacrificing his own integrity or attempting to influence Constance's beliefs. Unlike her, he could not accept literally the inviolability of the Church's teaching, although he believed in its underlying spiritual truth. The question whether their differences constituted an obstacle to marriage was laid, as many other problems had been, before his friend Charles Marson, who at that time had a London slum-parish. Marson promised to write to Constance as a priest and not as Cecil's friend. He did not disclose to Cecil what his priestly advice would be, nor did Cecil inquire, but two days later he wrote to Constance:

I cannot write a note of music and I begin to fear that Marson was quite right, and that it is sheer happiness which has nipped the current of my thoughts.

On 22nd August, the marriage took place at Clevedon in Somerset, and is thus described by Charles Marson in a letter to his wife:

The event came off today. I rose up at 6.30, better of my diseases, and turned up at All Saints where the 'furniture' is very gorgeous, and the altar very decently draped. The old curate served, and after the Credo I whipped off the casula and went to the steps, blessed the happy pair and exhorted them, and so finished the mass and the sign-ing. Then we drove all together to the 'Wilderness' and had a neat cold breakfast in the garden on a lawn amphitheatre, hewn out of the rocks. Above us waved holm oaks and arbutuses, and round were beds of bright flowers and pines, and overhead sailing white clouds – an ideal party some twenty strong. Then we chatted about, and pretty Evelyn told my fortune, and the father Sharp talked architecture. Then the bride came in neat grey and we drank their healths in champagne, and they drove away, and we walked off.

Their prospects were not brilliant. Cecil was reasonably sure of earning £350 a year and was hopeful of increasing this to £400, whilst Constance had about £100 a year of her own; but neither of them allowed finances to worry them. In discussing ways and means before their marriage, Cecil wrote:

Do not trouble your dear old head about the idea that working for money will injure my music. I am not likely to go money-grubbing mad. I think you would not like it any more than I should. There is that great comfort that we think and feel alike on all important things. I don't seem to have a shadow or fear that we shall ever quarrel over anything.

They never did quarrel, although they did not always think and feel alike. Constance's lot was not an easy one. Poverty, the ill-health of herself and her family, and the depressions and enthusiasms of her husband – she bore whatever came her way without complaint, and if at times she was worried she did not let Cecil see it. It was a great disappointment to her when he gave up composing for the sake of folk music, but she accepted his judgement as to its greater value, and she willingly shared the sacrifices which it demanded. Indeed, she was always ready to persuade him to give up remunerative work for the uncertain or negative financial return of folk music. She lived until January 1928, surviving her husband by three and a half years.

Their first child – Dorothea Margaret Iseult – was born in September 1894 at Clevedon. Two years later came a son – Charles Tristan;[1] and having thus paid his homage to Wagner, he called two more daughters Joan Audrey[2] and Susannah Angel Birch, respectively.

Shortly after Dorothea's birth, in 1894, they took a house in Manor Gardens, Holloway, where they remained until 1896. Before that they had lived for a short time in rooms in Margaret Street, one attraction being that it was close to All Saints, which Cecil described as 'an awfully nice church'. During this time there was a 'Box and Cox' arrangement whereby his brother Lancelot took possession of the Langham Chambers studio at night and Cecil used it during the day for his lessons and musical lectures.

The studio was also the scene of meetings to discuss philosophy, religion, politics and art. Each form of new thought he tasted thoroughly: it possessed him while he was trying to understand it. For a short time he delved into Christian Science, theosophy

---

[1] Charles died in 1952 and Dorothea in 1941.

[2] To Joan on her twenty-first birthday: 'I thought this morning before I got up of this day twenty-one years ago. I have very vivid recollections of what you looked like when you made your appearance, which by the way was so badly timed that it robbed me of half my summer holiday. But in those days I was only collecting wild flowers, not songs and dances, so that time was not so important. You were a nice little thing from the beginning and went on steadily getting nicer as you grew older, and I hope it will be long before the process ceases!'

and spiritualism. He was a vegetarian for his health's sake, and although in words he chaffed others with being 'carnivorous' as opposed to his own 'pure living', in deeds he was careful not to give trouble by his demands or discomfort by any implied criticism. Any display of singularity was displeasing to him; and he followed the conventions in behaviour as well as in appearance unless there was a very good reason for departing from them. 'It saves so much trouble,' he would say.

In politics Cecil Sharp was at no time a keen Party man, although he supported the Liberals and afterwards the Labour Party. He has described himself as a 'Conservative Socialist' and that will perhaps serve as well as any other label. He joined the Fabian Society in December 1900 and perhaps in order to maintain equilibrium he was at the same time a member of the Navy League. He expresses something of his views on Socialism in a letter written 26th June 1893:

The Christian Socialists are endeavouring to disseminate the grand and ideal truths of Socialism very wisely, as I think, leaving these principles to take concrete form themselves. Marson thinks you should begin by measures and work back to the underlying theories. We have had many an argument on this subject. To my mind the Fabians[1] have lost all the power they had through tacking themselves on to the Liberal Party. Socialists should keep clear of politics for there is as much or as little Socialism in the Liberals as the Conservatives.

He had a dislike of catchwords. For instance, he did not regard democracy as a fetish to be unreservedly worshipped, though he believed that in the long run the mob was usually right. In a letter to his son Charles from America, he writes:

31. 1. 1918
One of the evils of democracy is that it is liable to become ruled by a tyrannous majority . . . and one of the greatest problems that democracy will sooner or later have to solve will be how by majority rule to protect minorities.

[1] He resigned his membership of the Fabian Society in May 1913, apparently because he disapproved of its allying itself with a Party, but he withdrew his resignation at the request of Mrs. Sidney Webb, who thus justified the Society's action: 'It was felt that we had to take some part in the organization of a Labour Party, as perhaps the most important instrument for permeating working class opinion. I admit all the deficiencies of the Labour Party. But incidentally its establishment has had the effect of bringing about a forward movement both in Trade Unionism and in co-operation. Moreover the very fact of its existence means that the Liberal Party is more anxious to take up Collectivist measures.'

He was at all times an ardent social reformer and a strong opponent of capital punishment. He did not sympathize with the women's suffrage movement, but the definite opposition which he at one time felt and expressed was probably not so much to the principle of female suffrage as to the militant tactics of the suffragettes.

Cecil Sharp continued to read widely during his early married life and he amassed a large general library in addition to an extensive collection of music and books on music. He became immersed in Schopenhauer, and he was enthusiastic over Ibsen whom he regarded as 'the greatest and most fearless of modern prophets'. He was a not uncritical admirer of Cardinal Newman.

Cardinal Manning was a pigmy by the side of Newman, whom I reverence very much despite his lack of balance between faith, or conscience – whatever you like to call it – and head. It is bad, perhaps worse, for the conscience to rule the intelligence as vice versa.

In later years he was greatly influenced by the writings of Samuel Butler.

It was at the Langham Chambers studio that A. H. Fox Strangways first met Cecil Sharp. His memories of that meeting are given below in his own words:

The first thing that struck me, and that I still seem to see, was his eyes. They were extraordinarily kind, and they looked at you as if they wanted to 'see' what you were saying . . . We seemed to know one another quite well in a few minutes. It was talking to him and hearing about what he was doing that clinched an idea I had of working at Indian music, and I went to India the following year . . . He was an extraordinarily good listener. He gave the impression that what one had to say was just what he wanted to hear.

A recollection of Cecil Sharp's appearance[1] at a later date is given by Mrs. May Elliot Hobbs:

The first time I saw Cecil Sharp – in 1911 – as he came into Mrs. Arthur Sidgwick's drawing-room, he gave me an impression which has

---

[1] Several photographs and a portrait by Sir William Rothenstein are given in this book. Cecil himself liked the Rothenstein portrait because, as he said, 'that is the face I see in the mirror every morning when I shave'. This portrait reveals the visionary side of his nature – it is not perhaps fanciful to see in it a likeness to Teilhard de Chardin – but neither this nor the photographs give a hint of his geniality, without which he could hardly have promoted a popular movement so successfully.

III   Cecil Sharp as a boy

IV   Cecil Sharp in middle age

V Cecil Sharp in 1922

VI Cecil Sharp in his last days

never changed – the piercing blue eye – falcon-like – the strong nose, the firm set of the head on the shoulders, the superb carriage, which he retained even when more bent with increasing age. There was a controlled suppleness in the whole body, loosely knit without being wobbly and this it was that made his dancing unique in its grace and ease. It might be summed up in two words – line and carriage.

Two other pictures come before me. An early one of him seated at the piano in my room, pipe alternately in his mouth or on the music-stand, playing and singing shanties just collected in Somerset, the hands, with the slightly crooked little finger, looking the most unlikely 'piano hands', and yet bringing out the value of every note, just as he wanted it; and every now and again he would turn his head towards us, seated round and on the floor, with that characteristic one-sided pursing of the mouth and twinkle in his eye which always heralded a joke.

Another picture, much later, sitting rather crouched in his armchair by the fire, a brown Shetland shawl round his shoulders, the fine modelling of the head more apparent as the bones showed up in age – a real sculptor's head, the eyes still as compelling as ever, the whole frame becoming more and more but a shell for the still eager spirit, full of nervous energy, concentrated but never restless.

In 1896 Cecil Sharp became Principal of the Hampstead Conservatoire of Music.[1] The owner, who had no part in teaching, was Mr. Arthur Blackwood whom Cecil Sharp had met in Adelaide. Cecil Sharp greatly enjoyed his work at the Conservatoire, which gave him a splendid opportunity of infecting others with his enthusiasm and of imparting to them some of his great store of knowledge. He is said to have 'made the place hum'. He collected a first-rate Staff which included Edward d'Evry, Michael Hambourg, Medora Henson, Madame Fischer-Sobell and Auguste Wilhelmj. He himself conducted, took classes in theory and harmony and had a few private pupils.

Unfortunately the business side was not so satisfactory, and by 1904 the relations between the Principal and Mr. Blackwood had become severely strained. Apparently no formal agreement had been drawn up between them, there were doubts about the remuneration to which Cecil Sharp was entitled and his salary was in arrears. The more the matter was investigated, the further away they became from reaching agreement; and a correspondence

---

[1] The building was later converted into the Embassy Theatre.

lasting over a year, which was particularly acrimonious on Cecil Sharp's side, only increased the sense of irritation. In July 1905, the position became untenable and Cecil Sharp resigned, to the regret of pupils, parents and professors.

Soon after his resignation the family moved to 183 Adelaide Road, Hampstead, where they remained until May 1911.

III

The Turning Point
1899—1902

All Nature is but Art unknown to thee,
All Chance, Direction which thou canst not see.

ALEXANDER POPE, *An Essay on Man*

CECIL SHARP regarded the close of the century (1899) as a
turning point in his life. The reasons he gave were 'asthma,
Mattie Kay, and Headington'.

Asthma was a development of hay-fever, and he suffered from it
for the rest of his life. At first the attacks came only at a certain
period of the year, but gradually the disease became chronic, and
except for a short time in America and, later, in Switzerland he
seldom was able to draw a clear breath. It would not have been
surprising if he had given up the fight and subsided into the life of
an invalid; but he struggled on, a martyr though no saint. 'Please
let the announcement of my death read "after a long illness most
*im*patiently borne",' he once remarked. Asthma was not his only
trouble. Shortly after his marriage he developed severe attacks of
delirium, commonly supposed to be influenza, though said by one
doctor to be 'something of a malarial nature with a tendency to
congestion and pneumonia'. These attacks, usually followed by
extreme weakness and exhaustion, recurred at frequent intervals
throughout the rest of his life. In addition he suffered from a form
of gout in the eyes, which caused irritation and great pain, and
often blindness. Those who saw him at his work would not have

suspected that he suffered so much, but one who lived with the family at that time speaks of his 'uncertain temper' caused by illness and says that 'when he was not in the mood there was but little talk at table'.

Mattie Kay (later Mrs. Algernon Lindo) was a singer with a fine untrained contralto voice whom Cecil Sharp heard at a concert at Walton-le-Dale while staying with some relations in Lancashire. Mattie Kay was living in surroundings in which a musical talent could hardly develop and, with the help of friends, he at once made arrangements for her to come to London. He took her into his own home among his children, and put her under Medora Henson for singing. She was given a scholarship at the Conservatoire. He had no ulterior motive in doing this; he merely thought it was a pity that a voice of such quality, with such purity of diction and such an inexorable sense of rhythm, should miss the training which was its due. There is no sign of his having as yet thought of folk song, in which she eventually made her name. By singing at his lectures from 1903 onwards for many years, she repaid him many times over. The appreciation of the Hon. Neville Lytton, as expressed in a letter to Cecil Sharp, stands by no means alone:

Miss Mattie Kay is a wonderful singer. I don't think I have ever heard a more perfect pronunciation. I suppose her coming from the North accounts to a certain extent for the beauty of her accent. But she pronounces some words in a way that I have never heard anyone else pronounce them, notably the word 'milk' in 'It's dabbling in the dew makes the milkmaids fair'. English is nearly always sung abominably and said abominably by actors on the stage, especially in poetry. Miss Kay's English is very personal and very beautiful.

Another singer who often illustrated his lectures was that great artist, J. Campbell McInnes, who settled in Canada after the First World War. In later years, when Mattie Kay was not available, he occasionally availed himself of the services of Gwen Ffrangcon Davies, whose singing he greatly admired.

And now we come to 'Headington', the last of the three happenings which were to influence the course of Cecil Sharp's life. He and his family spent Christmas 1899 with his wife's mother, who was then living at Sandfield Cottage, Headington, about a mile east of Oxford. On Boxing Day, as he was looking out of the window, upon the snow-covered drive, a strange procession appeared: eight men dressed in white, decorated with ribbons, with pads of small latten-bells strapped to their shins, carrying coloured sticks and white handkerchiefs; accompanying them was a concertina-player and a man dressed as a 'Fool'. Six of the men formed up in front of the house in two lines of three; the concertina-player struck up an invigorating tune, the like of which Cecil Sharp had never heard before; the men jumped high into the air, then danced with springs and capers, waving and swinging the handkerchiefs which they held, one in each hand, while the bells marked the rhythm of the step. The dance was the now well-known Morris Dance, 'Laudnum Bunches', a title which decidedly belies its character. Then, dropping their handkerchiefs and each taking a stick, they went through the ritual of 'Bean Setting'. This was followed by 'Constant Billy' ('Cease your Funning' of the *Beggar's Opera*), 'Blue-eyed Stranger', and 'Rigs o' Marlow'. Cecil Sharp watched and listened spellbound. He had not been well; his eyes had been giving him pain and he was still wearing a shade over them, but all his ills were forgotten in his excitement. He plied the men eagerly with questions. They apologized for being out at Christmas; they knew that Whitsun was the proper time, but work was slack and they thought there would be no harm in earning an honest penny. The concertina-player was Mr. William Kimber, junior, a young man of twenty-seven, whose fame as a dancer has since spread far and wide. Cecil Sharp noted the five tunes from him the next day, and later on many others.

Cecil Sharp always pointed to the Headington incident as the beginning of the folk music revival and so indeed it was, though it was not immediately apparent, for the seed that was sown at Headington took time to germinate. His imagination had been fired by the dances, but he did not at first see what to do with them; and beyond harmonizing and orchestrating the tunes he made no practical use of his discovery.

For some time he had been feeling that the normal musical education, based on German music, did not supply all that was needed for young people; and we may believe that the encounter with the Headington Morris turned his mind towards seeking more music of this kind: good, strong, simple melodies which were essentially English in character.

It was not until a few years later that he thought of unearthing folk songs himself from the English countryside. His first step was to go to printed collections of folk songs and 'old English' songs, including William Chappell's *Popular Music of the Olden Time*. From these he compiled *A Book of British Song for Home and School* (1902).

The book is dedicated 'To the memory of Arthur Tempest Blakiston Dunn', the late headmaster of Ludgrove School; and Cecil Sharp acknowledges how much he owes to his knowledge, enthusiasm and kindly encouragement. Out of the seventy-eight songs, sixty-six are English. He calls them all 'traditional' as his predecessors had done before him; adding that 'being chiefly of folk origin [they] are of assured humanity'. This comment read in conjunction with his note that 'Mr. Chappell had worked, in the main, among books only, and had made no serious effort to gather those innumerable songs and dances which have been handed down among our peasantry from generation to generation, and are still to be heard in country places', shows that he was even at that time to some extent aware of the distinctive nature of folk song. The collection is a good one; and it was undoubtedly useful. It contains a fair sprinkling of genuine folk songs, and Cecil Sharp believed that this was the first time that folk song had been sung in the classroom.

As he worked on the material he came to realize the difference in character between the songs in their edited and modified book-form and those that had been faithfully transcribed from the lips of traditional singers, such as those in Miss Lucy Broadwood's collection. He therefore made up his mind to seek for himself the living tradition at its source, believing – and rightly so – that only in this way would he experience the real flavour of folk song. And his work in the collection of folk songs was to occupy him on and off throughout the rest of his life.

In order to place this work in its historical perspective it will be necessary to review briefly what had already been done when he came on the scene.

The publication of folk songs was, of course, no new phenomenon, either in this or in other countries. The texts of traditional songs and ballads are to be found in broadsides as early as the second half of the seventeenth century, e.g. the collections of Wood, Rawlinson, Douce and Pepys, and a few appeared in early eighteenth-century printed collections of songs. The first comprehensive collection was that of Percy's *Reliques* (1765), which, although it has been severely criticized on account of its literary embellishments, yet served its purpose in arousing enthusiasm for popular ballads. Bishop Percy's collection was followed by many others during the next fifty years, e.g. those of Ritson in England, and Herd, Scott, and Jamieson in Scotland. In these collections interest centred solely in the texts, and the accompanying tunes were ignored. A few traditional tunes are recorded in early eighteenth-century musical collections, but Johnson's *Scots Musical Museum* (1787–1803)[1] is the first publication to contain any considerable number of traditional tunes, though which of these are taken from traditional sources is uncertain. In the third decade of the nineteenth century a number of collections appeared – mostly Scottish – and those of Kinloch and Motherwell (both 1827) contain several airs said to have been recovered from tradition.

The first publication to be devoted exclusively to songs with tunes, noted directly from the lips of country singers is a small collection of sixteen songs, entitled *Sussex Songs*, by the Rev. John Broadwood (uncle of Miss Lucy Broadwood). This was privately printed in 1843 and was reprinted in 1899 with additional songs collected by Miss Broadwood. During the last quarter of the nineteenth century, nine collections of folk songs appeared, accounting for 640 tunes.[2] Among the collectors represented in these collections are J. Collingwood Bruce, John Stokoe, S. Baring-Gould, Frank Kidson and Lucy Broadwood. Following these collections, four numbers of the *Journal of the Folk-Song Society* appeared during the years 1899–1902, accounting for another 120 tunes. There are also two great store-houses in which the material is taken in each case from printed sources: William

---

[1] For an account of this and other Scottish collections, see *The Traditional and National Music of Scotland* by Francis Collinson (London, 1966).
[2] For a short bibliography of these and later collections, *see English Folk Song: Some Conclusions* by Cecil J. Sharp, edited by Maud Karpeles (London 1965), pp. 181–4; and for a full annotated list of collections published between 1822 and 1922, see *A Guide to English Folk-Song Collections* by Margaret Dean-Smith (Liverpool 1954).

Chappell's *Popular Music of the Olden Time* (1855–59) and Francis J. Child's *English and Scottish Popular Ballads* (1822–98).[1]

The Folk-Song Society[2] had been formed in 1898 with the primary object of 'the collection and preservation of Folk Songs, Ballads and Tunes and the publication of such of these as may be advisable'. It had the support of prominent musicians and scholars as may be seen from the names of the Committee[3] which was elected at the first General Meeting on 2nd February 1899. On that occasion, Sir Hubert Parry gave his memorable address.[4] The Society published an annual Journal in the years 1899 to 1902. Then came a period of inaction, in part due to the illness of its honorary secretary.

Cecil Sharp's first venture into the field was in the late summer of 1903 on the occasion of a visit to the Rev. Charles Marson. The story will be told in the next chapter, but since Father Marson played an important part in it during the first few years, we propose to give here a further account of his association with Cecil Sharp.

It was at Adelaide about 1889 that they first met. Charles Marson, who was a year older than Cecil Sharp, was curate first at Glenelg, a watering-place five miles to the south and then at St. Oswald's in the capital. He was rather a thorn in the side of his colonial bishop, to whom it was possibly a relief when, in 1892, he

---

[1] This work is concerned with the texts of the ballads and contains only fifty-five tunes in an appendix. It is now being supplemented by Bertrand Harris Bronson's *The Traditional Tunes of the Child Ballads with their Texts according to the extant records of Great Britain and America* (Princeton,1959, 1962 and 1966. In progress).

[2] For a short account of the Folk-Song Society and the work of its members, see 'The Preservation of English Folk Song in the *Journal* of the Folk-Song Society' by Margaret Dean-Smith (*Journal of the English Folk Dance and Song Society*, December 1951).

[3] President: Lord Herschell; Vice-Presidents: Sir John Stainer, C. Villiers Stanford; Sir A. C. Mackenzie, Sir Hubert Parry; Committee: Mrs. Frederick Beer, Miss Lucy Broadwood, Sir Ernest Clarke, W. H. Gill, Mrs. Laurence Gomme, A. P. Graves, E. G. Jacques, Frank Kidson, J. A. Fuller-Maitland, J. D. Rogers, W. Barclay Squire, Dr. Todhunter; with Mrs. Kate Lee as Honorary Secretary and A. Kalisch as Honorary Treasurer,

[4] In it there occurs that notable passage: 'True style comes not from the individual but from the products of crowds of fellow-workers, who 8ift, and try, and try again, till they have found the thing that suits their native taste; and the purest product of such efforts is folk-song, which, when it is found, outlasts the greatest works of art, and becomes an heritage to generations. And in that heritage may lie the ultimate solution of the problems of characteristic national art.'

left Australia to take up a curacy in Soho. Cecil Sharp left Adelaide that same year. When subsequently the Bishop was translated to the See of Bath and Wells, Cecil Sharp, who met him somewhere at dinner, rather gleefully told him that Charles Marson, who meanwhile had become perpetual curate of Hambridge, three miles north of Langport, was in his diocese.

The kind of thorn he was may be gathered from an incident or two. When the Bishop came to Hambridge on his diocesan visitation, Charles Marson, after placing him (on the warrant of Mark ii. 16, 17) next to the landlord of the public-house, presented to him after luncheon his report, in which he described his parish as 'forward at the public-house but backward at Mass'. The Bishop said he had nothing to object to in the report except, possibly, some of the nomenclature. This 'nomenclature' puzzled the parishioners, and Charles Marson explained it to them; to the caretakers of the church he said it meant the corners which were not properly swept; to the organist, that the Bishop had noticed that the choir was singing flat; and so on. Again at a diocesan conference Dr. Warre of Eton had been insisting with general approval on the need for gentlemen as ordinands. This atmosphere was rent asunder by Father Marson's speech:

The playing-fields of Eton have a large place in our history. It is there that most of our battles have been lost. But what the Church requires is bounders like Peter and Paul.

On one of the rare occasions when Cecil Sharp discussed religion, he said that he was converted from indifference to Christianity by finding a parson on a gate telling fairy tales to children.[1] This can only have been Charles Marson. His first book, *Faery Stories*, published at Adelaide and evidently written for Australian children, shows a fertile imagination with a simple and poetic style. He was a voluminous writer on Christian Socialism.

For the way he put these views in practice Father Marson was beloved by his parishioners; and the love he felt for them, and the knowledge he had of them, may be read in his *Village Silhouettes*.[2] In the Preface he writes:

See p. 6.
[2] Now out of print. It was published by the Society of SS. Peter and Paul in 1914.

These Village Silhouettes have a serious purpose. It is to bear some testimony to what the author has discovered – how shameful and blind to have discovered it so late! – the greatness, the sweetness, the unexpectedness and the cleverness of God's common people . . . How could anyone miss seeing what is so plain, so constant and so attractive to the sight? . . .

People were once kind enough to applaud the writer for his discovery of a great gold mine of beautiful song in Somerset: and he is glad to have discovered this; to have set ardent miners at work and to find the results of his discovery echoed from John o' Groat's beyond even the Land's End. The disbelievers are cured, or at least struck dumbly modest, and the apathetic public admit the genuineness of the metal. Now the prospector wishes to proclaim a far greater discovery. The graceful, manly and fine-wrought melodies are not separable accidents, they belong to lives and characters at least as interesting, as full of fine art and exquisite melodiousness, as are the songs we have discovered and valued. Not only is the expression great, but the life which is so delicately expressed is worthy of our utmost attention and admiration.

It was with Charles Marson's alert imagination, sincere conviction and Christian charity that Cecil Sharp was in contact for seventeen years and the friendship meant a great deal to both men. Cecil Sharp acknowledged that Charles Marson had exercised more real influence over him than had any other man.

IV
Folk-Song Collecting
1903 — 14

To such a mood I had come, by what charm I know not
where on that upland path I was pacing alone;
and yet was nothing new to me, only all was vivid
and significant that had been dormant or dead:
as if in a museum the fossils on their shelves
should come to life suddenly, or a winter rose-bed
burst into crowded holiday of scent and bloom.

ROBERT BRIDGES, *Testament of Beauty*

TOWARDS THE END of the summer holidays of 1903 Cecil Sharp
went to the small village of Hambridge in Somerset to search for
folk songs. His host, Charles Marson, was not optimistic, but as he
afterwards admitted (in the preface of *Folk-Songs from Somerset*,
vol. I):

The folk-song is like the duck-billed platypus in this particular, you
can live for years within a few yards of it and never suspect its existence . . . Eight years of constant residence in the small village of
Hambridge in Somerset had left him [the writer] in Stygian ignorance
of the wealth of art which that village contained. . . . Only one song,
and that by chance, had fallen on his untouched ears.

Charles Marson related (also in *Folk-Songs from Somerset*) that he
had mentioned this song to several musical friends of whom none
had shown great interest, but at last Cecil Sharp came to Hambridge, heard it sung and in a moment recognized its value.

31

The song was 'The Seeds of Love' and the singer was John England, the vicarage gardener. And it was through this song and this singer that Cecil Sharp had his introduction to the living folk-song.[1] It happened in this way. Cecil Sharp was sitting in the vicarage garden talking to Charles Marson and to Mattie Kay, who was likewise staying at Hambridge, when he heard John England quietly singing to himself as he mowed the vicarage lawn. Cecil Sharp whipped out his notebook and took down the tune; and then persuaded John to give him the words. He imme-diately harmonized the song; and that same evening it was sung at a choir supper by Mattie Kay, Cecil Sharp accompanying. The audience was delighted; as one said, it was the first time that the song had been put into evening-dress.

It seems almost prophetic that Cecil Sharp's first singer should have borne the name of John England, for he was the precursor of the many English men and women from whom Cecil Sharp was to discover our glorious heritage of folk song. He perceived imme-diately the value of what he had found and he spent the remaining days of his summer holiday exploring Hambridge and the neigh-bouring villages in search of further treasures. He was accompanied – or, one might say, introduced – by Father Marson, and together they noted some forty songs, Cecil Sharp taking down the tunes and Father Marson the words. Over half this number came from Mrs. Louie Hooper and her sister, Mrs. Lucy White, who between them eventually provided over a hundred songs for Cecil Sharp's

[1] On 10th June 1961, a plaque on the wall of the vicarage garden was unveiled by the present writer, the ceremony being attended by several hundred people from all parts of the country. The plaque bears the inscription:

> In the garden of this Vicarage in September 1903
> CECIL SHARP
> while staying with his friend and early collaborator
> CHARLES LATIMER MARSON
> Heard John England sing 'The Seeds of Love'
> This incident inspired the Folk Song revival in England

There has always been some uncertainty as to the exact date on which Cecil Sharp collected 'The Seeds of Love', because, contrary to his usual practice, he does not give this in his notebooks. For the first forty two songs there is only a general indica-tion, i.e. 'September 1903'(except for two which are undated). One had therefore assumed that they were all collected during that month. However, correspondence which has recently been examined suggests that 'Seeds of Love' may have been noted on 22nd August.

notebooks. Mrs. Hooper has told how when she was a child she used to love lying in bed and hearing the rain pattering on the roof, for 'it would always turn itself into a little song'. 'I was always full of music,' she added. It probably gave her as much pleasure to sing the songs to Cecil Sharp as it gave him to listen to them. She has related that when she told him that she had remembered yet another song, 'he would be dizzy until he had written it down'.

Cecil Sharp was deeply affected by the songs he heard during his short visit to Hambridge. He felt that a new world of music had been opened to him. From now on his course was set and he never turned back.

At the next opportunity, that is, in the Christmas holidays (1903–04), he returned to the scene of action, dividing his time between Somerset and North Devon. Incidentally, it may be mentioned that for the first seven years, until he gave up his other professional work, he could devote only holidays and occasional week-ends to collecting. And, of course, all expenses had to come out of his own pocket.

For the first three years, except for an occasional short excursion into Devonshire, Cecil Sharp's researches were practically confined to Somerset; and because of the large number of songs that were collected there it is sometimes supposed that it must have been a richer field than other counties. This is not necessarily so, although the rural nature of the country made it particularly fruitful, as did the cottage industries, such as shirt-making and glove-sewing, in which the workers were wont to gather together in one room and to lighten their labours by the exchange of songs. The later use of the sewing-machine, which caused the worker to be tied to her own room, put an end to this delightful practice.

In order to appreciate the task that Cecil Sharp had set himself it is necessary to consider for a moment the general attitude towards English folk music at that time. It can best be summed up by one word: ignorance. The ordinary townsman hardly knew of the existence of English folk music, nor were there many musicians who were better informed. As a wit of the day expressed it: 'if there were any English folk songs they were Irish.' And among the country people, folk song had gone out of fashion. Many of the older people still treasured them, often as precious heirlooms, but their memories were failing and they were sensitive to the ridicule of the younger generation. Folk song had not at that time been made respectable by the radio.

More than once it happened that Cecil Sharp would be sitting quietly with an old couple listening with enjoyment when the peaceful atmosphere would be disturbed by the noisy entrance of the grandchildren, who would be shocked to find their grand-parents singing their silly old songs to the gentleman, and would endeavour to reinstate the family reputation by turning on the gramophone with the latest music-hall records; songs of which one old man said: 'Can't make no idea to it, no more than that chair; 'tis a gabble of noise with no meaning to it.'

On one occasion when he called on an old gypsy-woman of eighty-three, he suffered even worse than gramophone records, as the following anecdote relates:

I called on Lucy one day . . . and found her hale and hearty, upright as a dart, and looking anything but her reputed age. This, of course, I told her; whereat she looked pleased and replied, 'I be old but of fair complexion,' using the last word in its Elizabethan and wider sense. A compliment is a good foundation to build upon, and we were soon chatting away in a most friendly fashion. 'And thee be vond of the music, do 'ee?' she said, and before I could stop her, she had impul-sively jumped up and set a–going a small musical box that was fixed in a clock that stood on the mantelshelf. 'There now!' she said proudly as the instrument started on the first lap of the only tune it could play, 'The Blue Bells of Scotland'. I feigned admiration, but at the end of the twentieth repetition or so mildly suggested that we might stop the music and proceed with the singing. My heart sank when she informed me, 'You can't stop he,' and intimated that we should have to wait until it had exhausted itself, and that that would take a full fifteen minutes 1 But she said, 'Thee won't hearken to it when I do zing,' and forthwith started off singing at the top of her voice. The song was a good one, but I couldn't take it down; the Blue Bells in a different key broke in at every pause. It was distracting. I caught up the box, wrapped it in a shawl, and deposited it in the next room. This was of no avail; the Scottish National Anthem pierced the woollen shawl as though it were of gossamer, while the lath and plaster partition, which separated the two rooms, seemed to give it added resonance. I felt I should go mad. Even Lucy began to show signs of weariness, for she presently suggested that we should take it upstairs and muffle it in her bed. Up-stairs, accordingly, we crept, the old gypsy-woman leading the way up the ladder with the musical box still playing its nauseating tune with unbroken energy. To bed it went, shawl and all, and pillow and bolster piled on the top. This put the musical box thoroughly on its mettle; for when we got downstairs the whole room was full of its music. And there we waited – there was nothing for it – until the fifteen minutes were up; a *mauvais quart d'heure*, if ever there was one! Even Lucy seemed depressed, for, with deep melancholy in her voice, she confided to me that she had bought it only a few days ago off a pedlar; adding wearily that if I cared to have it she would let it go at a reduction. . . . Then at last we set to work and I noted down several interesting songs.

And then as I got up to go away the old gipsy offered to tell my fortune; I produced the customary piece of silver and off she went. I had crossed the water twice . . . I had an enemy; he was short and dark and cunning and was plotting to do me great harm, etc., etc. I eventually tore myself away, and as I shook hands at the door of her cottage she put her face close to mine, looking me deep in the eyes, and whispered, 'When you are in trouble, you do think of the old gipsy-woman; she can help you, for she's a *seventh* daughter!

It will readily be appreciated that the utmost tact and patience were needed to extract the songs from the recesses of the singers 'memories and to overcome their shyness. 'Forty years agone,' said one, 'I'd a–zung 'un out o' sight.' 'When you come to me all at once I can't come at it,' said another, and the only way was to leave him 'to bide and stud'.

On the other hand, Cecil Sharp gives instances of wonderful memories. Reference has already been made to the two sisters, Mrs. Louie Hooper and Mrs. Lucy White, from whom he noted over a hundred songs and who would have given him three times as many had he wished to include composed songs. And an old man of eighty-two who was appealed to for a Robin Hood ballad was able to recall the tune and the complete ten stanzas of the song which he had learned as a child, although he had not sung it for over forty years.

Cecil Sharp has maintained that the mind of the English peasant is as good as anyone else's, but it moves more slowly. He knew well how to adapt his pace to theirs; and although naturally of quick action and conversational disposition he would be content to sit in silence for long stretches of time puffing at his pipe and waiting for the clearing of the throat which indicates that the song is about to begin.

To get a true picture of Cecil Sharp's work in the field and his relationship with the singers, one must know how completely he could enter into their thoughts and feelings. He never looked upon the singers as mere 'informants'. They were men and women; and through his appreciation of their songs he was able to meet them on an equal footing as fellow-artists. He believed, as did Charles Marson, 'that the graceful and finely-wrought melodies are not separable accidents' (see p. 30).

He was quick to recognize the qualities of the artist under a rough exterior. To Miss Anne Gilchrist he writes (26. 1. 1907):

> I sat one day from noon to four o'clock in a small lonely public-house on the peat moors with a dozen cut-throats – at least they looked it – and I heard nothing but modal tunes the whole while.

And to Mrs. Stanton of Armscote, Warwickshire, who gave him much assistance in collecting, he comments thus on the death of a singer who was, as he described himself, 'as good a whistler as ever cocked a lip':

> I was glad to have your letter despite its sad news. Poor old Tom. I was afraid his days were numbered, but I hoped he would last through the winter. He left quite a mark in my mind; there was something about him which raised him from his fellows and singled him out. A pathetic figure of one who was himself his only enemy. His very reck-lessness endeared him to me. Well, I fancy he got a deal out of life, more perhaps than many of us who live in a very different environment. He had the waywardness of the musician and a patience which enabled him to bear unruffled a querulous and slatternly wife – no mean perform-ance. I have been harmonising 'Nelson's Praise'[1] quite lately, so I have poor Tom in mind. What a gorgeous tune it is, and I can always hear his voice in it.

The love of the singers for their own songs and their apprecia-tion of Cecil Sharp's efforts in saving them from oblivion are shown by the following incident related by the Rev. W. Warren, at one time curate of Bridgwater, who used to give hospitality to Cecil Sharp and sometimes accompany him on his visits to singers:

> I can remember a man in the Bridgwater workhouse, who was re-ported to be a singer, receiving us with the utmost coldness, but end-ing by placing a fatherly hand upon Mr. Sharp's thigh as he taught his pupil at his knee and addressing him as 'my dear'. And when we rose to take leave, he clung to Mr. Sharp's hand and shed tears, so great had been his pleasure in finding one who would listen to the songs he so loved, and actually take them down on paper.

[1] *English Folk-Songs, Centenary Edition*, vol. ii, no. 38.

VII(a) Mrs Rebecca Holland,
folksinger (see pp. 42-3)

VII(b) William Bayliss,
a Gloucestershire carol singer

VII(c) John England, of Hambridge, Somerset, who
sang 'The Seeds of Love' (see plate II and p. 32)

VIII(a) John Short, chanteyman, of Watchet, Somerset (see p. 121)

VIII(b) Shepherd Hayden, of Bampton, Oxfordshire, folksinger

Often he would overcome suspicion with the humour and ready wit of which he had a great store, and when, after many a joke and much laughter, he had convinced them that he was a jolly good fellow, they would open out their hearts to him.

And in a letter to Cecil Sharp dictated by a Somerset singer we read:

I sometimes get an old line or refrain come into my head, and I think that's one of Granny's old songs, I wonder if Mr. Sharp has that; but it goes so quickly, and I have no one now to jot it down, I forget the dear old ditties.

Yet another incident has remained in the memory of one who heard Cecil tell it in a lecture given over twenty years earlier.

Cecil Sharp had heard that a song which he had not hitherto recorded was known in an out-of-the-way corner of England. Accordingly he rushed off to secure it. On arriving at the place he was told there was only one person who knew it and this was an aged woman. On arriving at her cottage he found she had gone out to work in the fields. After much difficulty he discovered her, engaged in gathering stones off the land. The day was bleak and there was a cutting wind; when the old woman heard Cecil Sharp's inquiry, she replied that she knew the song. 'Shall I sing it to you?' she said; and raising her old weather-worn face to his, taking the lapels of his coat in her hands, and closing her eyes, she sang 'The Lark in the Morn'[1] in her quavering yet beautiful voice, while he rapidly made notes. When the song was finished, she gazed into his eyes in a sort of ecstasy, and, in perfect detachment from herself, exclaimed, 'Isn't it lovely!'

There was a real bond of affection between Cecil Sharp and his singers and dancers. In December 1922, he wrote to a friend:

It has been a great rush this Christmas and I have croaked and wheezed in the streets buying Christmas presents for all and sundry. There are so many folk-singers and dancers I should like to send presents to, but I can only pick out one or two, which is rather sad. Of course, I don't rob them as I should if I bought their old tables and chairs – but still I feel under a great obligation to them.

And the other side of the picture is given by this letter from the son of an old Morris dancer.

I now take pleasure in writing a few lines to you in answer to your kind and welcome letter and father thanks you so much for the tobacco

---

[1] The writer's memory must be at fault with regard to the title of the song, because Cecil Sharp did not at any time note 'The Lark in the Morn' from a woman singer.

you sent him. He was so pleased with it. Dear Sir, father is very ill and has been for a long time. He has been under the doctor's hands. He has been in bed for a long time but he is just getting a little better. He tells me again to thank you for the tobacco and pipes. Father would have wrote before only he has been waiting to get you a little present. Then he had his downfall of being ill and he could not get it, but he says he will get you something as soon as he is able to get to work again. We all wish you a merry Christmas and a happy New Year when it comes.

We would also quote a letter from Mrs. Hooper which was addressed to Mr. Fox Strangways:

Hambridge, 12. 10. 1931

Sir, I was looking down the paper when I seen Cecil Sharp's name. And you wanted to know if anyone knew him. Now I must say I Louie Hooper and my sister Lucy White both of this place knew him quite well and spent many a happy hour singing to him at the Vicarage Hambridge with Father Marson his friend . . . He gave me a nice concertina. I would play it. And Mrs. Sharp gave me and my sister a new blouse each. I went to Ilminster Fair with him to hear the old people sing, and I remember quite well there was an eclipse of the sun the same day and he smoked a piece of glass for me to look and see it through.[1] And he had a nice concert at Langport and gave us a nice tea . . . I and my sister used to go to the Vicarage and he used to pay us very well. And we used to have our supper together. Mrs. Sharp was there sometimes. The last time I seen him was when Father Marson was buried. That was in March the same year as the War broke out. I am 72 years of age . . . He came to my house one Christmas time and took the photo of my dinner Christmas Day, and when I went to Langport to a lantern lecture that he gave I seen my Christmas dinner come through on the slide . . . He gave me a book of songs after he had mine and he said exchange was no robbery. And he wrote it in the book . . . I liked him very much, he was a very kind gentleman . . . He also gave the old men tobacco that used to sing to him. I often think of the days. It was a happy time. I often say I should like for someone to have the concertina in memory of him. He used to like to hear me play it. Now I hope you will be able to understand this letter that I have sent.

From Yours faithfully,
Louisa Hooper

[1] Mr. Fox Strangways has pointed out that reference to the eclipse of the sun fixes the date of Ilminster Fair as 30th August 1905.

Something should be said of his collecting methods and particularly of how he set to work to find the singers. He went everywhere on his bicycle. He could not afford to keep a motor-car and when urged to hire one for his journeys he would refuse because he was afraid that if he did so he might miss something on the roadside: a chance encounter with a stone-breaker, a farm labourer returning home from work, or a gipsy encampment. Sometimes he would call for information on the parson or the squire, who were always co-operative and sympathetic and the assistance of a number of them is acknowledged in the various volumes of *Folk-Songs from Somerset*. But more often he would make inquiries first from the village people, not for singers (that would normally have been useless) but for the names of the old people. One introduction would lead to another and ultimately, almost by a sixth sense, a singer would be found. Even then the song would not be immediately forthcoming for the social preliminaries would have to be gone through and the conversation brought round gradually to the subject of old songs. The traditional singer, as we know, does not distinguish between folk songs and other songs in his repertory, and he will produce first songs which he thinks his visitor will like best, which are fairly certain not to be folk songs. Then, various techniques will have to be employed. One may ask for 'old-time' songs, or for 'songs that have no music to them', for, to the traditional singer, music means the printed notation. In this he is reverting to the custom of the eleventh century when Guido d'Arrezo (d. 1050), who invented a form of musical notation, was called *inventor musicae*. But the best method will usually be to quote a familiar phrase, such as, 'As I walked out one May morning', or to sing a few lines of a well-known folk song.

Contrary to general opinion, Cecil Sharp has affirmed that the best folk songs are not usually obtained in village inns, but in a more secluded environment. Here are some of his experiences:

I once took down two excellent songs from a 'bird-starver'. It was his business to guard a patch of mangold seeds from being eaten by birds, and this he did by hammering a tea-tray. He was quite prepared to sing, but his conscience would not allow him to neglect his duty. So we arranged that he should hammer his tray between each verse of his songs, and thus combine business with pleasure; and we accomplished this to our mutual satisfaction and to the amusement of passers-by.

On another occasion I recovered a good song from the proprietor of a coco-nut pitch at Cheddar Cliffs, when business was slack; and I have many times sat by the side of stone-breakers on the wayside and taken down songs – at the risk, too, of my eyesight, for the occupation and the song are very often inseparable.

One singer in Langport could only sing a song when she was ironing, while another woman in the same court sang best on washing-day! I remember an amusing incident which happened to me at the house of the latter. I was in her wash-house sitting on an inverted tub, notebook in hand, while my hostess officiated at the copper, singing the while. Several neighbours congregated at the door to watch the strange proceedings. In one of the intervals between the songs one of the women remarked, 'You be going to make a deal o' money out o' this, sir?' My embarrassment was relieved by the singer at the wash-tub, who came to my assistance and said, 'Oh! it's only'is'obby.' 'Ah! well,' commented the first speaker, 'we do all 'ave our vailin's.'

He has told an amusing story of an encounter with a woman who had a great reputation as a singer. She lived in a mean street, which was inhabited – so he was told – by 'bad people'. She was out when he first called upon her, but was said to be at the public-house round the corner. As he approached the public-house he saw a group of women standing outside and chatting. 'Is Mrs. Overd here?' he asked. 'That's my name,' an elderly woman replied, 'and what do you want of me?' Cecil Sharp explained that he was hunting for old songs and hoped that she would sing him some; whereupon without any warning she flung her arms around his waist and danced him round and round with the utmost vigour, shouting, 'Lor, girls, here's my beau come at last.'[1] In the middle of this terpsichorean display Cecil Sharp heard a shocked exclamation, 'But surely that is Mr Sharp,' and looking round he saw the vicar, with whom he was staying, and the vicar's daughter, both gazing with horror on the scene. When asked what he did, Sharp said: 'Oh, I shouted to them to go away – and they went.'

It says much for the courtesy of the people that never once throughout his visits to their cottage doors was he asked what his business was. And their kindliness and generosity are exemplified by an old lady who was rather deaf and had not understood Cecil Sharp's preliminary inquiry about a certain song, but had only

[1] A quotation from 'Sweet Kitty', one of her own songs:
'He rode found her six times, but never did know,
Though she smiled in his face and said: There goes my Beau.'

heard his final appeal for help. Her response was, 'Well, we're poor folk, but if a penny will be any good to you, you are welcome.'

Cecil Sharp's collecting was, of course, done before the days of the tape-recorder and he used to take down the tune in ordinary staff notation and then write out the words. Occasionally he used a phonograph, but he did not much like it, as he thought it made the singer self-conscious. However, on one occasion the phonograph was the means of saving his life – or so he said. He was noting songs by phonograph from a gypsy woman in a caravan, when suddenly she stopped singing and, turning deathly white, announced that she heard her husband approaching and as he was of a jealous disposition she was afraid he would kill Mr. Sharp. Cecil Sharp did not want to be killed, and there was nothing for it but to present a bold face. Opening the caravan door, he shouted to the man: 'A happy Christmas to you. Stop a moment and listen. I've got your wife's voice in a box.' The man listened to the record of his wife's song and was so amazed and delighted that he forgot to kill Cecil Sharp, and instead they became great friends.

Another encounter with gypsies is worth recording, if only as an example of the persistence, accuracy and care which Cecil Sharp exercised when noting songs. In a letter to his wife from Minehead Vicarage, where he was staying with his friend, the Reverend Francis Etherington, 'as delightful a companion as man could have, witty and serious and most sympathetic', he writes (21. 7. 1907):

Yesterday we went to Simonsbath. We had decided to make our way over the moor to Withypool and were just wheeling our cycles up the hill when Etherington gave a penny to a very dirty but picturesque little child who took it and ran to a small cart that was under a tree down a little lane, and gave it to his father – evidently a gypsy. So I went up to him and chatted, and broached the question of songs. No! *he* didn't sing but his wife did, but she was in a house close by trying to sell some crockery. We waited, gave him baccy and played with a second child, a baby tied up in the cart. It was a peaceful little scene, and he showed us his stove and the contrivances for making a tent in which they camped out every night – only using his van during the winter. Presently out came the wife, Betsy Holland, aged 26, a bright, dark-eyed woman. The baby cooed with delight directly she appeared. We attacked her about the songs which she had learned from her grandmother. A little persuasion and she sat down on a stone, gave her baby the breast, and then began a murder song[1] that was just fascinating. Talk of folk-singing! It was the finest and most characteristic bit of singing I had ever heard. Fiendishly difficult to take down, both words and music, but we eventually managed it! I cannot give you any idea what it was all like, but it was one of the most wonderful adventures I have ever had. I photo'ed the baby and her, and she is mad to have the picture and told me they were making their way down to Cornwall via Bideford and Barnstaple. They will be at Bideford on Saturday, and I shall, I know, find it hard to keep away!

He evidently found it impossible, for four days later he wrote from Meshaw Rectory to Mr. Etherington as follows:

Well! I got to Barnstaple yesterday at four and then biked slowly on to Bideford keeping my eyes open, but seeing nothing of our draggle-taggles. Then I searched the waste places round Bideford till dusk, but could find them not, nor could I hear news of them from police, or other, people, nor from the post-office where I inquired. To bed, therefore, rather despondent in an expensive and uncomfortable hostelry . . . Then I made a plan of campaign and put it into execution this morning. I searched from 9 till noon, by which time I had got nearly five miles from Bideford. I then decided to give up chase, examined the map and took the road to Barnstaple, thinking perhaps they were still on the road. Directly I started, I found that the waste lands I had been examining extended along the road I was taking – a fact which I had not realized before. So I continued the search and there I found them!!!!
Tent up, three children (there was one asleep in the cart when we met them) rolling about in the grass, Betsy superintending the cooking over a large kettle, Henry eating a large dumpling with a pocket-knife. They received me quite quietly, both saying they were quite sure I would turn up! I stayed nearly an hour with them and they were perfectly delightful. She sang me three other songs which I noted down, but none comparable with the Simonsbath song. That she sang again to me, and I found I had noted it accurately, as I think it *can* be done in ordinary notation.
I enjoyed my visit to them immensely. . . . were very keen I should go and see her grandmother, aged 90, who still sings like a lark. They gave me a vague address in the neighbourhood of Honiton, 'Stafford Cottages'. Her name is Rebecca Holland. Rebecca may give me a different cadence to that tune: I have an idea it might end on A, not C, in which case it would be more regular; but I am not certain.

Rebecca was run to earth six weeks later, and although she had nearly forgotten the song she was able to sing enough to satisfy

[1] James Macdonald, (*Folk-Songs from Somerset*, 4th series).

Cecil Sharp that it was cast in the Lydian mode – the only example of that mode he had found in English folk-song.[1]

To conclude this chapter on folk-song collecting we give some personal reminiscences by the Reverend Francis Etherington which he wrote on the occasion of the centenary of Cecil Sharp's birth.[2]

My short experience of collecting with Cecil Sharp occurred over fifty years ago: it is strongly etched in my memory plates and is a great possession. In these few scattered reminiscences I should like to try to recapture some of the early freshness and expectant adventure of those primitive bicycling forays into unexplored regions where even a scare-crow in a cornfield might be expected to burst into unaccompanied song.

First let me describe the man as he is in my portrait gallery. He was graceful in movement with a slightly deliberate courtesy in greeting. His manner and bearing were such as to ensure a respectful welcome without destroying the lines of communication. But for me the great attraction was in his eyes which had that particularly focused expression that I always associate with sailors and their kind. Have you ever no-ticed the expression in the eyes of women who live in fishing villages and are used to standing before the cottage door looking out for the re-turn of the boats ? There is nothing restless or strained, but they are sure to pick up the first sign before the untrained observer is aware of the advent.

My part in the collecting was limited to that of introducer and 'taker down' of words. In this capacity I started out with him from my vicar-age at Minehead one fine sunny morning on a treasure hunt on Exmoor riding our well-loved bicycles. For me it was a real holiday. He was sufficiently my senior in years to make me conscious of a reverent thrill at being accounted a friend and he was already distinguished enough to make me proud to be in his company. We arrived at a cottage to visit an old farm worker who was said to have a store of old songs. We were expected, and the stone-floored kitchen was the reception room (praise

[1] Mr. Fox Strangways has supplied the following note to the song:
As this is the only song yet recorded which is quite definitely in the Lydian mode, it is worth mention that the melody is almost certainly not English. With a tonic C and an F# it emphasizes strongly the notes E and A, and so corresponds exactly with the well-known Indian Lydian, 'Hamir Kalian'. Sharp also records that it was 'fiend-ishly difficult to take down', a thing he has not said of any other song; and it seems likely that this was due to slides and graces that were almost certainly put into it. It has often been remarked that Hungarian gipsy music bears the same sort of relation to Indian that Romany does to Hindustani.
[2] *Journal of the English Folk Dance and Song Society*, vol. VIII, No. 4, December 1959.

be!) for granfer could only sing from his own chair by the sacred hearth. Otherwise we should have been chilled off in the small parlour with the horsehair sofa and the centre table with the family Bible and the wax flowers in a glass case surmounting it.

Granfer after the ritual preliminaries fixes his eyes upon the necessary point of vision and begins in a quavering voice which soon steadies down. Occasionally Sharp interrupts to secure a repetition, but when he learns that any such intervention invariably means a return to the beginning of the first verse he exercises strict economy in his demands for elucidations. In this particular case we were cumbered by the presence of a young male relative who was on a visit from a neighbouring town. He treated us as dealers in ancient scrap-iron and winked at us with a horrid suggestion of the sophisticated accomplice. When at last he insisted on producing a dreadful gramophone of his own with a record of the departure of a troopship Sharp's nerves gave way and with many apologies we escaped, making arrangements to return at a later date when the young man would have returned to his urban delights – and then a very rich harvest was gathered.

Occasionally it would be reported by a reliable scout that old So-and-so, who had a great store of songs and was withal a mighty man at the cider cask, might be persuaded to sing, but only when he had had the exact amount of stimulant necessary for intelligent expression. 'He's a cup too low' meant waiting; and 'a cup too high' meant packing up for that occasion. I have seen Sharp sitting in the bar parlour with his watch on the table waiting patiently till it was deemed the exact moment for another entry into the tap-room – tense with all the grave anxiety of a maternity doctor attending a difficult birth.

There were many disappointments as well as rich rewards for our labours. One afternoon we set out full of hopes in search of an Exmoor shopkeeper who was reported to be a good singer of old songs, but when we finally ran him to earth he proved his reputation to be built on 'The Anchor's Weighed', which he considered old enough to please any lover of the antique. He was, too, a talkative politician of a rather Jingo sort and drew an acid comment from Sharp as we hastily retreated from an unfruitful field. In my short experience this was the only occasion on which politics had any mention in our interviews. Sharp was himself a Fabian, but was, I think, more interested in life and people than in any formulated theories about them.

After that little explosion about the Boer War we cycled on in the mellow sunshine of the late afternoon into a roadside encounter with a gipsy woman who sang us the stirring murder song of 'James Macdonald' whilst she nursed her baby sitting on a heap of stones by the wayside. When we had noted the song and made friends with the various members of the family we cycled on to a village inn for rest and refreshment.

After our meal, Sharp with his straight pipe at that particular angle, which was as significant as the tilt of Lord Beatty's cap, went to the piano, and I had the treat of my life. From his pencilled notes he played the tune over slowly and very softly – then there was a swift sort of disentangling and a bold unharmonized statement emerged. Then came the accompaniment. It was like watching an Indian craftsman doing that delicate beating of filigree silver work. It was indeed the setting of a jewel. And Sharp said nothing, but he would glance at me every now and then over his shoulder with that indefinable droop of an eyelid that expressed complete satisfaction in a joy that he invited you to share. That was the man at his most complete: the reverent artist, finding fulfilment in putting a beautiful thing in its right setting so that it would catch the light and give reflections of its own fires.

That sunset hour in an inn parlour has much meaning for me. I witnessed there both a gathering in and a setting free of many mysterious forces, and the experience awakened in me a new sense of values. The courtliness of life in the country cottages was revealed to me and I was made aware of the contrast between the delicate refinement of the countryman's art and the heavy vulgarity of much that went by the name of enlightened entertainment.

This may sound like laboured sentiment, but for me it is not so. In the past I had heard many folk singers. I had lived in a remote country village where I had attended many rural festivities. I had – Sharp forgive me! – even used my experience of local folk singers as a small reservoir for sundry humorous items which I used to contribute to my small circle in town. I had at one time thought of the countryman much as he was featured on the stage and in the music-hall, and I had failed to discover any beauty in the songs as I had heard them rendered at club walkings and village feasts. I was only aware of the fixed glassy stare of the singer – of the curious mechanical jarrings of his vocal apparatus. Judge then of my overpowering sense of discovery and revelation when I saw the craftsman working at this despised thing and holding up a real jewel.

That moment has never deserted me: the sense of delicate freshness, the suggestion of some faraway dreamy thing, so beautiful as to be true.

V

Folk-Song Crusade
1903 — 06

Be not like the empiric ant which merely collects nor like the
cobweb-weaving theorists who do but spin webs from their own
intestines; but imitate the bees which both collect and fashion.

BEYOND PUBLISHING their 'finds' little attempt had been made
by the early collectors to make the songs widely known. In fact, the
prevalent approach to folk song during the first decade of the
century was slightly tinged with antiquarianism and there were
some who felt that these precious objects must be protected from
common usage for fear of their vulgarization. Cecil Sharp, as we
shall presently see, was entirely opposed to this point of view.

He had been quick to sense the implications of the discoveries
he had made at Hambridge and he returned to London in the early
autumn of 1903 resolved to fan the dying embers of folk song into
a mighty flame which would shine throughout the land. This
involved the two-fold task of further collection – and this must
not be delayed – and bringing the songs back into the everyday
lives of the English people.

He started the latter task by making use of the facilities that lay
ready to hand; and on 26th November 1903 he gave a lecture on
folk song at the Hampstead Conservatoire, the first of the many
hundreds that he was to give in all parts of Great Britain as well as
in America. His illustrations were taken from the songs he had
recently collected in Somerset, beginning with 'The Seeds of
Love'; the singers were Mattie Kay, Helène de Sérène, Walter

Ford and Leonhard Sickert, with Cecil Sharp and Edward d'Evry accompanying. His suite of Morris dance tunes, scored for strings, bassoon and horn was also played by the Hampstead Conservatoire Orchestra.

The lecture was widely reported in the press and notably in the *Morning Post* (at that time one of the leading London daily papers), which as well as giving a long account of the lecture devoted a leading article to the subject of folk song, stressing the urgency of its collection. This article aroused considerable response including a letter from Ralph Vaughan Williams.

Mr. T. Lennox Gilmour, the second leader-writer of the *Morning Post*, who was also Lord Rosebery's private secretary and a practising barrister, was a friend of Cecil Sharp. 'The Fates,' says Mr. Gilmour, 'who presided over my birth, unkindly denied me the gift of music, but they gave me some sense of historic values and a certain capacity to respond to contagious enthusiasm. And was there ever a more attractive enthusiast than Cecil Sharp! His sincerity was crystal clear; his egotism was not for himself but for the cause.' The two had a talk about this cause a few weeks later; and the next day Mr. Gilmour invited Cecil Sharp to come and see him. He thereupon read him his 'interview' of the day before. Cecil Sharp listened and bubbled with laughter as he recognised in the formal statement his own arguments and asides. In allusion, no doubt, to this occasion he said that a statue ought to be erected 'To one who himself unable to distinguish "God Save the King" from "Pop goes the Weasel" yet gave his life to the advancement of Music'.

The interview, together with a leading article, was published in the *Morning Post* on 18th January 1904. Briefly, the views advanced were that the county councils might ultimately be approached, but as this would take time and the collecting of the songs was urgent, there should be some *ad hoc* organization to appeal for funds unless, perhaps, some philanthropist would provide them. Many letters followed. Mr. T. L. Southgate (a member of the Musical Association) protested that there was no need for an *ad hoc* organization, for the Musical Association, to which belonged the professors of music at our universities, the heads of the great schools of music, together with prominent musicians and notable amateurs, was well qualified to undertake the work. Then there was the Folk-Song Society, although admittedly its operations did not appear to have met with any distinct measure of success. To this Cecil Sharp replied that 'the professors of music', etc., are just the very people who had hitherto shown the least interest in the subject, as was exemplified by the fact that since its foundation in 1874 no paper on folk music had been read before the Musical Association. As for the Folk-Song Society, there had been no meetings for two years; it was moribund.

The Folk-Song Society protested next day that it was alive but impecunious: while Lucy Broadwood wrote privately to Cecil Sharp that she was delighted with his 'pricks and pokes at our Folk-Song Society'. The persistent Mr. Southgate pressed his suggestion of a sub-committee of the Musical Association. Others turned it over in imagination to the Folk-Lore Society; others, again, said that the songs were not worth collecting.

When all had had their say, Cecil Sharp, supported by a leading article, presented his ultimatum (the *Morning Post*. 12. 2. 1904):

All your correspondents agree that if the old songs which are still being sung by the peasantry of England are now to be preserved for the benefit of future generations, they must be collected without delay. This general admission inspires the hope that at least some determined effort will really be made to complete a collection of English folk-song. The further point – as to the most suitable society to undertake the work – is of minor importance, so long as the work is done effectively and done quickly.

He criticizes the Folk-Song Society for its comparative inactivity and claims that it has done little to further the objects for which it was founded more than five years ago. He complains that no attempt has been made to systematize the private efforts of individual collectors, no appeal for public support has been issued, nor has any effort been made to popularise the movement.

On 8th February, 'An Outsider' (possibly the leader-writer mentioned above) suggested a meeting of the Folk-Song Society to which others, not members, should be admitted and the Society be reconstructed on a broader basis. The Society's answer to this broad hint was to put Cecil Sharp on the Committee and Miss Lucy Broadwood was appointed Honorary Secretary.

This was not the last of Cecil Sharp's press controversies, as will be seen in the following chapters. Meanwhile, he had reason to be satisfied with the present campaign, for it had brought folk song to the notice of the public and it had played a big part in galvanizing the Folk-Song Society into life. The Society resumed publication of its *Journal* in 1904 with a collection of folk songs from Yorkshire contributed by Frank Kidson, followed the next year by a volume of songs from Somerset contributed by Cecil Sharp. The Society continued to publish its *Journal* until 1931, the year preceding its amalgamation with the English Folk Dance Society (see p. 193). The *Journal of the Folk-Song Society* – eventually thirty-five numbers in six volumes were published – is an invaluable repository of English folk songs; and it also has some good collections of Gaelic songs from Scotland, Ireland and the Isle of Man.

Although Cecil Sharp proved to be the most prolific collector of English folk songs, he was by no means the only one, as is shown by the successive pages of the *Journal of the Folk-Song Society*. The names of Lucy Broadwood and Frank Kidson have already been mentioned. Others soon followed. Of these mention must first be made of Ralph Vaughan Williams.[1] He was a lifelong friend and supporter of Cecil Sharp and in their views on folk-song they were in entire sympathy. Vaughan Williams began collecting in earnest at Ingrave in Essex on 4th December 1903 when he heard 'Bushes and Briars'. This was only three months after Cecil Sharp had heard and noted 'The Seeds of Love'. It seems extraordinary that Vaughan Williams did not immediately tell him of his discovery – for fear of boring him! Others who made important collections and contributed to the *Journal* during the first quarter of the century were Miss A. G. Gilchrist, Percy Merrick, H. E. D. Hammond, Percy Grainger, G. B. Gardiner, George Butterworth and E. J. Moeran. Miss Gilchrist and Miss Broadwood were the two who made the greatest contribution to scholarship in the pages of the *Journal*.

The suggestion made by Cecil Sharp in his press campaign that the efforts of individual collectors should be systematized and assisted by public funds was not followed up; and collectors continued to work on their own and with their own resources. Some financial support would certainly have eased the burden of collectors and particularly that of Cecil Sharp who was without private means. The lack of systematization was not so serious,

[1] For an account of Vaughan Williams's work in connection with folk song, see Chapter III of *The Works of Ralph Vaughan Williams* by Michael Kennedy (London, 1964).

since at that time it was an unwritten law among collectors that they should not trespass on each other's geographical domain. In this respect Cecil Sharp was even more scrupulous than was demanded by the conventions of his day. For instance, the publication of his children's singing-games appeared under the joint authorship of Alice B. Gomme and Cecil J. Sharp, although the games are drawn entirely from his collection. The reason for this quixotic action was that since Lady Gomme was the recognized authority on the subject he was diffident of poaching on her preserve.

Cecil Sharp lost no time in publishing the songs he had collected, or rather a selection of them. The first volume of *Folk-Songs from Somerset* appeared in 1904. This was followed by four more volumes, the last published in 1909.[1] Cecil Sharp was entirely responsible for the music, including the pianoforte settings, of all five volumes. Charles Marson for the preface and the texts of the first three volumes only. For, unhappily, the friendship which had meant so much to both men came to an end at the close of 1906.

During the course of preparing their joint work for the press, they had been unable to meet often and correspondence had led to misunderstandings which were not confined to their joint authorship. Cecil Sharp makes complaints about the 'one-sided correspondence' and Charles Marson, probably irritated by his insistence, writes (2. 12. 1904):

The egg is hatching now and we must make the best of a horrid welter and try to keep our hair on in the pains of parturition, and not upbraid each other for the difficulties, when both instruct the printer and each other and all at full steam.

Charles Marson's name does not appear on Volumes IV and V of *Folk-Songs from Somerset*. He insisted on relinquishing all his rights to Cecil Sharp, because, as he wrote to him (7. 11. 1906): 'You have done the lion's share of the work and deserve any rewards there may be.' Cecil Sharp endeavoured to persuade

[1] The work was printed   and published as 'author's   property' by the Wessex Press, Taunton,   after   having been refused by several large publishing firms. It is now out of print, but most of the songs are to be found in *English Folk Songs*, Centenary Edition, 1959.

Charles Marson to change his mind, but he steadfastly refused and finally Cecil Sharp had no option but to accept the position.

The immediate cause of the breach was a well-intentioned but indiscreet move on Cecil Sharp's part in which, overstepping the bounds of friendship, he criticised and attempted to influence Charles Marson's conduct in a private family matter. Cecil Sharp admits (12. 11. 1906) that he may have written clumsily, 'but I am not master of the pen like you'. However, the break was irreparable. Cecil Sharp to Charles Marson (9. 11. 1906): 'There have probably been mistakes on both sides: our tempers are too individual and autocratic for us to run smoothly in harness.' They did not meet again and Cecil Sharp went to Charles Marson's funeral early in 1916.

In 1905, Cecil Sharp collaborated with the Reverend Sabine Baring-Gould by undertaking the musical editorship of the fifth edition of *Songs of the West*, a book of 121 songs collected in Devonshire and Cornwall by S. Baring-Gould, H. Fleetwood Sheppard (who died in 1901) and F. W. Bussell. Cecil Sharp is responsible for about two-thirds of the accompaniments.

Sabine Baring-Gould, born of an old Devonshire family, became rector of Lew Trenchard in North Devonshire in 1881. His interest in folk-song represents only one corner of an alert mind. Miss Priscilla Wyatt-Edgell, a friend of the family has written:

In his song-collecting I think he used to get the tunes along with the words, but said he was much hampered by not being more of a musician. Mr. Sharp said that after he had altered or added to the original words, as often happened, because they were 'outway rude' or fragmentary, he was apt to forget that his alterations were not part of the real song.

It was a funny household at Lew. They were an amusing family: I only knew Daisy, Veronica, Barbara, Cicely, Diana, Joan, Felicitas, John and Julian; but there were lots more than that – twenty altogether, they said. 'All regular English girls,' said Mr. Sharp, 'and each one prettier than the other.' He was wrapt up in his books, and sometimes forgot the names of his children; they were wrapt up in 'Papa' and did not always trouble to learn the names of his books. If the girls could not get to a meet in any other way, they would ride the cart-horses; and it was said in the county that nothing kills a Baring-Gould. A horse that kicked their dogcart to pieces was objected to by them only because they said they could not take Papa out with it again. The lake at Lew, with precipitous, rocky sides, was the place where the elder children used to amuse themselves setting the younger ones adrift in tin baths. None of them could swim. 'And Papa used to sit in his study and say he knew we should all be drowned.'

I think he was a very kind squire. I have stayed there for one of his village dance evenings, and he walked about and talked to them all, and saw to it that they all had cider afterwards.

He did not care only for old things: in his church he had a good new carving as well as old. He set an artistic daughter to paint the panels of the screen with Saints of whom no one but himself had ever heard. The Service was perfectly plain; no music except a hymn, and, as a contrast, a sort of plain-song Creed which he sang himself.

The following year (1906) the collaboration between Sharp and Baring-Gould resulted in the publication of *English Folk-Songs for Schools*. The songs are drawn from their collections; and the Introduction explains that 'this collection has been made to meet the requirements of the Board of Education, and is composed of melodies strictly pertaining to the people, to which words have been set as closely adhering to the original as was possible considering the purpose of the book'. Cecil Sharp was not very happy about the texts in this volume, although he had given his approval to them. But he felt, rightly or wrongly, that the all-important thing was to get the songs with their beautiful melodies introduced into the schools, and if a slight bowdlerization of the words would assist that object, then the end justified the means.

Cecil Sharp and his contemporaries have been criticized by a later generation for not printing the texts exactly as they noted them, as was their invariable practice with the tunes. Some explanation is necessary.

In their preface to the first volume of *Folk-Songs from Somerset* the editors explain that:

the collection is presented as nearly as possible as it was taken down from the lips of the singers; in the tunes with exact fidelity. We have not tried to reproduce by spelling the Somerset dialect, because such attempts are useless to those who know, and merely misleading to the ignorant. Anything like a peculiar use, archaisms, and rare words, we have carefully kept. In a few instances the sentiment of the song has been softened, because the conventions of our less delicate and more dishonest time demand such treatment, but indication has been given, and we plead compulsion and not desire in these alterations. We have corrected obvious slips of grammar, and reluctantly changed the weak perfects into strong ones.

The words and tunes in Sharp's autograph are in the Library of Clare College, Cambridge.[1] When this is compared with the printed version it will be seen that some alterations were inevitable. First, there are songs in which there is an irregularity of rhythm in the corresponding lines of the successive stanzas. In the original, the singer has probably altered the tune to fit, but when it comes to publication it is usually not practicable to print more than one form of the tune and variants have to be omitted. Secondly, there is the case of incomplete or obscure texts. The latter are often the result of the singer's having substituted for an unfamiliar, and to him meaningless, expression one that is more familiar to him. This accounts for the startling announcement made by a gypsy singer in the opening bars of a carol that 'God went to France on Sunday': in other versions, 'God made a trance on Sunday'.

Thirdly, as has already been mentioned, there are songs in which the sentiment was too outspoken for the conventions of the early part of this century. In the present day there would be little to give offence. For, contrary to general belief, obscenity as distinct from forthrightness is rare in English folk song; and in the few cases in which it does occur it is due, in Cecil Sharp's opinion, to the influence of the broadside ballad. The delicate and often poetic symbolism which occurs from time to time in English folk song is very far removed from sophisticated *double entendre* and it cannot in any sense be regarded as indecent.

Cecil Sharp's principle in editing the texts was not to 'improve'; he restricted himself to slight verbal alterations when words and tune did not fit, to the correction of grammatical errors and to the collation of different versions of the text when the single example was incomplete or unintelligible. He recorded in his published notes the changes he had made.

Charles Marson set out with the same conscientious purpose of keeping as closely as possible to the original texts, but occasionally his poetic mind got the better of him; and here and there his literary lines are as incongruous as hothouse orchids in a bunch of

[1] There ate also photostat copies in the Harvard University Library and the New York Public Library, and microfilm copies in the libraries of the University of California and Cecil Sharp House, London.

wild primroses. In later editions, Cecil Sharp reverted to the original words or made a closer adaptation wherever possible.

Cecil Sharp was scrupulous in presenting the tunes as he had heard and noted them, yet in the songs that were published for general use, as distinct from those for scholarly purposes, he added pianoforte accompaniments. His action in so doing needs no apology although some comment may not be amiss.

The older generation of traditional singers in England, and also in America, always sang without instrumental accompaniment. In fact, they have on occasion been known to fail to recognize one of their own songs when it has been harmonized. English folk song was conceived as a melodic entity and does not need harmonic support, although many of the tunes have harmonic implications. However, Cecil Sharp's aim, as we know, was to get the songs known and widely sung; and in the early days of the revival no one outside traditional circles would have thought of singing a folk song without accompaniment. Indeed, such is the domination of harmony in the present century that many will mentally supply their own harmonization on hearing or reading an unaccompanied tune; and if not versed in the folk-song idiom this 'mental' harmonization may well have the effect of disguising the essential qualities of the tune.

In setting the songs, Cecil Sharp's aim was not to add embellishment to them, but to make explicit what was implicit in the melody itself. As he wrote to his friend, Francis Etherington: 'I get right inside these beautiful melodies when I try to translate them into harmony, and the further you dive into them the more seductive and glorious they appear.' He always had in mind the voice of the singer and the effect that the singing had made on him. He kept his harmonization to the mode in which the melody was cast and avoided modulations and chromaticism.

His accompaniments have sometimes been criticized as being amateurish, halting and devoid of workmanship. This might possibly be true of some of his earliest attempts, but his technique improved with experience and it is interesting to compare his later settings with those of the earlier period. Praise has outweighed criticism. In 1906 Vaughan Williams wrote (in the *Morning Post*):

Those who study Mr. Sharp's accompaniments will realize how rich in suggestion the folk-song may be to a well-equipped and sympathetic musician.

And in 1932:

It has sometimes been questioned whether Sharp had the creative impulse in music, but his accompaniments to my mind clearly show that he had. His creative impulse came from the tune he was setting. That is why his settings are often better than those of more technically gifted arrangers, because they come to the task as composers and let the suggestions started by the tune run away with them, and so forget the tune itself . . . In all the best of Sharp's accompaniments it is the tune that counts and the arrangement falls into its proper background. In some cases his accompaniments look wrong, and sometimes even when played by themselves seem awkward, but they stand the important test that they make the tune sound right. It is true that Sharp had little of the conventional technique of pianoforte accompaniment, as taught by professors of composition, but he developed a technique of his own whose complete success was only hindered, I think, by his fear of the harmony professor.

Again, Bernard Shaw in a letter to Cecil Sharp, asking if the idea of a topical *Beggar's Opera* would interest him, writes:

Many of your accompaniments are both ingenious and exquisite; but that accomplishment is not really so rare nowadays as your power of finding out the strength of a melody and giving it its value in a simple and sure way without rich, thick modern chords – you know what I mean unless you are a deplorably modest man.

Cecil Sharp had definite views on folk-song accompaniment. He wrote at one time to Balfour Gardiner (20. 10. 1907): 'I am not against chromatic treatment if it can be used without destroying what seems to me to be the essential nature of the folk-melody. But I feel it is very difficult – for me impossible – to use modern chromatic harmonies without going astray.' He was, however, broadminded enough to be able to appreciate methods other than his own. 'I do not always like his way of harmonizing,' he wrote after studying a book of folk-songs,[1] but it is always musicianly and the rest is a matter of taste.' Again, he made a point of meeting Mr. Howard Brockway – hitherto a stranger to him – for fear that some remarks he had made about his accompaniments might have annoyed him. He told Mr. Brockway frankly that he had criticized his settings of Kentucky songs[2] as being too sophisticated, but he

---

[1] *Songs from the Hills of Vermont* collected by Edith R. Sturgis, music arranged by Robert Hughes (New York, 1919).
[2] *Lonesome Tunes*, Loraine Wyman and Howard Brockway (New York, 1916).

wished him to know that he admired his musicianship, which, he said, far surpassed his own.

He very rarely used his right of veto in the arrangement of folk tunes collected by himself and certainly never when it was intended to treat the tune as a theme for composition. On one of the very few occasions on which he declined to allow the songs he had collected to be treated with 'rich thick modern chords', his correspondent questioned his right of refusal. In reply, Cecil Sharp said:

> The law protects the product of the man's brain, not the thing on which he exercises his wits. . . . A collector who takes down a song from a folk-singer has an exclusive right to his *copy* of that song . . . It is always open to someone else to go . . . to the same source, exercise the same skill and so obtain a right to *his* copy.

This incident is worth mentioning if only because it is so often claimed that the collector claims copyright in the song; and if that were true it would seem grossly unjust that a song which belongs to the nation, if to anyone, should be held to belong exclusively to one member of it. But it is not true. All that the collector claims, and has, is the right in the copy that he himself has made, which has involved him in time and money as well as wits.

The first volume of *Folk-Songs from Somerset* is 'dedicated by permission to Her Royal Highness the Princess of Wales' – later Her Majesty Queen Mary.

During the years 1904–07 Sharp had the honour of giving musical instruction to the royal children at Marlborough House. The class consisted of Their Royal Highnesses The Prince of Wales, Prince Albert, Princess Mary,[1] and nine other children, and later, Prince Henry.[2] It was held twice a week during the summer and the lesson lasted for three-quarters of an hour. This covered notation (on the blackboard), rhythm by clapping, pitch (scale solfeggi), instruction in breathing and enunciation and the singing of rounds, national songs and folk songs. In his annual report for 1905 Cecil Sharp writes:

> that both Prince Edward and Prince Albert have keen ears for a tune will be apparent if reference is made to the appended list of fifty songs which

[1] Later, the Duke of Windsor, King George VI, and The Princess Royal.
[2] Afterwards the Duke of Gloucester.

they are now able to sing. The speed with which they will fasten upon and learn a new tune has continually surprised me and I consider that Prince Edward and Prince Albert are both possessed of a musical instinct and ability far above the average.

The following letters are among his correspondence:

York Cottage,
12th November 1905

Dear Mr. Sharp,
   Thank you very much for the book of songs you were kind enough to send me. I shall be glad to learn some of them when we go back to London. I can play the first page of the book you got for me. I like it very much.

With kind remembrances I remain
Your little friend
Mary.

York Cottage,
2nd February 1907

Dear Mr. Sharp,
   Thank you so much for the nice singing books you sent us. It is very kind of you. We learnt two new carols at Christmas. David[1] had learnt them at Osborne. We shall have to learn some of the songs out of it. We are coming up at the beginning of March. Please give my respects to Mrs. Sharp.

We remain,
Yours very sincerely,
Albert
Henry

[1] The Prince of Wales.

VI
Definitions
1906—07

Just as a doctrine only needs to be defined after the appearance of some heresy, so a word does not need to receive attention until it has come to be misused.   T. S. ELIOT, *Notes towards the Definition of Culture.*

CECIL SHARP'S ambition was to give to every English man, woman and child the opportunity of getting to know the songs. He was not content merely to bring them to the notice of scholars and musicians; he wanted them to be part of the everyday lives of the people no matter what their walk in life might be. He was convinced that the best way of achieving this end was to introduce the songs into the schools and he had for some time been advocating this. We have seen that in 1906 he published in collaboration with Sabine Baring-Gould *English Folk-Songs for Schools*; and two years later he started on a more ambitious venture when he persuaded Messrs. Novello & Co. to publish in their School Series a number of inexpensive books of folk-songs.[1]

However, as will be shown in the following pages, there were many stormy passages before the recognition of the genuine folk song and its widespread practice in the schools were assured.

In July 1905, the Board of Education had published a Blue-book entitled *Suggestions for the Consideration of Teachers and others concerned in the Work of Public Elementary Schools* (Cd. 2538) which included a

---

[1] The songs in this series were also published separately, the price at that time being as low as 2d. per copy.

chapter on 'The Teaching of Singing'. After discussing the various educational advantages to be derived from the singing of wisely chosen songs and the musical experience that is thereby gained, the practice of national or folk songs is recommended, as being

the expression in the idiom of the people of their joys and sorrows, their unaffected patriotism, their zest for sport and the simple pleasures of a country life. Such music is the early and spontaneous uprising of artistic power in a nation, and the ground on which all national music is built up; folk-songs are the true classics of a people, and their survival, so often by tradition alone, proves that their appeal is direct and lasting.

In the Appendix, lists of songs are given to which the attention of the teacher is invited.

When the Blue-book came to his notice, Cecil Sharp immediately rose to the challenge. In the hospitable columns of the *Morning Post* (19. 4. 1906) he gives a preliminary airing of his views, stating that 'while the precept of the Board of Education was admirable, its practice was deplorable' for after showing the great educational value of folk-songs it had published a list of songs suitable for use in schools in which there is scarcely a single genuine folk-song. He returned to the charge a month later in the *Daily Chronicle* (22. 5. 1906), contending that

To call such songs as these folk-songs is an abuse of language. They possess none of the peculiar glory of the folk-song . . . Whoever is responsible for the article and lists of songs has failed to distinguish the national song from the folk-song . . . Schoolmasters, in the belief that they are teaching folk-songs, will give the children the songs suggested in the Blue-book. The results, which folk-song enthusiasts have confidently predicted, will not of course follow. The experiment will be noted a failure, and folk-songs, without even a trial, will be branded as unfit for school use.

Sir Charles Stanford hotly defended the action of the Board in the *Daily Chronicle* on the following day and delivered this attack:

Archaeologists who have personally dug up an antique are apt to glorify it at the expense of those which have been dug up by their predecessors. This is the key to Mr. Cecil Sharp's reckless and unjustifiable attack upon the list of songs issued by the Board of Education. It issued a list of songs which are folk-songs, are songs of the people, and are songs of and for the nation, but which in his eyes have the disadvantage of having stood the test of a long life in the public ear; and if he wished his more recent discoveries of songs to reach the schools also, there is no better way than to begin with a list of those which have long been acknowledged as the back-bone of national music.

Apparently, Mr. Sharp thinks that folk-songs grew like trees in the fields, and national songs came out of human brains. He will find it hard to convince any musician of such nonsense . . .

Mr. Sharp is making the common error amongst archaeological musicians of mixing up practical necessities with interesting investigations. If he will stick to his excavating, we may be the richer for some antiques, but he need not, in order to exhibit them, relegate the Elgin marbles to the hayloft.

The following day (24. 5. 1906) Cecil Sharp replied:

Sir Charles has mistaken my contention. I agree, of course, that 'Tom Bowling' is none the less 'a people's song, because we know Dibdin to have written it'. But I deny, not that it is a people's song, but that it is a folk-song; that is, a song made by the people, as well as sung by them. The distinction is not academic; nor is it archaeological. It is intrinsic, for it distinguishes between two kinds of music that are fundamentally different from one another. And to this even Sir Charles Stanford must agree, unless he is prepared to place 'Tom Bowling' and 'Heart of Oak' in the same category as 'The Golden Vanity' and 'The Seeds of Love', or to couple 'Sir Patrick Spens' with Tennyson's 'Revenge' . . .

I am sorry that Sir Charles Stanford should credit me with believing that 'folk-songs grew like trees in the fields, and national songs came out of human brains'. 'Brains created both,' no doubt; but while the national song is the product of the individual, the folk-song has been evolved by the brains of countless generations of folk-singers and composers. The one is individual, the other communal and racial. They differ not only in the manner of their birth, but in the finished product.

Among the subsequent correspondents who supported Cecil Sharp's views was Ralph Vaughan Williams who 'as a collector in a small way' was delighted 'to see the distinction between the genuine folk tune and the "composed song" so clearly stated'.

A month later (28. 6. 1906 and 29. 6. 1906) Cecil Sharp again contributes articles to the *Daily Chronicle*, in which he gives a further exposition of the distinction between folk music and composed music, and stresses the importance of folk music in general musical education.

One reason why we have in England no national school of music is because we have so unaccountably neglected our folk-music . . . Little or no effort to repair this deficiency is made . . . at the musical colleges . . . Our younger musicians are now studying English folk-music, and . . . their compositions already reflect the new and inspiring influence; but how much better it would have been if . . . they had absorbed it in their young days.

Some light relief to the heated controversy was provided by an article in *Punch* (30. 5. 1906) in which fictitious correspondents express their disapproval of the songs recommended. One of them reads:

Why should the Board of Education go out of its way to affront that large and constantly increasing section of the community which has foresworn meat food by including that disgustingly carnivorous paean 'The Roast Beef of Old England'? (Signed) G.B.S.

(It was, of course, well known that Bernard Shaw was a vegetarian.)

Public controversy again flared up later in the year, sparked off in the first instance by an article of Miss A. E. Keeton in the *Morning Post* (22. 8. 1906) with the provocative title, 'Why England has no Folk-Songs' and its equally provocative content in which she claims that England has no national school of music because she has no folk songs. Cecil Sharp (who at the time was reaping a rich harvest of folk songs in the Quantock region of Somerset) and many others, including Lucy Broadwood and Vaughan Williams, refuted Miss Keeton's statements. So also did Dr. (later Sir) Arthur Somervell (5. 9. 1906), who was at the time Chief Inspector of Music to the Board of Education and bnod out largely responsible for the controversial *Suggestions for the Consideration of Teachers*. He fastens on the concluding paragraph of Miss Keeton's article in which she criticizes the two volumes of *Folk-Songs from Somerset* which had recently appeared. But why, asks Dr. Somervell, are these the only books to have been chosen? He twits Mr. Sharp with being a newcomer in the field and invokes the names of older collectors: experts such as Mr. Kidson,Miss Broadwood and Baring-Gould (the very people whose work had been referred to by Cecil Sharp in his recent letter to the *Morning Post*). Turning to the vexed question of the distinction between 'national' and 'folk'-songs, he declares that:

for the purposes of musical classification there is a distinction. For the purpose [of] . . .the widespread education of the coming generation, resulting in the power of musical self-expression, there should be none.

And as a parting shot:

> Mr. Sharp is constantly condemning the work of all collectors save those of a special school of recent origin – though he has curiously enough included in a song-book for schools[1] the best known of the very class of songs, the use of which he now deprecates.

Cecil Sharp (on 18. 9. 1906) answers the charges that have been brought against him and once again denies the assumption that he is averse to the use of national songs in the schools: his objection is to their being labelled folk songs.

Most of those who had collected or had made a serious study of folk song were in general agreement with Cecil Sharp's views, but few were willing to support him in his uncompromising con-demnation of the Board's action. The Folk-Song Society, in particular, was opposed to his attack on the Board and various members feared that his over-violence would result in stiffening the backs of those in authority. The matter came to a climax when Cecil Sharp learned that at a committee meeting, at which he had not been present, the following paragraph had been adopted for inclusion in the Committee's Report to the General Meeting of the Society:

> During the past year a very important step has been taken by the Board of Education, who, in their *Blue-book of Suggestions for the Consideration of Teachers* (1905) have for the first time recorded the im-portance of our National and Folk Songs in the musical training of children, and urge earnestly that such songs shall be taught throughout our country. This scheme, if consistently carried out, must become a powerful means towards cultivating a healthy musical taste, and cer-tainly claims the support of all who believe in the enormous influence exercised by Folk Music upon composers of all nations.

Cecil Sharp protested to the Honorary Secretary, Miss Broad-wood, about what he termed 'an unqualified blessing of all that the Board had done'. Miss Broadwood and other members of the Committee endeavoured to persuade him that there was no difference of opinion as to the general scheme and nothing had been said in the Committee's Report about the offending Lists of

[1] This refers to *A Book of British Song* (1902).

Songs. Cecil Sharp was obdurate and he forwarded an amendment to be brought before the General Meeting of the Society proposing certain alterations in the paragraph. This amendment was later withdrawn in favour of another moved by Dr. Vaughan Williams, proposing that the comment on the action of the Board of Education be referred back to the committee for reconsideration. This was not carried.

It would seem that Cecil Sharp had placed himself in the wrong by not making allowance for the fact, which had been emphasized by Miss Broadwood and others, that the lists in the Appendix of the Blue-book were headed 'Lists of Songs' and not 'Lists of Folk-Songs'. He appeared to the majority of the members of the Folk-Song Society to be dogmatic and to be forcing the pace – as indeed he was. Certainly, he showed himself to be lacking in diplomacy; but he was convinced, rightly or wrongly, that this was not the time for diplomacy. It was all-important, particularly at the outset of the folk-song revival, that there should be no mistake about the nature of the material that was being promulgated. He had also laid himself open to criticism in that he was fighting for a definition which he had himself ignored in his *A Book of British Song*. But that had been written four years earlier before he had come into contact with the living folk song and had become fully aware of its distinctive qualities.

Other folk-song collectors were likewise aware of these qualities, but since most of them were not vitally concerned with the promulgation of folk song they did not feel called on to take action. Also, since he was only one collector among several, and a particularly successful collector, he seemed to some to be aiming merely at self-advertisement. Nothing could have been further from the truth. It is significant that in later years when folk song and folk dance had become generally accepted as part of the national culture, he rarely took part in any Press controversy. 'Once you have gained your point it does more harm than good to keep on rubbing it in' was his advice to others and to himself.

Seven years later in 1913, when a revised edition of 'Suggestions for the Teaching of Singing' was being prepared by the Board of Education, Cecil Sharp was invited to offer his criticisms and suggestions.

One good result of the controversy was that it brought home to Cecil Sharp the necessity of giving full expression to the faith that was in him. This faith is made manifest in *English Folk-Song: Some Conclusions*, which appeared in October 1907.[1] 'I felt,' he said, 'the book *must* be written, and I went straight home from the meeting of the Folk-Song Society and wore out three fountain pens.'

The contents of the book have been thus summarized by A. H. Fox Strangways:[2]

All forms of mental activity proceed from the development by education of qualities that are natural and inborn. We shall, therefore, best gauge the musical potentialities of a nation by the utterances of those who are least affected by extraneous influences. Folk music is created by the common people, art-music is composed by the educated. 'Common' means 'unlettered' (not 'illiterate'), and the common people were once more numerous and more homogeneous than they are now. Was it the man or the community that invented the *words* of a song? Sir Walter Scott said, the man; the brothers Grimm said, the community; Böhme (*Altdeutsches Liederbuch*, 1877, pp. xxii, xxiii) said, 'one (nameless) man sings a song (words and tune) and others sing it after him *changing what they do not like*'. It is these italicized words that constitute the difference between communal and individual authorship. The individual composer, a nameable man, invents and criticizes, and his last draft may be very unlike his first. Communal invention is analogous: a nameless author and a succession of nameless singers, who criticize by the way they perform the song, correspond to the composer's successive drafts, and the final result may be very different from the original.

This joint authorship, or communal creation, is made possible by two things. It is open to anyone to sing a melody, but not everyone can play a sonata and no one man can play a symphony; and, sonata and symphony are fixed by notation, but the song is not. But if the song can thus be altered, may it not be spoilt as often as improved? It may. But the poor song dies out, nobody wants to sing it; the successes remain. The song is, in fact, evolved. Evolution has the three stages of persistence, variation, and selection. The folk-singer's well-known and remarkable memory makes for persistence, his fancy for variation, and the community selects. The process may be compared to the behaviour of a flight of starlings. The flock 'persists' in its unanimous course, individuals dart out from that and 'vary' it, and the flock 'selects' which, if any, individual it will follow. The flock of starlings is looking for a suitable place to roost in; the singing community is looking for a song which shall satisfy its understanding and its sense of beauty.

[1] Having failed to find a publisher, he published it himself with Barnicott and Pearce (The Wessex Press) as printers.
[2] *Cecil Sharp*, 1st and 2nd editions, pp. 64–6.

The chapter on the Modes is written to show two things: (a) that a melody which is in a mode need not be, and is not in folk-song, old in spirit (like the Church tones), though it may happen to be old in time; and (b) that if harmonization is employed, it ought to confine itself to the mode of the song. That on English Folk-scales sums up a large practical experience; it is concerned with the general behaviour of non-harmonic tunes, the identification of the tonic, and with the sense in which modal melodies modulate. That on Rhythms and Melodic Figures gives a probable explanation of some apparent irregularities.

The singer and his song are dying out, and what is to happen now? It is not too late; some thousands of songs are on record, and we might sing them and know them.

When every English child does so as a matter of course then, from whatever class the musician of the future may spring, he will speak in the national musical idiom. He will not write English music by going to English folk-song for his themes, though that would be all in the right direction. We must wait till the younger generation has absorbed folk-song. The publication by Bishop Percy in 1765 of forty-five ballads killed at a blow the cold formalism of the preceding age, as Wordsworth and Sir Walter Scott bore witness. Is it unreasonable to suppose that the present collecting and publishing of English folk-song will lead to a similar revival in music?

The book had been written in ill-health: some of it had had to be dictated owing to blindness caused by gout in the eyes. And he was fearful that his lack of skill in writing would fail to do justice to the subject. 'It is not much of a book,' he wrote to Miss Gilchrist (with his fourth fountain pen?) 'but it contains something that should be said; and although I realize that I have said it all very clumsily, yet on the whole I think it should be said so rather than not said at all.'

Many tributes reached him. Professor F. B. Gummere, whose *Popular Ballad* was published at about the same time as Cecil Sharp's *Some Conclusions*, wrote:

It is the sort of work that you have done which really counts. It is an unspeakable comfort to have a man who knows folk-song at first hand write such words about it as you have written.

And Gavin Greig (author of *Folk-Songs of the North-East of Scotland* and, posthumously with Alexander Keith, of *Last Leaves of Traditional Ballads collected in Aberdeenshire*, Buchan Club, 1925) addressed Cecil Sharp as:

the greatest dynamic in the folk-song world. You have been doing a magnificent work. Some of the older school would theorize without first-hand material and the discipline that comes from collecting it, while some of your younger enthusiasts do nothing but collect and cannot see the wood for the trees. What we chiefly want is workers who both collect and can generalize.

The press reviews make interesting reading. 'A bombshell amongst musicians' (*Guardian*, 27. 11. 1907) might serve as a general heading for them. On the whole, one might say that they are respectful but sceptical, or at least that the reviewers have reservations. 'His "conclusions" may not be everybody's but he has written a vigorous book which cannot be lightly laid aside,' writes Frank Kidson in *The Musical Times* (1. 1. 1908). The only really hostile criticism was provided by *The Times Literary Supplement* (23. 1. 1908) which, belittling the author as a 'late-comer' in the field, asks what he could know of folk song in England when he had examined only Somerset (suppressing the fact that he had found more there than anyone anywhere), accuses him of confusing modes and tones (when he had carefully distinguished them) and concludes with the comment that 'as a collector Mr Sharp deserves both praise and support, but he might well leave to others the work of analysing the treasures he has found'.

The book is probably not perfect – the pages on harmonization were written before he had had much experience – but it shows remarkable prescience. It was considerably in advance of anything that had appeared at that date; and it has not yet been superseded.

One cannot refrain from quoting here from a review of the 1954 edition by Professor B. H. Bronson, the outstanding authority on the 'Child' ballad:

Looking back, it seems almost incredible that these basic revelations are only a generation old. The twelve brief chapters of this extraordinary book, published less than fifty years ago, were like the first accounts of a voyage to a new world, and almost every page was news.

Re-reading now in historical perspective, one is deeply impressed by the book's vitality. What was news now quietly commands general assent as accepted doctrine. Sharp puts his case with the utmost simplicity, economy and clarity – and in a spirit that can only be called one of Faith.[1]

[1] *Journal of the International Folk Music Council*, Vol. VII, 1955.

Cecil Sharp's views on nationalism in music which are forcibly expressed in the penultimate chapter of his book were hotly contested by Ernest Newman some years later in *The English Review* ('The Folk-Song Fallacy', May 1912; followed by 'A Reply' by Cecil Sharp, July 1912, and 'A Rejoinder' by Ernest Newman, August 1912). 'What is the national musical idiom?' asks Ernest Newman and proceeds to disprove its existence. To which Cecil Sharp replies:

Art can only be built from below; the instinct for music cannot suddenly appear for the first time when civilization has attained the flowering stage; it must be innate in the nation and be present, therefore, in some form or other in all the earlier periods of its development.

Or as Vaughan Williams has put it:

How it can be imagined that it was of the slightest use to practise the art of music in a country where its very foundations were absent, passes my understanding.[1]

The struggle of Cecil Sharp and Vaughan Williams for the recognition of folk song as the foundation of national music had its counterpart in Hungary where already in the early part of the century Béla Bartók and Zoltán Kodály were collecting the folk music of their country and fighting against what Kodály has called musical colonization.

Among others who have supported Cecil Sharp's views on nationalism in music there was Sir George Dyson who has pointed out that 'cosmopolitanism is generally the overwhelming prestige for the time being of a particular national brand'.[2]

And of interest is a letter (1. 3. 1906) which Cecil Sharp received from Prince Kropotkin, the Russian geographer, writer and revolutionary, who was living in exile in England. In acknowledging *Folk-Songs from Somerset* which Cecil Sharp had sent him, he writes:

The work of collecting songs from the people . . . seems to me the very best way for creating some day a national music in this country. Without that preliminary work – under the present separation between town and country – the growth of national composers would not be possible.

[1] *English Folk Songs* (The English Folk Dance Society, 1912).
[2] *Cecil Sharp*, 1st edn., pp. 114–15.

VII
The Morris Dance
1905 — 10

Hark hark I hear some dancing
And a nimble morris dancing;
The bagpipe and the morris bells
That they are not far hence us tells.
Come let us all go thither
And dance like friends together.

THOMAS WEELKES

WE MUST NOW revert to the folk dance: first, the Morris Dance
which since that memorable occasion at Headington in December
1899 had been lying more or less dormant in Cecil Sharp's mind.
At that time his only experience of dancing had been ballroom
dancing – he was a first-rate waltzer – and the Alhambra ballet
which he had enjoyed as a young man; but these were no more
than pleasurable entertainments. At a later date he was a great
admirer of Ruth St. Denis and of the Diaghilev ballet; but the
Headington Morris was his first intimation that dance was an art
comparable with that of music. Still, he felt that it was outside his
province and he was in any case fully occupied with the songs. In
the circumstances some special incentive was needed to spur him
into action.

In September 1905, he had a visit from Miss Mary Neal, the
Honorary Secretary of the Esperance Working Girls' Club,
Cumberland Market, St. Pancras, the members of which were
mostly seamstresses. Music, dancing and acting were among the

IX William Kimber, Headington Morris dancer

X William Wells, Bampton Morris dancer and fiddler. From a
drawing by Sir William Rotherstein

activities of the Club, but they had come to the end of their resources, when their musical director, Mr. Herbert MacIlwaine,[1] chanced to read an article in the *Morning Post* on Cecil Sharp's work in the collection of folk-songs. Miss Neal has described her interview with Cecil Sharp in a pamphlet, *Set to Music* (undated) which is dedicated to

I went to see Mr. Cecil Sharp to ask his advice as to whether these songs would be suitable for a Working Girls 'Club. In ten minutes we were deep in the subject of Folk-Song, and I was told that I should be surprised at the way in which English boys and girls would understand and appreciate their own Folk music.' They will learn it,' said Mr. Sharp, 'by a sort of spiritual sixth sense'. . . I went away having made up my mind to the experiment, although I confess that the music looked to my inexperience very difficult. In a fortnight I wrote to Mr. Sharp telling him that I could only express the result of the first few lessons by saying that the Club had gone mad, that they were perfectly intoxicated with the music.

After this rapturous reception of the songs Miss Neal's next step was to find dances 'which would fit in with the spirit of the folk song'. Cecil Sharp was only too ready to help and he told her of Mr. William Kimber. Without delay Miss Neal visited him at Headington and arranged for him and a cousin to come to London and teach the Morris Dances to the girls. This was also a great success. In two evenings they had learned enough to be able to give a performance at their Christmas party of Morris Dances, folk songs and singing games: these last from Mrs. (later Lady) Gomme's collection. At Laurence Housman's suggestion, the performance was repeated at the Small Queen's Hall on 3rd April 1906, when an introductory lecture was given by Cecil Sharp. This aroused great interest and Miss Neal was besieged with inquiries as to how the songs and dances could be learned.

---

[1] Herbert C. MacIlwaine was the son of Canon MacIlwaine of Belfast Cathedral. He spent some years in Australia on a cattle-station and in journalistic work. He returned to England about 1895 and devoted himself to literary work, publishing several novels in which the scenes are laid in Australia. He became Musical Director of the Esperance Club in 1901 when Miss Pethick, who had been responsible for the singing, gave it up on her marriage to Mr. (later Lord) Pethick-Lawrence. As Mrs. Pethick-Lawrence, she was a well-known leader of the suffrage movement. Mr. MacIlwaine retired in 1908 and was succeeded by Mr. Clive Carey. He died in middle age on 1st October 1916.

Arrangements were made for some of the club members to give instruction in the dances; and performances continued to be given in London and also in the provinces. Cecil Sharp was delighted at the turn of events. Although he had no official connexion with the club he co-operated with it whenever opportunity offered and often lectured at its performances.

In July 1907, Cecil Sharp published in collaboration with Herbert MacIlwaine, *The Morris Book*, Part1; and the accompanying music with pianoforte arrangements by Cecil Sharp was issued as *Morris Dance Tunes*, Sets 1 and 11. *The Morris Book* is dedicated to 'our friends and pupils, the members of the Esperance Girls' Club' and the authors give credit to Miss Mary Neal who 'not only made the venture possible in the beginning, but with her powers of organization gave it a reach and strength that neither of us could have given'. The book contains the description of eleven dances, eight of which are from Headington. The Introduction, of which the literary style seems to be that of MacIlwaine rather than of Sharp, informs us that the book is not 'primarily for the information of the archaeologist and scholar, but to help those who may be disposed to restore a vigorous and native custom to its lapsed pre-eminence'.

The historical account of the dances, supporting faint-heartedly the theory that the Morris is Moorish in origin and was brought to England in the reign of Edward III, does not show signs of deep research, and it was revised and rewritten by Cecil Sharp in a second edition published in 1912. In this later edition extensive alterations were also made in the technical description of the dances in view of the wider experience gained, and three dances from Bidford, now thought to rest on insecure authority, were discarded, though full credit was given to Mr. D'Arcy de Ferrars for his revival of them in 1886.

In the first edition the notation was based partly on the dancing of the Esperance Club girls. This was obviously unsatisfactory and in the second edition the Headington dances were noted solely and directly from William Kimber, while the rest of the dances were noted similarly from the traditional performers: a practice from which Cecil Sharp never deviated in subsequent folk-dance collections.

The Headington dances and tunes collected by Cecil Sharp, eventually numbering some twenty, were all noted from Mr.

William Kimber, who had played the concertina at Headington when Sharp first saw the Morris in December 1899. The Headington 'side' had been disbanded in 1887, and revived again in 1899 at the instigation of Percy Manning, whose scholarly researches have contributed much valuable information on the subject. The 'revived side' included four dancers from the old team. William Kimber was not one of them, but his father, who had danced as far back as 1847, had been foreman of the 'side', and with his fiddle and concertina had often understudied the regular fiddler.

It was from his father that William Kimber had learned the tunes and most of the dance movements, and it was no doubt from him that he inherited his love of the dance. The following account of a visit to his father is taken from a letter which William Kimber wrote to Cecil Sharp in February 1915, sending him at the same time an old drinking-cup:

He was in the best humour I have ever seen him. We had talked some time about one thing and another, and all at once (I wish you had been there) he says, 'I think I have got something you can have that you can turn into a bob or two.' Of course I wondered what it was going to be. He went to the same old place where he had taken out the old peeling horn and brought out this cup. This is his version:

'You see this! Well this is one of the oldest relics of Headington; Morris and Wheatley. This cup belonged to old Mr. Hall of Noke, him that used to play the whittle and dub for us to dance. It was made from the horns of some animal out of Holton Park. When old Hall finished, this cup was left at the pub at Wheatley, and the old Benefit Club took care of it till it was broken up. Then one of the Wheatley men knowing that I should prize it brought it to me. I remember drinking out of it before I knew your mother – that's over fifty years ago. Old Tom Carter wanted it, so did Joe Trafford, but I kept it. But you can have it now, we shall never see such times again.'

I wish you had been there to have seen him holding this cup and talking to it just as if it were human and very dear indeed to him. I told him where I was going to send it, and he said, 'Perhaps I may tell him that cup's history some day when we meet.' I asked him its age and as near as he can say, according to old Mr. Hall's version, it is no to 150 years. I think you are entitled to all this old stuff, but if it is no good let me have it back.

William Kimber has been described as 'a bricklayer by trade and a dancer by profession', but above all he was an artist, and that no doubt made the bond of friendship between him and Cecil Sharp – a friendship which continued unsullied for twenty years.

Shortly before *The Morris Book* was published William Kimber wrote to Cecil Sharp as follows:

Last week I heard a piano playing opposite where we are working, and I listened, and to my astonishment it was playing 'Country Gardens'. I could not work. I had to lay my trowel down and listen. My mates said, 'What's up, Merry (my nickname)?' Of course they did not know the tune. I said, 'Wonder where they got that from.'

One man said, 'It was "Vicar of Bray"', but, as I told him, there was a lot of difference in 'Country Gardens' and 'Vicar of Bray' – as much as chalk and cheese. . . .

Well, the young lady kept on playing for ten minutes, so I just gave them a turn on the planks, up close to the chimney, for we were just preparing to build the chimney stack. . . . I had a good mind to ask her where she got it from but another thought struck me. I wondered if the book was out, so I thought that by writing I should know for certain.

His frequent letters to Cecil Sharp always drew sympathy and often opened a helping hand.

I was delighted to hear from you and to hear of your splendid luck in the matter of pigs. May they thrive and grow up handsome and profitable pigs,

Cecil Sharp writes at one time; and at another, when the luck had not been so good,

I am indeed sorry to hear that you are in the wars again. Things do seem to have gone awry with you of late. Never mind, cheer up and perhaps some day the clouds will roll by. I am quite sure that if a man sticks to his job through bad as well as fair weather somehow or other things come right. But he's got to stick to it. Let him grumble if it lets off steam. I often do this! In the meanwhile I send you a small present in the hope that it will help things a little.

The correspondence which is a big one is, however, mainly concerned with their mutual interest in the dancing. The philosophy of folk dancing has perhaps never been better expressed than by Kimber, when in a letter to Cecil Sharp (11. 4. 1921) he inquires how the dancing is progressing and adds:

I was reading the other day how they are going to modify classic dancing. I thought to myself, 'Ours doesn't want any modifying at all – they are now what they were and always will be.'

And that same year he writes bemoaning the fact that he is spending such a quiet Christmas time:

> Not a single step of any sort. I was only thinking the other morning as I passed Sandfield Cottage and looked at that room where you and I had our first tune, it doesn't seem all that time ago. Yet, it's too true, a great many things have happened since then. And the old saying of bricklayers crossed my mind, 'And you, old boy, have at last wound up your line' – which makes a fellow feel just a bit down. As I always said, when I could not have a dance, I hope it would soon be over; for if ever one loved a certain thing in this world, the one thing I loved was the Morris.

But the time had not come for William Kimber to 'wind up his line'. He lived another forty years and made friends far and wide through his fine dancing and his native wit. He died on Boxing Day 1961 in his ninetieth year, just thirty-two years after his first meeting with Cecil Sharp. His coffin was borne to his grave in the snowbound church at Headington by a younger generation of dancers wearing their Morris Dance regalia.

We must now leave for a time this engaging personality and return to the Esperance Club whose activities loomed large on Cecil Sharp's horizon for the next few years. Its work continued to prosper and by 1908 a number of Club girls were being employed in teaching. The chief teacher was Miss Florrie Warren, an exuberant and vital dancer, whose help in noting the dances is acknowledged by the authors of *The Morris Book*.

On 14th November 1907, Miss Neal called an informal Conference at the Goupil Gallery 'to talk over plans for putting at the service of all who wish for it, this great possession of English folk music in which it has been our good fortune to be the means of reviving active interest'. At the meeting, which had received the blessing of *Punch*, Mr. Neville Lytton took the chair.[1]

Cecil Sharp had grave misgivings about the proposed plans and he urged that any organization which might be formed should not include collecting as one of its objects since that was a matter for experts. A resolution was adopted that a Society be formed for the development and practice of folk music and a provisional committee, which included Cecil Sharp, was appointed to draw up

---

[1] Also present were Mr. Laurence Bradbury (proprietor of *Punch*), Mr. E. Burrows (H.M. Inspector of Schools for Sussex), Lady Gomme, Mrs. Pethick-Lawrence, Lady Constance Lytton, Miss Neal, Mr. Sharp and others.

rules. He proposed to this committee that the Society should be representative of all who were associated with the subject and that its rules should allow for the periodic retirement of the members of the Executive. He did not carry the committee on these points; and it did not report to another meeting. A Society, with which Cecil Sharp was not associated, was formed the following year, with the title of the 'Association for the Revival and Practice of Folk Music', under the Presidency of the Earl of Lytton, with Mr. Neville Lytton as Chairman, Mr. Laurence Bradbury as Honorary Treasurer and Miss Neal and Mr. MacIlwaine as Honorary Secretaries. Mr. MacIlwaine retired shortly after his appointment.

There appears to have been some misconception in the public mind concerning the scope and purpose of the Association; and Miss Neal wrote in the *Saturday Review* (11. 4. 1908) in reply to a letter from Mr. John Runciman that the Association did not propose to do the work of collecting folk music 'which is being done so admirably by experts such as Cecil Sharp'.

In the course of noting and describing the dances, Cecil Sharp had obtained a deeper understanding of them; and he had become correspondingly more critical of the standard of dancing and teaching as practised by the Esperance Club. There was a fundamental difference of attitude towards the dances between him and Miss Neal. He was fretted by her lack of artistic discipline and she, no doubt, considered him to be unduly repressive. Throughout 1908, relations between the two became increasingly strained, though they still co-operated on several occasions, notably at an entertainment at Stationer's Hall, organized by the Worshipful Company of Musicians.

In May 1909, at the instigation of Mr. Burrows, folk-song and folk-dance competitions were held at Stratford-on-Avon at which Cecil Sharp was invited to adjudicate, as the sole adjudicator in the singing and together with members of a panel, which included Miss Neal, for the dancing.[1] The day after, Miss Neal wrote to Cecil Sharp to tell him that while he had been talking to the children she had been vividly reminded of the early days of their friendship. She grieved at the misunderstandings which had arisen and

[1] Incidentally, this was the present biographer's first acquaintance with folk dance and song. My sister Helen and I, who were attending the Shakespeare Festival, visited the competitions out of curiosity, and we stayed the whole day, spellbound by what we saw and more particularly by what we heard. The dancing was crude, but the music, the like of which we had not heard before, enchanted us.

hoped that they might be able to continue to work together. Sincere attempts were made on both sides to find a *modus operandi*; and Mr Burrows and Mr Lytton, both of whom ultimately resigned from Miss Neal's Association, did what they could to promote co-operation. They both realized that Cecil Sharp had the knowledge and the musicianship, but they hoped that use could be made of Miss Neal's enthusiasm and organizing ability.

It was a great disappointment to Cecil Sharp that he was unable to continue his collaboration with Miss Neal. He was however convinced that her lack of artistic sensibility would always prove a stumbling-block. Her interest was centred in her club and she approached the subject entirely from the philanthropic point of view. So long as young people were getting enjoyment from the dances, the standard of performance mattered little or nothing. As he wrote to a friend early in 1910:

> Enthusiasm that is uninformed seems to me to be capable of working more harm in the world than anything else. The fact is, philanthropy and art have nothing in common, and to unite them spells disaster.

Meanwhile the need for a body of trained teachers had become urgent, for the Board of Education in its revised syllabus of Physical Exercises (1909) had given official recognition to the Morris Dance. We may believe that Cecil Sharp was partly instrumental in bringing this about. Mr. E. A. G. Holmes was then Chief Inspector to the Board. He has been described by one who knew him as 'an educationist of the first order, a poet and a man of broad sympathies . . . Perhaps the greatest Chief Inspector the Board has ever had since the days of Matthew Arnold'. Mr. Burrows arranged for Cecil Sharp to meet Mr. Holmes and we are told that he made the most of the opportunity and that Mr. Holmes was favourably impressed.

It had not originally been Cecil Sharp's intention to play an active part in the teaching of the dances, but he had under-rated the difficulties and dangers of popularization. He now realized that it would be impossible to safeguard the tradition unless he himself had direct control over the teachers. In the Physical Training Department of the South-Western Polytechnic Institute (later the Chelsea Physical Training College) he found an organization which would supply him with a potential body of trained teachers;

and in September 1909 a School of Morris Dancing was established with Cecil Sharp as Director. Its objects were:

(a) to form classes in morris dancing;

(b) to train, examine, and grant certificates to teachers of morris dancing;

(c) to keep a register of certified teachers, lecturers, etc., and to give advice and disseminate information respecting folk-dances, folk-songs, children's singing-games, etc.

The Head Mistress of the College was Miss Dorette Wilkie, a woman of imagination and broad outlook. She at once perceived the practical value of Cecil Sharp's gospel and throughout their association her encouragement and sympathy were of real help to him. She gave him a free hand and he made good use of it. He gave personal instruction to the College students and members of the staff, assisted by occasional visits from William Kimber; and by the time the School opened Cecil Sharp was provided with a competent body of teachers. Also he was able to draw on the students[1] to illustrate his lectures.

My sister Helen (afterwards Mrs. Douglas Kennedy) and I were among the outsiders who attended the classes. At that time I was in charge of a children's 'Guild of Play' connected with the Mansfield House Settlement in Canning Town and my motive in learning the dances was to pass them on to the children. But with the very first step of the very first dance I knew that this was something which concerned me personally. Cecil Sharp, who was always on the look-out for likely disciples, immediately spotted my sister and me and fanned our enthusiasm by his words of encouragement.

Other members of the class were Miss Maggie Muller and Miss Peggy Walsh (later Mrs. Kettlewell). After a few months we felt that we needed more scope for our energies than were afforded by the Chelsea classes and so the four of us and a few other friends got together for weekly practices. These took place at the drawing-room of our house in Westbourne Terrace; and our long-suffering parents stood by while we rolled back the rugs and removed the

---

[1] Several of the students who taught and danced for Cecil Sharp at that time continued to work for him after they left College. These included Miss Helen Kennedy (Mrs. Kennedy North), Miss Olive Lett (Mrs. Cranko) and Miss Marjory Sinclair who has only recently retired from active teaching.

surface of the slippery parquet floor with a plentiful supply of Vim.

In April of next year (1910), we formed ourselves into a Folk-Dance Club, hired the Portman Rooms in Baker Street and gave a performance at which Cecil Sharp lectured and Mattie Kay sang. For the occasion we bullied some male cousins and other acquaintances into letting us teach them a few country dances and, with some apprehension on the part of their instructresses, they appeared with us on the platform. The success of its first venture, which drew an audience of five hundred, encouraged the Folk-Dance Club to further activities. It gave a number of small private performances and, in November 1911, a public performance at the Kensington Town Hall. In addition, the Club conducted classes in folk dancing. Cecil Sharp gave a general blessing to the Club and kept its activities under his supervision. These eventually led to the formation of the English Folk Dance Society, an account of which will be given later.

VIII
Controversy
1910—12

οὐ καλὸν ὦ φίλε πάντα λόγον ποτὶ τέκτονα φοιτᾶν,
μηδ᾽ ἐπὶ πάντ᾽ ἄλλῳ χρέος ἰσχέμεν· ἀλλὰ καὶ αὐτὸς
τεχνᾶσθαι σύριγγα· πέλει δέ τοι εὐμαρὲς ἔργον.[1]

BION, *Frag.*

THE YEAR 1910 was a critical one for Cecil Sharp. Now that he was actively concerned with the dance as well as the song, pressure of work had become very great. So at the end of the summer term, persuaded by his wife, he resigned his post at Ludgrove, which he had held for eighteen years, and henceforth he devoted himself entirely to folk music. It says much for his faith in the movement and for Mrs. Sharp's self-sacrificing devotion to her husband that this step was taken when the Ludgrove teaching was his only regular source of income. Apart from that he had only royalties and lecture fees to depend on, and many lectures were given *gratis*.[2]

It is interesting to note that Cecil Sharp never sought a change of work merely for the sake of change. As he wrote much later to his daughter Joan:

[1] You want a pipe made? Well then, try my plan:
   Don't hand it over to another man
   To make; make it yourself. You'll find you can.
[2] Mrs. Lindo (Miss Mattie Kay) wished it to be known that her fee was always paid after these lectures, even if it left nothing, or less than nothing, for Cecil Sharp.

On principle I do not believe in change. In this matter I have always allowed events to dictate to me rather than attempt to control them myself. I can think of but few cases in my own life when I have deliberately forced a change – perhaps it might have been better if I had. But . . . it seems to me that normally change waits on development; I mean that as one gains experience in one's work extension of opportunity is natural – and pretty sure to offer itself – and then being natural the change is of the best kind.

During 1910, lectures both on the song and the dance greatly increased. The latter were illustrated mostly by students from the Chelsea Physical Training College supplemented by members of the Folk-Dance Club.

The attendances of the Chelsea classes also continued to grow. The one that was chiefly prized by those who were chosen to attend it was the Tuesday evening 'Experimental' class conducted by Cecil Sharp himself, when he used to try out the various dances that he had recently collected. From week to week we eagerly awaited this class, never knowing what exciting experience might be in store for us. When the School first opened, its repertory of dances was very small, being restricted to the Morris Dances from Headington and a dozen or so Country Dances. The major part of Cecil Sharp's dance collecting (of which an account will be given in the next chapter) was done between the end of 1909 and 1914.

Miss Neal was equally busy at this time with classes and performances. Altogether, folk dancing was very much in the public eye. The press was flooded with articles and interviews and with letters on the subject, not only from the two principals but also from their adherents. The Association for the Revival and Practice of Folk Music had been superseded by the Esperance Morris Guild, thus emphasizing the close connexion between the Esperance Club and Miss Neal's general dance propaganda. In order to correct a false impression Cecil Sharp wrote to the *Morning Post* (1. 4. 1910), disclaiming any connexion with the Guild and urging that the dances should be accurately taught by accredited instructors. Miss Neal's response is:

It behoves those of us to whom has been entrusted the guidance and the helping of this movement for the renewal of beauty in life to tread reverently, and to see to it that the blighting touch of the pedant and the expert is not laid upon it. As the folk music and dance and drama are communal in their origin and the work of no one individual, and have come from the heart of the unlettered folk, so the handing on of them and the development should also be left in the hands of the simple-minded and of those musically unlettered and ignorant of all technique (*Vanity Fair*, 14. 4. 1910).

And in an interview in the *Morning Post* (5. 5. 1910), after denying that it is a personal matter between Mr. Sharp and herself, she says:

It is merely an example of a deeply rooted, age-long controversy which is always going on. It may be described as the difference between the form and the life, the bookman and the workman, between the pedant and those in touch with actual life itself. Certainly it is necessary to be possessed of technique and experience in collecting folk-songs, but, in my opinion, any average person of intelligence can collect a Morris Dance, and, having seen a traditional dancer, is quite able to say whether the dance has been handed on in a correct form. To me it seems as unreasonable to talk about an expert in Morris Dances as to talk about an expert in making people happy.

Cecil Sharp's response was to criticize the exposition of Morris Dances as given by the Esperance Club and to point out the difficulties by which the collector is beset and the need for expert knowledge, in order to 'appraise the traditional value of the revived dance, to detect the faked dance, or to exercise a wise discrimination with regard to corrupt dances'. And so it went on. Even the technicalities of the Morris step were publicly discussed, the subject being raised in the first instance in the *Westminster Gazette* (May 1910) by 'Oxoniensis' who, having seen the Morris performed at Headington 'in all its traditional dignity' with a straight leg and a spring from the ankle, was critical of the step as danced by the members of the Esperance Guild. Miss Neal protested that the members were performing the step correctly. Cecil Sharp on the other hand denied that there was any traditional authority for raising the thighs and moving the legs violently up and down after the manner of a high-stepping horse. Thereafter, 'straight' and 'bent' legs were bandied about almost as party cries.

Some months later, in October 1910, Miss Neal endeavoured to strengthen her position by seeking evidence which might throw doubt on the infallibility of Cecil Sharp's expert knowledge. Accompanied by Clive Carey, Francis Toye and a shorthand writer, she visited Headington and talked to some of those who had previously danced in the Morris. Her inquiry was directed towards finding out (1) whether in the Morris step the free leg should be straight or bent; and (2) whether William Kimber, Junior, was an authentic traditional dancer. On the first point the evidence was conflicting; on the second, it showed that Kimber had danced not with the old team but only after the revival had taken place. This was true, but it leaves out of account that he had learned the dances from his father (see p. 71). Miss Neal sent her notes[1] to Cecil Sharp, who wrote in acknowledgement that there was nothing in them that threw any doubt on Kimber's authenticity and that 'in technical matters it is far better to go by what dancers *do* than by what they *say*'. William Kimber's comment to Cecil Sharp was:

> Please keep up your spirits. I will stick to you like a leech, and would like to stand in any hall in London and face the biggest audience so as to explain the truth.

The notes were also sent to the Governors of the Shakespeare Memorial Theatre at Stratford-on-Avon, but apart from a lengthy correspondence involving a number of busy people there were no direct consequences. But the incident added to the distress of mind which Cecil Sharp was already suffering on account of the prolonged controversy. He knew he was on firm ground, but he dreaded 'a long wordy warfare which no one will understand'.

In the summer of 1910, the Governors of the Shakespeare Memorial Theatre invited the Esperance Guild to hold a Summer School, with public performances, at Stratford-on-Avon in connexion with the Shakespeare Festival. The intention of the Governors was to make this an annual event, believing that it would attract visitors to Stratford. The question then arose as to who should direct future Schools: Miss Neal or Mr. Sharp. Mr. (later Sir Archibald) Flower and Mr. (later Sir) Frank Benson who was responsible for the theatrical performances considered the matter. Both were impressed with Miss Neal's organizing ability, but they feared that the inaccuracy with which her dancers had been charged might sully the reputation of the Festival. At Frank Benson's suggestion they tried to draw up a definition of the

---

[1] A copy of the notes and Cecil Sharp's comment on them are to be found in his manuscript Dance Notes, i. pp. 247–255.

Morris step for Miss Neal and Cecil Sharp to sign. This, of course, came to nothing.

The ultimate decision rested with Mr. Flower and for the next eighteen months or so he was besieged on all sides by the warring elements. One can but admire his patience and composure. Cecil Sharp had great esteem for him. He described him to a friend as 'one of the nicest men I have come across for a long while. He is a man of great capacity, modest, as honest and straight as an English-man should be, and a man of strength of purpose, fearless and courageous'. Mr. Flower's chief advisers were Mr. Lee Mathews, a musician and businessman, who was strongly in favour of Cecil Sharp, and Mr. Benson who was equally strongly in favour of Miss Neal. Mr. Flower invited Cecil Sharp to meet them both at Stratford-on-Avon in November 1910. It seems that they were favourably impressed by what he had to tell them, but no definite decision was made until some months later.

At the beginning of 1911 Cecil Sharp talked of throwing up every-thing and emigrating to Australia. He was in poor health with his asthma getting steadily worse; his eldest daughter Dorothea was seriously ill; the family was in straitened circumstances; and the prospect of effecting a lasting revival of English folk dance seemed to be dwindling owing to the misconceptions and misunderstand-ings that had arisen.

Prospects gradually brightened. In May the family moved to Uxbridge on Dorothea's account, where she slowly recovered her health. Cecil Sharp had a fine, large room for his study and enjoyed digging in the garden when he was at home, but the constant journeys to and from town were tiring.

In July he was told he had been awarded a Civil List Pension of £100 a year in consideration of his services in the collection and preservation of English folk songs. This was a welcome addition to the family income, which was then £500 a year, including his wife's patrimony. A friend who was instrumental in getting the pension wrote to him:

I wish you could have seen the document we sent to the Prime Min-ister. It was the most remarkable collection of distinguished names I have ever seen – about 30 in all – and I am certain more would have signed if they had been asked, only we were advised that with such a list we need go no further. . . . You have admirers in all sorts of unexpected quarters.

This recognition was all the more gratifying seeing that the professed musicians as a body ignored him; and even the article on Folk-Song in the 1910 edition of Grove's *Dictionary of Music and* Musicians had no mention of his name.[1]

Meanwhile Cecil Sharp went on with his propaganda and continued to give all over the country lectures illustrated by students of the Chelsea Physical Training College and the Folk-Dance Club. In July 1911, at the Festival of Empire held at the Crystal Palace, London, he gave a series of lectures and organized demonstrations of dancing and singing-games, the latter being performed by children from the Brompton Oratory School brought by Father Kerr. A suite of Morris Dances for military band was arranged especially for the occasion by Gustav Holst. This was by no means Holst's first arrangement of English folk music. Already in 1907 he had written the *Somerset Rhapsody* for orchestra based on tunes collected by Cecil Sharp, which had been written at Sharp's request and was dedicated to him; and in 1909 Holst's pianoforte accompaniments to *Folk-Songs from Hampshire* collected by George B. Gardiner were published in the *Folk-Songs of England* series edited by Cecil Sharp.

At the Crystal Palace performances and at some others about this time, men took part in the country dances and performed solo Morris jigs, but there was as yet no complete Morris team or 'side', as it was called. Morris dancing by women is completely contrary to the tradition and it may seem strange and illogical that he who was such a stickler for tradition should have countenanced it. George Butterworth used to say of Cecil Sharp that he had a genius for compromise; and that in a sense is true. Although an idealist he did not allow the absence of ideal conditions to stultify his actions. At the time, women were available and men were not.

[1] When in 1918 Cecil Sharp was asked if he would allow his biography to appear in the American Supplement, he replied: 'It is nice of you to wish to include my name, but I do not quite see what I have to do with the American volume, seeing that I am an English musician and am merely temporarily a visitor here. If my name and work were worthy of mention in the *Dictionary*, the proper place would, of course, have been in the English volume. The only part of my work which might, perhaps, be mentioned in your part of the publication is that which I have done in the way of folk-song collecting and publishing in America and that, it seems to me, could be mentioned under the heading of folk-song or folk-dance.'

In any case, he did not condemn women's Morris – and in that he had the backing of William Kimber. He always explained that it was not the real thing but a translation of it; and it could be a very beautiful thing in itself. There was, too, the practical aspect. He was dependent on women teachers. In the early days, most men dancers had been taught by women and certainly one could not complain of the results. Classes for men had been started at the South-Western Polytechnic during 1910, but it was not until the beginning of 1912 that a men's Morris side appeared in public. It was always more difficult to attract men to the ranks than to gain women adherents and right up to the time of the Second World War the revival suffered from a grave lack of proportion between men and women dancers.

A later illustration of what George Butterworth called Cecil Sharp's genius for compromise was his action in having gramophone records made of the dance tunes, thus enabling them to reach a far wider public than they would otherwise have done. He even agreed to the tunes being arranged for piano-accordion.

Miss Neal spent the early part of 1911 lecturing in America. She found on her return to England that she no longer had the whole-hearted support of the Governors of the Shakespeare Memorial Theatre. She therefore resigned her position as Honorary Secretary of the Festival Association pending a conference which the Governors proposed to call for the purpose of discussing the divergent views on folk dancing. In June 1911, Cecil Sharp's programme was substituted for Miss Neal's. He describes the opportunity as 'a grand one and I mean to make the most of it'.

The School was held for four weeks in August. It was an unforgettable experience for those who took part in it. I was fortunate enough to be there as a member of the teaching staff; others were Miss Mattie Kay (for the singing), Miss Helen Kennedy (sister of Douglas Kennedy and now Mrs. Kennedy North), Miss Peggy Walsh (now Mrs. Kettlewell) and my sister Helen (now Mrs. Douglas Kennedy). For about five hours each day, sixty or seventy people met in the seclusion of the 'Parish Parlour' and the Council schools for classes in Morris, sword and country dances and singing-games. There were also lectures, a daily gathering for

XI(a) Henry Cave,
a Gloucestershire fiddler

XI(b) Another Gloucestershire fiddler

XI(c) Henry Taylor, Longborough
Morris dancer

XII   Charles Benfield, of Bledington, Gloucestershire.
A portrait drawn by A. van Anrooy, R.I. (see p. 97)

folk songs directed by Cecil Sharp from the pianoforte;[1] and a country dance party was held at the end of each week. Weekly performances (or demonstrations as we used then to call them) were given in the Memorial Theatre Gardens. Among the visiting dance groups who took part were a traditional country dance group from the neighbouring village of Armscote; a rapper sword dance team trained by Mr. Phillips Barker; and a group from my children's club in Canning Town. These children had hitherto been no farther afield than Epping Forest and I was glad to be able to give them the delight of this outing. It was a very small return for their having been indirectly the cause of my discovering the joys of English folk dancing.

The School was repeated for one week during the Christmas holidays. 'I wonder if ever we shall have just such another week,' wrote Cecil Sharp to Mr. Flower; and George Butterworth, who was one of the students, pronounced it as one of the few occasions when he had lived in a really musical atmosphere. It is difficult to convey the enchantment of those early Vacation Schools at Stratford-on-Avon when with Cecil Sharp as pilot we found ourselves embarking on undreamed voyages of discovery.

Towards the end of 1911, Cecil Sharp felt the time had come to form a national organization which would be independent of any other body. He therefore suggested to the members of the Folk-Dance Club that it should be dissolved, making way for a bigger and more representative society and that a public meeting should be called to bring this society into being. The main responsibility of carrying out this plan fell on my sister Helen and myself. We had had very little experience of organization and while we were highly flattered at the honour that was being paid us we felt quite inadequate and the thought of the public meeting

---

[1] It was of such a gathering that W. D. Howells wrote in his *The Seen and Unseen at Stratford-on-Avon* (Harper, New York, 1914): '. . . One of the ballads was so modern as to be in celebration of the *Shannon's* victory over the *Chesapeake* in the War of 1812, when the American ship went out from Boston to fight the British, and somehow got beaten. It had a derisive refrain of 'Yankee Doodle Dandy O', and whether or not the lecturer divined our presence, and imagined our pain from this gibe, it is certain that the next time he gave the ballad to be sung, he adventurously excused it on the ground that it possibly celebrated the only British victory of the war. Nothing could have been handsomer than that, and it was the true Shakespearian spirit of Stratford where fourteen thousand Americans come every year to claim our half of Shakespeare's glory.'

filled us with alarm. However, Cecil Sharp left nothing to chance and he planned and discussed with us every detail of the preparations.

On 6th December 1911, a public meeting was held at St. Andrew's Hall, Newman Street, with Mr. T. Lennox Gilmour in the Chair. At this meeting the following resolution, proposed by Cecil Sharp and seconded by Lady Gomme was adopted:

That a Society, to be called The English Folk Dance Society, be established, having its headquarters in London, with the object of preserving and promoting the practice of English folk-dances in their true traditional form.

Cecil Sharp emphasized the artistic character of the movement and the importance of a high standard of teaching and execution, and summarized its objects thus:

The instruction of members and others in folk-dancing; the training of teachers, and the granting of certificates of proficiency; the holding of dance meetings for members at which dancing shall be general, and of meetings at which papers shall be read and discussed; the publication of literature dealing with folk-dancing and kindred subjects; the foundation, organization, and artistic control of local branches in London, the Provinces and elsewhere; the supply of teachers and providing of lectures and displays to schools, colleges and other institutions ; the technical and artistic supervision of the Vacation Schools of Folk-Song and Dance at Stratford-on-Avon, organized by the Governors of the Shakespeare Memorial Theatre.

A committee[1] was appointed. A guarantee of £112 was promised, but was not called upon. Mr. Wilfred Mark Webb (of the Selborne Society) offered the Society temporary accommodation at his offices in Bloomsbury Square, and this was accepted for a period of six months.

We now propose to depart from the chronological sequence of events and to defer to Chapter X the story of Cecil Sharp's direction of the English Folk Dance Society. We must, however, mention here that the Stratford-on-Avon Summer Vacation

---

[1] Mr. Hercy Denman, Mr. A. D. Flower, Lady Gomme, Miss Maud Karpeles, Mr. Perceval Lucas, Mr. Cecil Sharp, Mrs. Arthur Sidgwick, Mr. G. J. Wilkinson, Dr. R. Vaughan Williams and Miss Helen Karpeles (Hon. Secretary). Subsequently Mr. George Butterworth and Miss D. Wilkie were added to the Committee; Captain Kettlewell was appointed Honorary Treasurer and Miss Walsh (Mrs. Kettlewell) Secretary.

School of 1912 was again directed by him and was held under the
auspices of the Society. During the course of the School, on 12th
August, the long-awaited conference was convened by the
Governors of the Shakespeare Memorial Theatre. With Mr.
Flower in the Chair, the speakers included Mr. (Sir Amherst)
Selby Bigge (Secretary to the Board of Education), Dr. (Sir)
Arthur Somervell, Mr. (Sir) Frank Benson, Dr. Ralph Vaughan
Williams, Mrs. Mary Davis, Lady Margesson, Miss Neal and Mr.
Sharp. The Chairman opened the meeting by saying that he hoped
the Conference would assist the Governors to find points of
agreement on the three following questions:

(1) Was it wise to establish the School of folk-dancing?
(2) If so, what standards should be set?
(3) Had Stratford special opportunities for encouraging such
a school?

Cecil Sharp said that the subject attracted ethnologists, educa-
tionists, scientists and philanthropists; that the most important
aspect was the artistic, and that every other aspect of the subject
was subservient to this. He looked upon collectors and teachers as
trustees whose duty it was to take these arts of folk song and
dance from a small body of the peasantry and to pass them on to
the whole nation as accurately and as reverently as possible. 'Have
your ideal clear and try to carry it into effect' was his guiding
principle.

Frank Benson pointed to the danger of over-emphasizing the
art side at the expense of the unconscious joy side. Their way,
according to him, lay 'between the Scylla of academic perfection
and the Charybdis of the untutored joy of the savage'. Miss Neal
had been working in wildernesses of bricks and mortar and had
brought joy and gladness to many hearts. He hoped that the
Conference might result in drawing these two leaders more closely
together.

Ralph Vaughan Williams held the view that every art, if it is to
be of value, must be based on something that is natural to the
human being and that if we are faithful to the tradition we shall be
teaching something which is spontaneous and sincere. The
Reverend Francis Hodgson proposed that a National Board of
Folk Song and Dance should be formed with Mr. Sharp and Miss

Neal on the directorate; and Miss Neal replied that she was prepared to assist in putting such a scheme into action.

The Chairman, in summing up, said that if a School of Folk Dance were to be established it was essential that the instruction given should be accurate. No one dissented from this view. The Conference may have cleared the air somewhat, but, as one would have expected, nothing tangible came of it; and Miss Neal and Cecil Sharp continued to work independently through their own organizations. The Esperance Club continued its activities until 1914, but during the war these lapsed and were not afterwards revived.

As an epilogue to the controversy we would mention that, in 1921, Cecil Sharp invited Miss Neal to a Festival which was being given by the English Folk Dance Society and at the same time he wrote:

I have not forgotten that you and I started this business together many years ago . . . nor do I forget the pleasant way in which for the first few years we worked together. It is true that afterwards we found it necessary to part company owing to a difference of opinion, which I am quite sure was as sincere on your part as it was on mine. Nevertheless I prefer to dwell on the period when we co-operated and to relegate to the back of my mind the subsequent happenings.

Miss Neal was unable to attend the festival, but she wrote a friendly letter in reply. Their paths did not cross again[1]

A great many pages of this book have been filled with the conflict over the presentation of the Morris Dance; and the reader may very well be asking himself whether it was a matter of such vital importance and whether Cecil Sharp might not have been less adamant. It must, however, be remembered that in collecting and reviving the dances and songs he felt he was discharging a solemn trust. He considered it more important 'to appeal to a small percentage in the right way than to the whole of the nation in the wrong way'. His insistence on accuracy was not mere pedantry. As an artist he realized that form and spirit are bound together and that to tamper with the form might easily destroy the content.

It was not always understood by his contemporaries that he was

[1] Miss Mary Neal died in 1944. In 1937 she was appointed Commander of the Order of the British Empire (C.B.E.) for services in connexion with the revival of folk songs and folk dances.

fighting for the establishment and recognition of a standard and not necessarily a uniform conformity to that standard. As he wrote to a fellow folk-song collector:

I think it is very easy to be too touchy about the vulgarization of things like folk-songs which one loves. A lover of Beethoven's music must feel the same if ever he thought of the way his favourite composer's music is being rendered in Crouch End, Hornsey, etc. If anything good is to be made popular, many things will happen which will shock the sensitive feelings of the elect. This is inevitable and must be accepted. I accept it in this case because I believe so sincerely in the innate beauty and purity of folk music that I am sure it cannot really be contaminated, but that it must and will always do good wherever it finds a resting-place.

And when, later on, after the dance was established, an enthusiastic dancer asked him in horrified tones whether he realized how badly it was taught in the—shire schools, he was sympathetic but unmoved. He merely asked her if she was aware how much bad teaching of Shakespeare and of arithmetic there was in these same schools. But to his own staff he showed the other side of the picture. He pointed out that the scraping and scratching of a street-fiddler could do no harm to music, because no one, however unmusical, would be likely to mistake that for the sort of thing that was to be heard in the Queen's Hall; but in the absence of a generally accepted standard of folk dancing any shortcomings on their part would be attributed not to themselves but to the art which they were presenting.

Incidentally, the contention of his critics that accuracy and joy were incompatible would be immediately refuted by anyone who had been taught by him or who had danced under his direction. It was perhaps not so much a question of accuracy as truth. With the eye of an artist Cecil Sharp was able to differentiate between the essentials and accidental accretions. Of his notations of the songs, Professor B. H. Bronson has written: 'There has never been a collector with such quickness and tact in seizing and accurately reporting essential melodic characteristics from individual singing. His copy strikes a mean between the typical and idiosyncratic that is almost ideal.'[1] He exercised the same understanding in the folk dance.

The last few chapters have shown that on more than one

[1] *The Traditional Tunes of the Child Ballads*, vol. I, p. xxii (Princeton, 1959).

occasion Cecil Sharp was in conflict with his fellow-workers and the impression left in the mind of the reader may be that he was of a quarrelsome disposition. Those who knew him well would emphatically deny this. He was a fighter and a fearless one; and during a great part of his life he was faced with issues that had to be fought, but these issues never arose from mere touchiness on his part. Dogmatic he may have been, as are most who hold strong convictions, but he was never unreasonable and he was always ready to listen to criticism. It must at the same time be admitted that his polemics were often vehement and were occasionally enlivened with a kind of schoolboyish invective. During the last twelve years of his life, although he had many difficulties to contend with, his passage lay through calmer waters and he was able to devote himself to the work that lay before him without the distraction of any major controversy.

IX
English Folk Dances and Folk-Dance Collecting 1906—14

Dauncing (bright Lady) then began to be,
When the first seedes whereof the world did spring,
The Fire, Ayre, Earth, and Water did agree,
By Loues perswasion, Natures mighty King,
To leaue their first disordered combating;
And in a daunce such measure to obserue,
As all the world their motion should preserue.

Since when they still are carried in a round,
And changing come one in anothers place;
Yet doe they neyther mingle nor confound,
But euery one doth keepe the bounded space
Wherein the Daunce doth bid it turne or trace:
This wondrous myracle did Loue deuise,
For Dauncing is Loues proper exercise.

SIR JOHN DAVIES (1569–1626), *Orchestra*

IN THE FOREGOING chapters we have been guilty of putting the cart before the horse, for, with the exception of the Headington Morris, we have given no information about the dances that Cecil Sharp was propagating nor about his methods of collecting them. In the present chapter we shall endeavour to repair this omission.

As we have seen, he first encountered the Headington Morris on Boxing Day 1899 and he started to note the dances some six years later. In the years to follow he brought to light many more examples of the Morris Dance as well as other types of English folk dance; and the wealth of material that he eventually gathered must have surpassed his fondest imagination.

The dances fall into two main categories: (1) ritual and ceremonial dances and (2) social dances. The dances in the first category, which embrace the Morris Dance, the Sword Dance and certain Processional Dances, are performed traditionally at certain prescribed seasons of the year by picked teams consisting of men only wearing special costume. The Country Dances, which comprise the second category, are performed by men and women together on any occasion when they meet for social recreation.

Although the folk dance appealed to Cecil Sharp mainly as a form of artistic expression, he was also deeply interested in its anthropological and folkloristic implications and in its historical background. He did intensive research on these aspects of the subject and the various introductions to his folk-dance instruction books contain much valuable information concerning the origin and history of the dances. One can but regret that he did not live long enough to achieve his ambition of writing a definitive work on the English folk dance.

He has said that the folk dance constitutes 'a riddle of which the answer, if we could but read it, would materially add to existing knowledge of the religious ideas and ceremonies, the dim faiths, fears and aspirations of our remotest ancestors.' It is not possible to give here a full account of his attempts to answer the riddle: speculations which he did not claim to be either final or original. Briefly, the theory he propounded was that the dances had grown out of primitive religious ceremonies which were associated in some occult way with the fertilization of all living things, animal and vegetable.

The central feature of these rites consists of a ritual killing and subsequent sacramental eating of a victim. Traces of this rite are to be seen in the customs which were at one time associated with the Morris Dance, such as the procession at Kidlington in which a live lamb was decorated, paraded through the village and afterwards killed, cooked and eaten at a feast, the Whit-hunt at Field Town, the Lamb-Ale at Kirtlington, and so on. At Bampton, and formerly at other villages, the Morris dancers are accompanied by a Cake and Sword Bearer, i.e. a man carrying a flower-decorated sword on which a cake is impaled. This is supposed to have magical properties and it is said that a girl placing a piece under her pillow will dream of her sweetheart. Cecil Sharp suggests that in this custom can be seen the vestiges of a fertility rite in which the animal victim has been replaced by the products of the vegetable world in the sacramental feast. In the dance itself he saw possible traces of mimetic magic in the high leaps, referred to by Shakespeare – 'I saw him caper upright like a wild Morisco' – which might be intended to encourage the crops to spring up and grow tall. Again, the sound of the bells on the dancers' legs might have had for its purpose the arousing of the earth spirit or the driving away of evil.

The ritual significance of the Sword Dance, presently to be described, is more apparent, for here a mimic decapitation of a human being is performed before our eyes in the course of the dance. And any doubts we might have are laid aside by the Play which used to accompany the dance. In this, the dead man is brought to life, after suitable observances have been performed, by a 'doctor' or clown. The Sword Dance is performed at Christmas or the New Year and the interlude referred to can well be interpreted as the dramatic representation of the cyclic death of the old year and the re-birth of the new year.

The Sword Dance has many features in common with the Mummers 'Play which is known all over England. It is perhaps significant that 'Morris' is used by the folk as a generic term to cover not only the Morris Dance proper but the Sword Dance and the Mummers' Play. Cecil Sharp was of opinion that these three forms were survivals of different aspects of the same rite; and he thought that the nomenclature of the folk might perhaps point to the lingering memory of their common origin. He writes (*The Morris Book*, Part 1, 2nd ed., 1912, p. 12):

Little more than a cursory examination is needed to see that the same central idea permeates all three of them. Originally expressions of religious belief, in which the idea was as essential as the form, they have passed by various stages and along devious paths into the inspiriting dances and quaint dramas with which we are familiar. . . . Out of the debris of ancient faith and cult have issued three forms of folk-art. In the Morris Dance proper we have a dance of grace and dignity, instinct with emotion gravely restrained in a manner not unsuggestive of its older significance, full of complex co-ordinated rhythms of hand and foot, demanding the perfection of restrained muscular control. In the Mummers'-play the feeling for drama, the world-old love of personification, has been the determining factor; while in the Sword-dance, with its elaborate dexterity of evolution, its dramatic accompaniments of song and interlude, we find drama and dance combined.

Cecil Sharp totally rejected the hypothesis which he had at first put forward (see p. 70) that the Morris Dance might be of Moorish origin, and he accepted the view that it was 'a development of a pan-European or even more widely held custom'. He considered that the term could be explained by the blackened faces of the dancers which was formerly often practised. The black face was a form of disguise: an important element in maintaining the impersonal characters of the actors in a ritual drama. The tradition has died hard, for when Cecil Sharp encountered a dancer who had put a small smudge of black on his face and asked him his reason for doing so, the answer came pat: 'So that no one shan't know you, sir.' To our forefathers, the typical black man was the Moor and, to quote Sir Edmund K. Chambers, 'The faces were not blackened because they represent Moors, but rather the dancers were thought to represent Moors because their faces were black.'[1] It should be added that the term 'Morisco' was also used in connexion with court entertainments for dances of a grotesque character performed by dancers dressed in bizarre costumes and often having blackened faces. It is possible that these dances were inspired by traditional dances, but Cecil Sharp thought that the reciprocal influence, if any, was negligible.

In England, the significance of the Morris and other ritual dances has been almost forgotten, but there still remains the vague feeling that they bring luck. Cecil Sharp tells a story which illustrates the reverent way in which the older dancers regarded the traditional customs. There used to be an elaborate ceremony at Ducklington (Oxfordshire) connected with the raising and decorating of the Maypole and it was the custom for the Morris dancers to dance certain figures around the pole before proceeding on their rounds. One day the dancers omitted to perform this ceremony; they passed the pole and were processing down the lane away from the village. Whereupon an old man suddenly

[1] Another possible theory is that the term Moorish was used as being synonymous with Pagan (see Rodney Gallop: 'The Origins of the Morris Dance' in *Journal of the English Folk Dance and Song Society*, 1934).

stood up and shouted in a loud and angry voice: 'Come back.' The dancers returned and said, in reply to the old man's question, that they were on their way to dance at a neighbouring village. 'Very well,' said the old man, 'when you come back you'll have no pole to dance round, because I shall cut it down.' This reminded the dancers of their omission and without further ado they danced round the pole.

The Morris Dance in its most characteristic form is restricted to the Midland Counties and Cecil Sharp's investigations were made chiefly in the counties of Oxfordshire, Gloucestershire, Warwickshire and Northamptonshire, although the notation and publication of some interesting dances from Winster in Derbyshire should be mentioned.

Each village in which the Morris Dances have survived has its own tradition, i.e. its own dances and its own methods of performance. However, as Cecil Sharp explains (The Morris Book, Part III, 1st ed., p. 11):

Throughout all the numberless changes to which the Morris is subject, the type obstinately persists. In general appearance, in form and structure, and in all that is really essential, the Morris is unvarying. The normal Morris step, for instance, is practically the same everywhere. . . . while in character, in spirit, and in its emotional content the dance varies little. It is in the use of special figures, or combination of figures, in the preference for this or that step or hand-movement, and in the small and almost indefinable subtleties and nuances of technique that, in the main, the tradition varies.

What are the essential characteristics of the Morris? Over and over again Cecil Sharp has stressed that it combines grace with vigour. He writes:

To dance the Morris ungracefully is to destroy it. It is true that the dance is vigorous or nothing; but vigour and grace are not incompatible. . . . The impression [it leaves] is first of beauty, solemnity and high restraint, then of vigour.

'Plenty of brisk but no excitement,' as one Morris dancer put it.

It is fortunate that the dances of the Headington tradition were the first that Cecil Sharp saw and noted, for in William Kimber he was able to see the style and technique of the Morris Dance at its best. One has a vivid memory of his perfect carriage, the dignity of his bearing, his loose-limbed yet controlled movements and, above all, the sparkle of his step, which is one of the glories of the Morris Dance.

In addition to Headington there were only two villages in which Cecil Sharp saw a complete Morris team: Bampton (or Bampton-in-the-Bush, to give it its older name) and Eynsham, both in Oxfordshire. In all other cases he had to get the dances from individual performers.

Bampton is the only village in England in which the Whitsun Morris has been performed without a break (except for the war years) from time immemorial down to the present day. 'That it has escaped the fate of other villages in the neighbourhood,' writes Cecil Sharp, 'is largely owing to the enthusiasm of Mr. William Wells who, when the aged pipe-and-taborer died some years ago, was promoted from the office of Fool to that of Musician and has since by tact and skilful fiddling kept the side together.' William Wells, relating his early experiences, has said: 'I used to follow the Morris men as a child and I could hear the bells [worn on the legs] for days after, so when I started I had an insight and could play some of the tunes on a penny whistle at the age of ten.' It was from William Wells that Cecil Sharp noted the tunes and got the details of many of the steps and figures, but for the style of dancing he relied on the older generation and particularly on Mr. Charles Tanner, of whom it was said that a woman could place her fingers under his feet when he was dancing without fear of injury. When on Whit Monday 1910 Cecil Sharp conducted a small party of his Chelsea students and others, including Ralph Vaughan Williams, to Bampton, he warned us that we should not see the dances performed in the way that he had taught them, for already they had seriously deteriorated. But we had an insight into what the Bampton Morris must once have been from the few steps of a solo Morris Jig which were performed for our benefit by Charles Tanner, frail and infirm as he then was. Though the dancing of the Bampton side has technical imperfections, it has qualities which are not to be despised. It is blessedly free from showmanship and it has a real sense of purpose. A chance motorist, the owner of a small London retail shop, who came upon it a year or two ago said: 'I felt that here was England: the real England that has always been and always will be.'

As an annual event, the dancing at Eynsham ceased many years ago, but Cecil Sharp saw a 'scratch' side in 1908. This is the description he gives:

> The dancers met me one dull, wet afternoon in midwinter in an ill-lighted upper room of a wayside inn. They came straight from the fields in their working clothes, sodden with rain, and danced in boots heavily weighted with mud to the music of a mouth-organ, very in-differently played. The depression which not unnaturally lay heavily upon us all at the start was, however, as by a miracle dispelled immedi-ately the dance began, and they gave me as fine an exhibition of Morris dancing as it has ever been my good fortune to see.[1]

They had only one dance, i.e. so far as the steps and figures were concerned, but they performed it to different tunes, and so closely is the dance associated with the music in the minds of traditional dancers that they were fully under the impression that they were doing different dances – and in a sense they were.

Cecil Sharp published in all eighty-three Morris Dances from the Midland Counties (about half the number he collected), represent-ing fourteen different traditions. Headington, Bampton and Eynsham accounted for twenty-four dances and the remaining fifty-nine were obtained from individuals. His best chance of getting the dances was to find the man, if he was still alive, who had acted as foreman, i.e. had danced as No. 1. Cecil Sharp would stand at his side as No. 2, and the other dancers had to be imagined. Then while he hummed the tune they would together go through the movements of the dance, Cecil Sharp watching and imitating as best he could while he hummed the tune and jotted down a few pencil notes. In all cases the first thing was to note and learn the tune, for no Morris dancer can reproduce the movements unless he has the tune in mind. Even then he will seldom be able to analyse or explain what he is doing.

He cannot dissociate his movements from the tune; and it is a continual surprise to him that it does not similarly connote the dance to others. The playing, too, is an instinctive business. Cecil Sharp once presented a bow to Charlie Benfield of Bledington, an old fiddler whose own bow had been broken some years pre-viously, since when he had been unable to play his fiddle. The old man tuned up and played over a few tunes with his new bow, but the result did not please him. Thoughtfully he examined and

---

[1] *The Morris Book,* Pt. iii, p. 83 (1924).

fingered the bow, and said: 'It looks all right, and it seems a nice bow, but somehow it won't keep time with the other hand.'

The dancers were not always in agreement among themselves either in practice or precept. Cecil Sharp's principle was to note what he actually saw, afterwards to compare the variants, and finally to select for publication those dances, steps and movements which seemed to him the best and most representative. He made no attempt to combine different variants.

The Morris Dances often have very fine tunes. Those that Cecil Sharp noted were played mostly on the fiddle or concertina, or sometimes in the absence of a musician they were hummed or whistled by one of the dancers. Formerly the accompanying instruments were the pipe and tabor (whittle and dub), i.e. a small three-holed wooden pipe and drum, played by one man. Cecil Sharp only once heard the instruments played but he managed to secure two specimens and 'in a manner learned how to manipulate them'.

Cecil Sharp gave a careful description of the costumes which are worn by the dancers. These vary from village to village, but they are nearly always decorated with fluttering ribbons and the hats are ornamented with flowers and ribbons. The pads of bells which are worn on the dancers' shins are an indispensable part of the regalia. Of the several attendants who accompany the dancers, the Fool is regarded as an important personage and the dancers call him 'Squire' as a term of respect. He was probably at one time a sort of high-priest. He usually carries a short stick with a calf's tail at one end and a bladder attached to a string at the other; with this he belabours the dancers and prevents the crowd from encroaching on them. A Morris side dressed in full regalia is a gay spectacle.

We must now turn to the Sword Dance. In Part 1 of *The Sword Dances of Northern England* (1st Edition), Cecil Sharp refers to the many accounts of Sword dancing which used to be, and still is, practised in many countries of Europe.[1] He writes:

A comparison of the foregoing records with the descriptions of existing dances in this book will show that the sword-dance has altered little in the last four hundred years, and differs little locally, considering

[1] Since his death extensive research has been made on the Sword Dance and many other European examples have been brought to light, some of them very close to the English dances.

the wide area in which it has been found. Some of the features of the ancient dance have no doubt disappeared, and others have been modified, but many of its most typical figures have come down to us practically unaltered, and its essential unity runs through variants separated, in point of space, by half a continent.

Incidentally, it should be mentioned that the dance has survived in England to a greater extent than the Morris and even at the present day there are a number of traditional teams which still practise the dance.

The English Sword Dance, which bears no relation to the Scottish solo dance, is a team dance in which five, six or eight men take part. The dance is one of great complexity, demanding strength, skill, and, above all, fine team-work. A false movement on the part of any one performer will throw the whole into confusion, for the dancers are linked together in a ring by their swords, each holding the hilt of his own sword in one hand and the point of his neighbour's in the other. Without breaking this link they perform the most elaborate evolutions, twisting under the swords, jumping over them, turning the ring inside out, breaking it up into smaller rings, and so on. The climax of the dance is invariably brought about by the plaiting of the swords into a star (commonly called a Lock, or Nut, or sometimes Rose, or Glass) of five, six, or eight points, according to the number of dancers. The plaited swords are then held aloft by the leader, and afterwards placed, as a rule, round the neck of one of the dancers or of an extra character. At a word from the leader each dancer releases his sword by drawing it towards him; whereupon the victim suffers a mimic decapitation and, falling down, feigns death, from which he is afterwards miraculously brought to life.

Cecil Sharp saw his first Sword Dance at Kirkby Malzeard, Yorkshire, in July 1910. The dance had been performed in 1886 at the Ripon Millenary Pageant and it was from Mr. D'Arcy de Ferrars, the Master of the Pageant, that Cecil Sharp had heard about it. When he first interviewed the dancers they said that they had not performed the dance for some time and they were doubtful whether they could put it together again. Cecil Sharp asked them to think about it, and to practise, saying he would come back in a week's time, which he did. The men told him that they had at first despaired of remembering it, but at their last practice it had all suddenly come right. He thereupon noted the dance, and at a later visit verified it. Those who have seen a Sword Dance will realize the difficulties that were involved. Cecil Sharp has said:

When first I saw the dance performed it looked to be one continuous movement. It was not until I had seen it repeated that I realized it to be really compounded of a series of distinct and separate figures, like beads on a string.

Cecil Sharp used normally to try out newly collected dances at his Chelsea 'experimental' class, but the Kirkby Malzeard Sword Dance was collected during the holidays, and so the experimenting had to be done within the family circle, children included. It was only on the days when the charwoman came that a complete team could be got together; and when finally the dance was performed in public she was one of the most appreciative and critical members of the audience. In order to have a completely adult team on which to experiment, Cecil Sharp invited my sister and me and some other members of the Chelsea class to his house in Hampstead one afternoon. After a hasty tea we were ushered into the garden where we awaited instructions, but owing to some misunderstanding the swords were not forthcoming. However, a search brought to light umbrellas and walking-sticks up to the number of six and we set to work on what can only be described as a somewhat painful operation in which we got tied up in knots while trying to follow the directions which Cecil Sharp read from his notebooks. It seemed almost impossible that a dance could ever emerge from our physical contortions, but much to our delight it eventually took shape.

The visit to Kirkby Malzeard was the prelude to many more excursions to the north of England in search of Sword Dances, in some of which he was accompanied by George Butterworth. As a preliminary, he sent a reply-paid postcard to the incumbent of every parish in Yorkshire, Northumberland and Durham asking if they had ever seen or heard of any such dances.

It should here be pointed out that there are two distinct types of Sword Dance in England: the Long Sword, peculiar to Yorkshire, of which the Kirkby Malzeard dance is an example; and the Rapper or Short Sword Dance, which is to be found in Northumberland and Durham. In the latter dance, which is performed by five men, the implement used, which is called a rapper, is a short strip of flexible steel with a wooden handle at each end.[1] The flexibility and shortness of the rapper swords have the effect of massing the dancers more closely together and the movements of the dance are even more intricate than those of the Long Sword Dance. It is a breath-taking experience to see a team of men, whose average age might be around sixty, go through the complicated and strenuous movements of this dance as though possessed by some inner driving force.

Cecil Sharp was a man of prompt action and if his morning correspondence contained any likely clue, he would be off with his bicycle by the very next train, provided his engagements permitted. His promptness was sometimes justified: the old man who gave him the Escrick Sword Dance died just two days later – not as the result of his exertions, Cecil Sharp was relieved to hear.

Cecil Sharp published fourteen Sword Dances – nine Long Sword and five Rapper – and his notebooks contain further examples and fragments. In the case of four of the Yorkshire dances the teams had been disbanded and he had to get the dance from one or more individuals. One man can, of course, give little idea of the Sword Dance by his individuals movements, but fortunately the dance is not such an instinctive business as is the Morris. Anyhow, with the help of bottles and china ornaments, etc., moved about on a table, the sword dancer would usually be able to indicate the movements sufficiently clearly for Cecil Sharp to reconstruct the dance.

A further difficulty in collecting a dance from individuals lies in tracing them when they have moved from the district. Cecil Sharp would often spend a whole day toiling along on his bicycle in an endeavour to follow up clues, only to find that the man he wanted was living within just a few miles from where he had started his search. 'Well,' he said one day after arriving home tired out, wet, cold and hungry, 'I am not likely to have many competitors at this job.'

One of the most rewarding instances of this detective work was the finding of the Ampleforth Sword Dance, and its associated Folk Play which had not been performed for many years. A visit

---

[1] The origin of the implement is puzzling. The name suggests that it is derived from rapier, but this is hardly a weapon with which the dancers would have been familiar. Nowadays the generally accepted theory is that it is derived from an instrument used in scraping hides.

to Ampleforth brought to light only one man who knew the play, and he could remember only a few lines; but Cecil Sharp was told of an older man who had left the village and would probably remember more, since he used to dance and at times play the part of the Clown. His name was said to be George Wright, and his present address, 'No. 4, Darlington'. That seemed vague, but Cecil Sharp, knowing the habits of our people, asked leave to examine a china ornament on the mantelpiece and found it stuffed with old letters, among them being one with the old man's address, 'No. 4, The Bank, Darlington'. Calling there next afternoon he was told by a young woman that she had just put grandfather to bed with a poultice to keep him comfortable, but she would get him up if the gentleman wished. Glad to be got up, the old man described the dance and gradually remembered the lines of the play he used to act fifty years before.

The play, already referred to on p. 93, is a somewhat crude affair in which the dialogue is confused and the action difficult to follow. Yet, it captures the imagination and when performed it grips one's attention throughout in some strange, mysterious way. The central motif of the play is the death and resurrection theme in which a stranger is killed by the dancers by means of their locked swords. The 'doctor' who is called in to cure the dead man fails to do so and after he has indulged in much high-flown nonsense, he is pushed aside by the Clown who after making some mystical signs immediately brings the dead man to life.[1]

This is the only example of the Sword-Dance Play[2] discovered by Cecil Sharp, but, in other dances noted by him, relics of their association with ritual drama are to be seen in the extra characters which accompany the dancers. Among these, in addition to the Clown, are personages such as the Man-Woman (Bessy, Betty, Besom Betty or Dirty Bet, to give some of the names by which he is known), a King and Queen, etc. Many of the dances have a 'Calling-on' song in which the dancers are severally introduced by the captain of the team. At Earsdon, after the dancers have been introduced in the guise of various fictitious characters and sundry witticisms have been levelled at them, the apparently

---

[1] For the text of the play, see *The Sword Dances of Northern England*, Pt. III.

[2] Other versions of the play, usually in fragmentary form, have been found in association with the Sword Dance. The earliest known version is the Revesby (Lincolnshire) play which was recorded in 1779 (see *The English Folk-Play* by E. K. Chambers, Clarendon Press, 1933).

irrelevant announcement is made by the captain that he is going to kill a bullock. This intimation, the animal insignia which often appear on the coats of the dancers, the pieces of fur on their caps, all give a hint of some long-forgotten totemistic rite.

The finest of all the Sword Dances comes from Handsworth, a suburb of Sheffield. As with many of the Sword Dance teams the dancers are miners; 'artists every one of them', was Cecil Sharp's pronouncement on those from whom he noted the dance. This was no exaggeration. I had the good fortune to accompany Cecil to Sheffield on Easter Monday of 1913 when the dancers were performing in a parade for the benefit of the local hospital. They had arranged to give a special performance for us and a few friends and we repaired to a sordid public-house in a mean street in which a noisy crowd was disporting itself. It seemed an unlikely setting for a display of artistry, but as soon as the dance started one was caught up in its rhythm and the material world around ceased to exist. The dancers were oldish men, but they moved with the ease and sureness that come of experience, each dancer contributing slight individual variations on the basic movements with an unconscious grace which enriched without distracting from the unity of the whole.

Inaddition to the Morris and Sword Dances Cecil Sharp collected a number of Processional Dances which had their origin in the seasonal lustrations round the village. In one of the best known of these dances, the Furry Dance, which is still performed annually at Helston in Cornwall at the beginning of May, the dancers, men and women in couples, process through the streets and in and out of the houses. Formerly the dancers used to bear freshly picked flowers and greenery.

Of all the Processional Dances the most interesting and the most mysterious is the Horn Dance which is still performed at Abbots Bromley, Staffordshire, in the month of September. The company consists of six men, each bearing an enormous pair of reindeer antlers, accompanied by other curiously garbed persons; and the sight of this procession, half human, half animal, as it moves in serpentine patterns alternating with a challenging forward and backward movement by two confronting lines of antler-bearers, seems to carry one back almost to the beginning of time.

Other age-old ceremonies with connotations of fertility rites are the festivities at Minehead (Somerset) and Padstow (Cornwall) where the Hobby Horse can still be seen cavorting with his attendants on May Day.[1]

The Country Dance has for many generations been danced purely as a means of social and artistic recreation. Cecil Sharp believed, however, that it had its origin in the processional and circle dances which at one time formed part of the May Day ritual. The Country Dances are not peculiar to any region. Those that Cecil Sharp collected in Devonshire, Somerset, Warwickshire, Surrey and Derbyshire are all the 'longways for as many as will' variety; the main type that has survived into the twentieth century.

For the Country Dances of an earlier period Cecil Sharp went to John Playford's *Dancing Master*, which went through eighteen editions from 1651 to 1728, the first edition being entitled *The English Dancing Master*.[2] During the three-quarters of a century covered by these eighteen editions the dance appeared in many modified forms; and while some were dropped, others were constantly added. Of the earlier editions John Playford was not only publisher but probably took a share in editing the dances.[3]

Cecil Sharp worked for many months in the British Museum on the Playford collections. It was not an easy task. The directions are laconic for the book is addressed to those who already have some knowledge of the dances and need only a reminder. In his interpretation of the steps and style of the dances Cecil Sharp was guided both by the musical accompaniment and by the traditional dancing he had seen in the villages. He made no attempt to give an exact reproduction of the style of dancing that may have been current in the seventeenth century, but allowed the style to be gradually evolved. The re-creation which was thus effected was a thing of great beauty: lovely to behold and completely satisfying to the dancers.

---

[1] Cecil Sharp's accounts of these ceremonies are to be found in his manuscript notebooks. There is also a considerable literature on the subject.

[2] The first edition was entered in the Stationers' Register, 7 November 1650.

[3] For some further particulars of *The Dancing Master*, see articles entitled '"The Dancing Master" 1651–1728' in *Journal of the English Folk Dance and Song Society*, Vol. IV, Nos. 3, 4 and 5 (London,1944–6) and *Playford's English Dancing Master 1651*, a Facsimile Reprint with an Introduction, Bibliography and Notes by Margaret Dean-Smith (London, 1957).

Although Playford was the first to give us a technical description the dance was known at least a century earlier. In *Misogonnus*, *c.* 1560, two Playford dances, 'Putney Ferry' and 'The Shaking of the Sheets', are mentioned. Unlike the Morris and Sword, the Country Dance does not appear to have been the exclusive possession of any one class of society. The Earl of Worcester in 1602 writes to the Earl of Shrewsbury: 'We all frolic here at Court; much dancing in the Privy Chamber of country dances before the Queen's Majesty, who is extremely pleased therewith'; and Pepys describes the performance of a Country Dance at the Court of King Charles in 1662, where it took its place amongst the Branles, Corantos, and other French dances.[1] At the beginning of the eighteenth century, and perhaps earlier, the English Country Dance travelled abroad, was danced at many European Courts, and enhanced our reputation as 'the dancing English'.[2] During the eighteenth century the dance held its sway together with the Minuet, which occupied the first part of the programme at the Assembly Rooms.

Many of the dances in the Playford collection are not pure folk dances though they may be said to rest on a traditional basis. Some of the tunes – particularly those in the later editions – are popular composed tunes of the day which were pressed into the service of the dance, or some may have been written expressly for it. Cecil Sharp believed that the older dances in the collection were deeply rooted in tradition, though certain features may have been added at a later and more sophisticated period; while others owe a great deal to the creative efforts of John Playford's contributors. This conscious manipulation of traditional material by those who were immersed in the spirit of the dance brought forth some beautiful results, but the creative development was not sustained. During the eighteenth century, under the influence of the dancing-master,

---

[1] A quotation from Selden's *Table Talk*, 1689, may also be given: 'In our Court in Queen Elizabeth's time gravity and state were kept up. In King James's time things went pretty well, but in King Charles's time there has been nothing but Trenchmore and the Cushion Dance, omnium gatherum, tolly-polly, hoite come toite.'
[2] In 1717 Lady Mary Wortley Montagu writes from Vienna: 'The Ball always concludes with English Country Dances to the number of thirty or forty couples, and so ill-danced that there is little pleasure in them. They know but half a dozen and they have danced them over and over these fifty years. I would fain have taught them some new ones, but I found it would be some months' labour to make them comprehend them.'

whose opportunity came with the rise of the middle class,[1] the dance became formal and sophisticated. Its fashion moved towards the 'longways' form,[2] which lent itself more easily to decorous treatment; the 'rounds', 'square eights', and other forms gradually disappeared. In the early nineteenth century the 'long-ways' dance itself was displaced from popular favour by the waltz and quadrille, since when it has survived only in a few English villages and in trans-Atlantic form on the continent of North America.

In his choice of dances – he published 158m four volumes – Cecil Sharp was guided by aesthetic considerations and by the practical problem of accurate deciphering, but he gave preference to the earlier versions of the dance in which the traditional element was strongest.

In poring over the Playford collections, as he had over a period of many years, Cecil Sharp felt that he had come to know the man intimately and he conceived something like a fellow-feeling for him. He wrote:

> There are many ways by which men may become great and win the honour of posterity. Some achieve greatness through the possession of unusual intellectual or inventive faculties; others, like John Playford, without any special nature gifts, by patient work performing a greatly needed service for their own generation and doing it well and truly. This to plain people like ourselves is no small comfort. No one, I imagine, of his contemporaries would have been more surprised than John Playford if he had been told that nearly three hundred years later his name would be a household word in towns and villages throughout England.[3]

The question is sometimes asked why Cecil Sharp should have paid so much attention to the Playford dances seeing that they were not of pure folk origin; and it may seem all the more sur-

---

[1] 'Even the wives and daughters of low tradesmen, who like shove-nosed sharks prey upon the blubber of those uncouth whales of fortune, are infected with the same rage of displaying their importance and the slightest indisposition serves them for a pretext to insist upon being conveyed to Bath where they may hobble Country Dances and Cotillions among lordlings, squires, counsellors and clergy.' – Smollett's *Humphrey Clinker* (1771).

[2] Out of 104 dances in the first edition 38 are longways; whilst in the last edition there are 914 out of 918.

[3] From a lecture given at Aldeburgh Vacation School, August 1923.

prising when we reflect that he gave such a firm ruling about 'traditional' song. If an explanation is needed, we can say only that he was satisfied that the dances were the outcome of tradition; and they were beautiful. Had he done no more than to bring back into common currency these lovely tunes that had been preserved by John Playford and his successors, Cecil Sharp's life would not have been spent in vain.

Inthepromulgation of the dances Cecil Sharp was handicapped by the absence of a scientific and generally accepted system of dance-notation. The most notable systems of the past are to be seen in Arbeau's *Orchésographie* (1588) and Feuillet's *Chorégraphie* (1701). The latter, which is said to have been invented by Beauchamps, dancing-master at the Court of Louis XVI, is an elaborate system of symbols and diagrams, which owing to its complexity is of little practical use. On the other hand Arbeau's notation is, so far as it goes, clear and explicit. Cecil Sharp studied them both. In particular he got from Arbeau the idea of indicating the timing of the steps by showing on which notes of the accompanying melody they fall. In his Morris Dance books the movements are shown by printing under the melody a line of abbreviated symbols for the steps and a lower line for the track, whilst the hand-movements are placed above the melody. The system which he evolved with the help of Herbert MacIlwaine proved not only serviceable at the moment but capable of extension for the description of the many forms of Morris Dance which he afterwards collected. In the Sword and Country dances, which unlike the Morris have no great variety of steps, the figures are made clear by a description of the relative tracks of the dancers and, in the case of the Sword Dance, by defining the position of the swords. From 1911 onwards Cecil Sharp submitted all the drafts of his dance books to Dr. E. Phillips Barker, and acknowledged more than once the assistance which he got from his clear and analytical mind.

In the list of Cecil Sharp's publications which appear on pages 201–7, it will be seen that Herbert MacIlwaine's name does not appear on the title-page of *The Morris Book*, Part IV (1911). In the Preface, Cecil Sharp regrets that pressure of work has prevented Mr. MacIlwaine from taking any part in the compilation of the new volume. He would have left his name on the title-page, but to this Mr. MacIlwaine would not agree and Cecil Sharp was compelled with reluctance to respect his wishes. Herbert MacIlwaine had, as a matter of fact, played little or no part in the preceding volume, Part III.

For *The Morris Book*, Part V (1914) Cecil Sharp found another collaborator in George Butterworth, who assisted him in the collection of the Bledington, Bucknell and Badby traditions, being himself the first to discover the Badby dances. George Butterworth also arranged some of the tunes for pianoforte. He undertook the task without serious apprehension and arranged the tunes to his own satisfaction as a musician, but then discovered that his settings were entirely unsuitable as dance-accompaniments and that the only satisfactory solution was to scrap them and adopt Cecil Sharp's method. This he did with such success that Cecil Sharp himself could not later remember which were his own arrangements and which were George Butterworth's.

Cecil Sharp exercised great care and discrimination in the selection of the dances and songs that he published. Of actual dances (movements and figures) he noted over two hundred and published (excluding one hundred and fifty-eight dances from Playford) one hundred and fifty. The position with regard to the tunes – both dance and song – may be seen from the following table:

| | *Published* | | | |
	with accompaniment	*without accompaniment*[1]	*Unpublished*	*Collected*
English {Song	291	209[2]	2,313	2,813
English {Dance[3]	148	0	334	482
Appalachian Song	62	909[4]	711	1,682
Total	501	1,118	3,358	4,977

[1] These numbers do not include tunes which were also published with accompaniment.
[2] Including forty-one posthumously.
[3] Excluding transcriptions from Playford.
[4] Five-hundred and ninety-six of these posthumously.

X

The English Folk Dance Society
1912–14

Totter dantse is meer van doen
Dan het draeghen van ros schoen.[1]

Old Dutch Saying

THE ENGLISH FOLK DANCE SOCIETY was founded at the end of
1911 (see p. 86) and during the next three years, until the outbreak of the First World War, the dances were Cecil Sharp's main
pre-occupation. This did not mean that his interest in the songs
had weakened. On the contrary, they probably always remained
his chief love; and he continued his work on them: lecturing,
collecting and publishing. But whereas a knowledge of folk song
can be given by means of publication, this is not so with the
dances. In the absence of any general knowledge of the genre,
it is necessary to supplement notation and description by precept
and practice.

The sketchy account of the dances given in the last chapter will
have given some idea of the rich heritage that Cecil Sharp had
found lingering on in the English countryside. He had no intention of allowing these treasures to remain hidden in his notebooks.
He knew that the dances, though for the most part lying dormant,
were not moribund; and he threw all his energies and talents into
reviving the tradition so that it might take its rightful place in our
national culture. He was convinced that he could achieve this

---

[1] It takes more than a pair of red shoes to make a dancer.

ambition now that he had his own organization. It needed only hard work, patience and time. Of the first two he had an unlimited supply, but not, alas, of the third.

He set about the task of restoring the dances in a practical manner, building up the necessary machinery and at the same time the man- (and woman-) power wherewith to run it. He realized that the scope of the movement was limited by its teaching powers and that educational work must keep pace with propaganda. The Vacation Schools probably provided the most effective means of training teachers. These were at first held at Stratford-on-Avon each year for four weeks in August and for one week during the Christmas holidays. They were joyful occasions combining seriousness and gaiety as was in accordance with the subject of our studies. The students were by no means all prospective teachers; they came from all walks of life with a good sprinkling of professional people including musicians and university dons. But there were few, once they had been initiated, who did not feel the urge to pass on their experiences to others.

The dance instruction, which was of a purely practical nature, was supplemented by Cecil Sharp's lectures. As for the daily singing period, it could hardly be called instruction: Cecil Sharp sat at the piano and played, and the rest of us sang. There was a daily dance demonstration given by the staff and a public performance each week. Some of the most pleasurable events were the Country Dance parties when we met and danced solely for enjoyment. In the summer of 1912, Ralph Vaughan Williams was in charge of the music of Frank Benson's Shakespeare performances and when theatre engagements permitted Vaughan Williams would attend these parties and dance with great zest. We were also honoured by a weekly visit from Frank Benson. Unfortunately, the glamour of his personality was somewhat marred for us by his vague and almost incomprehensible addresses which were unkindly parodied by a member of the staff with her description of a dance movement as 'three bars of life rhythm and a joyaunce'.

In addition to the Vacation Schools, numerous classes were held regularly in London and the provinces. An examination syllabus was drawn up in 1912, and by 1914 nearly two hundred certificates of proficiency had been granted.

To ensure that the movement should be nation-wide, a plan for the establishment of branch societies was initiated and local correspondents were appointed.

In the Society's first Annual Report, which comes from Cecil Sharp's pen, we read:

[The Committee] realize the magnitude of the work that lies before them and the responsibility which is attached to it; and they know that if that work is to have permanent results it must be wisely directed and done slowly and thoroughly. They have no desire to create a mere splash.

'No desire to create a splash,' wrote Gordon Craig on applying for membership of the Society, 'but you have created it. A splendidly designed and proportioned splash. It has been to me more than all the skill of the Russians.'

To a certain extent Cecil Sharp adopted Fabian tactics and he accepted certain conditions as insuperable barriers. For instance, although he lectured on song and dance (with illustrations) in nearly every boys' public school in England, he made no serious endeavour to get the dances generally taught in the public schools, knowing that the curriculum would not allow of it; but he hoped that the dances would be introduced gradually whenever there were individual members of the staff who were keen on the subject. He felt that the main value of arousing interest in the public schools was to pave the way for a later period when the men would come across the dances at the university or elsewhere. Actually, at Dr. Rendall's instigation, Cecil Sharp taught the Kirkby Malzeard Sword Dance to six athletes of the Sixth Book at Winchester (see plate xiv).

In all the varied and sometimes complex matters of organization Cecil Sharp took an active part. He was conscientious over details and he took as much trouble over the drafting of a circular as he did over the noting of a tune or the description of a dance. He certainly made the most of every opportunity that came his way. He would answer letters promptly and carefully, whether to a learned professor or to a village schoolmistress. 'You never know what may come of it,' he would say. In the early days of their acquaintance, Dr. Phillips Barker paid him this compliment:

I begin to regard you as a shining example of what one often hears: that if you want questions answered or business done promptly and completely you must apply to the busy man. I ask you questions which might conceivably, had you been an idle person with plenty of time, have been answered on a postcard or on one side of letter-paper; you reply by treating the subject fully in a long, interesting and informing letter.[1]

The direction of the Society was a whole-time job, but not a lucrative one, for Cecil Sharp received no honorarium. He was able to earn a little by his lectures on folk-song, but he insisted on all fees for folk-dance lectures being paid to the Society. During 1913 his earnings amounted to about £500 (£400 from royalties and £100 from lecture fees). In 1914 he accepted after much persuasion a present of eighty guineas subscribed by some members of the Society, and in expressing his gratitude, he wrote:

> It is nice to feel that there are so many kind people in the world, and that I am now able to contribute something more to the needs of those who are dependent upon me. After all it is they who have suffered from my restricted income far more than I.

It is significant of Cecil Sharp's lack of self-seeking that in the organization of the Society it had not occurred to him to create the office of a Director, and that he himself had intended to take no more prominent a position than that of an ordinary member of Committee. Indeed, it was only after some persuasion from his fellow committee members that he agreed to accept the post of Honorary Director. Whatever his position, he would, as a matter of fact, have had things his own way on the committee because no one could miss his clearness of vision or run counter to his intensity of purpose. But in any difference of opinion he never rode rough-shod over other people's objections, and in any important step he would postpone action whenever possible until the committee was unanimously behind him.

There was nothing pretentious in Cecil Sharp's leadership. As Plunket Greene said of him: 'Like all big men who work with single-mindedness he had no fireworks or grand ceremonial in his make-up.' In whatever company he found himself he was at his ease and made others feel so. Many would agree with the old Morris dancer who spoke of him as 'an understanding gentleman'. The shy, or the taciturn, or the dull, opened out to him. He got the best out of people, because he detected their latent possibilities.

[1] The left-hand corner of the envelope was always marked C # a habit he adopted in Australia, in order to distinguish between private and official letters. Hence the cover of this book.

This is illustrated by the following letter written after a lapse of many years:

He came to Reading to judge a Folk-Dancing Festival. There was one class for Women's Institute teams in which my own Institute entered. It was not a good team; they had only had a very few lessons, were none of them under forty (to put it kindly!) and were all busy working-women; but they had so thoroughly enjoyed their classes that it would have appeared too discouraging not to let them enter. The teams against them were composed of quite young women, for the most part light of foot and prettily dressed. My own old ladies were in thick serge skirts and full blouses! When it came to giving the awards and criticisms of the teams I trembled for what might come, but Cecil Sharp, with his wonderful charm and courteousness, said: 'I should like especially to congratulate this team. I understand it is composed entirely of – a little hesitation here as I think he nearly said "grandmothers" – married ladies. I can only hope that their husbands were here to enjoy watching them as much as, obviously, they enjoyed dancing. They have learned to appreciate one of the greatest charms of folk-dancing, namely that it was not intended only for the young, but for the recreation of the workers of the world, as it has the power like nothing else of taking their minds off the daily drudgery which must fall to their lot. The dancing of this team showed that in this respect it had completely fulfilled its purpose.' If my team had been awarded the first prize, it could not have been more delighted, and many of the onlookers who were inclined to make fun, rather maliciously, were completely silenced. For an act of graceful tact, I think this cannot be beaten, and I have always felt grateful to Cecil Sharp for his charming handling of a trifling situation.

Arthur Batchelor, too, a sympathetic and discerning friend, has written:

It was that delightful gift of sympathy and understanding, combined with his obvious sincerity, which gave him the entrée straight into the hearts of the shyest of peasants or the silliest of patricians. I have been privileged like Mr. E. V. Lucas in *London Lavender*[1] to accompany him 'collecting', and have marvelled at the ease with which he managed and made a personal friend of the most secretive and intractable possessor of a folk-song. I have also been amazed at his masterly handling

[1] *See London Lavender* (Methuen, London, 1912), pp. 220–4. An account is here given of a visit which the author together with Cecil Sharp (referred to as 'the Director') paid to Mr. Eli and Mr. Will Rolfe, the two surviving members of the Bucknell Morris side. Their dancing and the pipe-and-tabor playing of Mr. Jim Pole are described.

of that incredibly foolish type, the well-meaning 'county' Lady Bounti-
ful with undigested views of her own on what she called 'olde worlde'
dances. In half an hour and without relaxing an inch of what he very
rightly regarded as essential he had that lady in the palm of his hand, and
converted one who, artistically, was a public danger, into an enthusiastic and valuable ally. These were the qualities which gave him such
influence on both sides of the Atlantic.

It was natural that Cecil Sharp should have gathered around
him a loyal and enthusiastic band of workers. It would be impossible to give a complete list, but a few must be mentioned. First
and foremost, there was the Society's President, The Lady Mary
Trefusis, whom Cecil Sharp had known in Australia as Lady Mary
Lygon. [1] He was anxious that the office should not be filled by a
mere figure-head and for this reason the presidency was left vacant
until he was able to persuade Lady Mary to accept it. This she did
in September 1913. Something of what her personality and work
meant to the Society may be gathered from the following note
contributed by A. H. Fox Strangways:

> She was the eldest daughter of the sixth Earl Beauchamp and, until
> her death in 1927, Woman of the Bedchamber to Queen Mary. In
> Cornwall, where she married Colonel Trefusis, she threw herself into
> Diocesan work, and sat on the committee which issued the valuable
> pamphlet, *Music in Worship* (1922). She edited for her brother, a member
> of the Roxburghe Club, the musical works of Henry VIII (1912). In
> 1920 she organized the Cornwall Branch of the English Folk Dance
> Society, and the first big open-air folk-dance festival was held at St.
> Austell (1921), when over a thousand took part. She brought success to
> everything she touched because she cared, and because others, seeing
> this, were ashamed of not caring enough. She had a clear head; at
> Sharp's death, when it was not certain how matters would be with his,
> and her, Society, she made every necessary inquiry, then acted unob-
> trusively, and the thing was done, and done right. She was a first-rate
> player of the dances, and quite tireless; she would often play at a
> country dance party for a whole evening.

Her sister, Lady (Margaret) Ampthill (later the Dowager Lady
Ampthill) succeeded Lady Mary as President of the Society.

Of the many others whose work contributed to the welfare of
the Society in the early days, there were the members of his staff

---

[1] Michael Kennedy has pointed out to me that she is the subject of the 13th of
Elgar's 'Enigma Variations' wherein he celebrates her voyage to Australia.

and his 'demonstration team' of whom more hereafter. In the organization of the Society there were Captain and Mrs. Kettlewell for many years Honorary Treasurer[1] and Secretary, respectively; Mrs. Arthur Sidgwick (of Oxford), Mrs. Robert Hobbs (of Kelmscott) and Mrs. Bruce Swanwick (of Cirencester), all of whom did yeoman work, particularly in the branch organization; and finally Helen Karpeles (married to Douglas Kennedy in 1914), the Society's Honorary Secretary from its inception until 1922,[2] on whom fell the burden of keeping the Society going during the war years.

And always in the background, ready to take an active part when called upon or when the need arose, was Ralph Vaughan Williams, a lifelong friend of Cecil Sharp. The encouragement and sound advice that he gave cannot be over-estimated. He was an active member of the Committee, both of the Folk-Song Society and the English Folk Dance Society and it was he who was largely responsible for the amalgamation of the two societies in 1932. After Cecil Sharp's death, Ralph Vaughan Williams helped to steer the English Folk Dance Society through uneasy waters, becoming with Douglas Kennedy and myself a member of the Board of Artistic Control; and when in 1936 that ceased to exist, he accepted the office of Musical Adviser and in 1946 that of President, keeping a fatherly eye over the affairs of the Society until his death in 1958.

The Society made its debut at an At Home at the Suffolk Street Galleries, London, on 27th February 1912, when the men's Morris side made its first appearance. On 6th June a public performance was given at the Kensington Town Hall at which Steuart Wilson sang folk songs and Violet Gordon Woodhouse played folk tunes on the harpsichord. These were among the many performances that were given by the Society's demonstration team in London and in the provinces from that time onward until the outbreak of war.

On these occasions Cecil Sharp not only lectured but accompanied the dances on the pianoforte. It has been said that there were no fireworks in his make-up and certainly there were none in his playing. There was nothing showy about it, but it had a magnetic quality. The touch of his fingers on the piano aroused an

---

[1] Mr. Walter Rea, M.P. (later Lord Rea), succeeded Captain Kettlewell as Treasurer.
[2] After her retirement I held the office of Honorary Secretary until 1930.

immediate feeling of elation and from start to finish the dancers were carried forward by his compelling rhythm. At the Summer School of 1912 and from then onward, Elsie Avril added her violin to his piano-playing and proved herself a worthy partner.

Some people have found Cecil Sharp's dance accompaniments difficult to play. It is true that he could have made them technically easier, but had he done so they would not so successfully have met the requirements of the dance. Anyone who plays the accompaniments exactly as written will be almost bound to portray the rhythm and shape of the tune to some extent even if he is not an expert performer. [1]

In 1913, Cecil Sharp developed neuritis in his right arm and for a time had to give up playing: a loss which was severely felt by the dancers. It was on account of this neuritis that I offered my services as amanuensis and from that time until his death in 1924 I was closely associated with his work. At first I used to pay daily visits to Uxbridge from London and afterwards I lived for the most part with the family.

Cecil Sharp's dancers were, of course, all amateurs. The women who normally took part in the performances were Marjory Sinclair, Helen Kennedy (Mrs. Kennedy North), Olive Lett (Mrs. Cranko), Maggie Muller, my sister Helen (Mrs. Douglas Kennedy) and myself. The men dancers were Douglas Kennedy, Claude Wright, A. J. Paterson, Percival Lucas, George Wilkinson and George Butterworth; and the only spare was Reginald Tiddy. During the two and a half years preceding the outbreak of war, there were very few week-ends in which we were not giving performances, the usual plan being to start off on Friday evening and return on Sunday. With additional week-day performances, particularly during the holidays, we covered a wide area and many thousands were given the opportunity of seeing the dances and hearing about them.

The following thumb-nail sketches of some of the dancers were contributed by A. H. Fox Strangways: [2]

Douglas Kennedy is well known to folk-dancers of the present day as Director [3] of the English Folk Dance and Song Society, but Lucas,

---

[1] See also comments on George Butterworth's accompaniments (p. 108).
[2] *Cecil Sharp*, 1st edition.
[3] Douglas Kennedy retired in 1961 from the Directorship of the Society (since 1932 the English Folk Dance and Song Society). In 1963, he and his wife, Helen, were appointed Vice-Presidents.

XIII(a) The Bampton Morris dancers

XIII(b) Cecil Sharp's first men's Morris team

XIV Winchester men in the Kirkby Malzeard sword dance (see p. 111)

Wilkinson, Butterworth, and Tiddy, to whom Sharp was also looking to carry on his work, were all killed during the British offensive (in the Battle of the Somme) of August 1916. Their loss to Sharp personally and to the folk-dance movement generally was a great one. Perceval Lucas was a younger brother of E. V. Lucas and, like him, a writer of charm. He edited the first two numbers of the *Journal of the English Folk Dance Society*. He was a delightful companion and he brought to the dancing, as to everything else he did, a gaiety and frshness of out-look which was very stimulating to his fellow-dancers Sharp has said of him that he was the first man who really understood what the folk-dance revival meant. George Jerrard Wilkinson, a professional musi-cian, succeeded Sharp at Ludgrove. He was a beautifuldancer – neat and finished in his movements; as a teacher, his sense of form and the clarity of his exposition did much to develop the echnique of the dancing.

Reginald John Elliot Tiddy was twenty years younger than Sharp. He went to Tonbridge and University College, Oxford; he was elected to a prize Fellowship there in 1902, and three years later to one at Trinity, where he lectured on classics. English literature was his real subject, and a 'great work' he projected at the age of twenty-five was to have been on Anglo-Saxon. Sprung from the folk – his father was a yeoman and his mother a farmer's daughter – he turned instinctively to folk-poetry, and to this end he read and knew every scrap of song or play he could lay hands on, down to the Elizabethans and beyond. The dance was much more than his hobby: nothing made him more deeply happy than to be teaching it to and learning it from the villagers of Ascott-under-Wychwood, near Woodstock. They were all his friends: he talked their dialect with them, not at them. To his Oxford friends, he quite as easily talked *their* 'dialect', and his genial cynicism and un-affected wit made him everywhere at home. Into his dancing, eye-wit-nesses say that he put a world of quiet fun. The 24 th Oxfordshires went out in May 1916. On 10th August Tiddy was killed instantaneously by a shell.

Some brilliant essays introduce his collection of *Mummers' Plays* (Clarendon Press, 1923). Cecil Sharp read them in October 1923 and called them 'quite wonderful – by far the best contribution that has yet been made to the subject, as, in my opinion, it is the first written by one who really knew and had felt what he was writing about . . . Nothing can compensate us for his loss and that of George Butterworth. I felt when the dreadful news came that I didn't want to carry on any more and I still have the same feeling . . . I found the memoir entrancing and very difficult to read with dry eyes'.

George Sainton Kaye Butterworth, born (12.7. 1885) in London, fell at Pozières near Albert on 10th August 1916. He called himself a

Cockney, but belonged in spirit to Yorkshire. He spent a boyhood at York and went to Aysgarth, to Eton (as a scholar), and to Trinity, Oxford. He had carried a notebook about at Eton to jot down musical ideas, and it became clear to him after Oxford that music in some form must be his life's work, and music meant, for him, composition. But in what form? He tried teaching (at Radley) and criticism (on *The Times*), but found neither congenial. He spent a year at the Royal College of Music in order to fit himself for a musical post. He then found occupation in collecting and arranging folk-song and-dance (see p. 108), but this did not solve the problem of a livelihood. The war came, and there was no need to inquire further. He enlisted in the Duke of Cornwall's Light Infantry in August and was given a commission in November.

A colleague at Radley wrote of him: 'He had strength of character, opinions and the courage of them, a rugged directness of manner coupled with a gift of keen criticism and an absence of heroics. Few men can have been worse at making an acquaintance or better at keeping a friend.'

The music he left behind is small in quantity but great in merit. It is not on the grand scale – that would have been to come – but it is true, delicate, and often poignantly beautiful. His use of the folk-music idiom was no conscious pose; he had absorbed the language so deeply that it had become his natural mode of expression.

The Society had its great opportunity when on 2nd December 1912 the Savoy Theatre, London, was lent by Miss Lilian Mc-Carthy and Mr. Granville Baker for a matinée performance. This was during the run of their production of *Twelfth Night* and the white décor of the stage made a perfect setting for the dances. Cecil Sharp disarmed criticism by his programme note:

The theatre is not, perhaps, the ideal place for an exhibition of folk-dances . . . Nevertheless, it is the only place in which the dances can be advantageously seen by a large number of people. It is not contended that a succession of dances, however beautiful each individually may be, necessarily constitutes a spectacle of a high order. The aim of The English Folk Dance Society is, rather, by setting a high standard of performance to exhibit the dances in such a manner that others may be encouraged to learn and practise them, not with view of giving public entertainments, but for the sake of the dances themselves. Indeed, it is hoped that a few years hence an exhibition such as this will be as unnecessary and uncalled for as, at the present time, would be a public demonstration of waltzes, polkas, and other drawing-room dances.

The press reports were most enthusiastic and a full-page cartoon appeared in *Punch* with the caption: 'The Midgley-Tomlinsons, in order to be in the movement, hurriedly decide among their house-party to introduce Morris Dances at a ball at their little place in the country.' A slightly captious notice by E.A.B. (E. A. Baughan) to the *Daily News* drew a letter from Miss May Morris, daughter of William Morris, who was herself an enthusiastic dancer and had done much, with her friend, May Elliot Hobbs, to introduce the dances to her native Kelmscott. 'I cannot allow "E.A.B." not to admire some of these dances,' she writes:

> I want to talk to him firmly till he sees the beauty of the Earsdon sword-dance . . . I invite him to my own village on some day of the Festival; then . . . let him look me in the eye, if he can, and declare he has not felt a thrill of pleasure, of sympathy and recognition, as it were, before a dance that, now just a gay and beautiful pastime, has its roots away back in a world that was young, whose warriors danced in worship before the altars of their gods.

E.A.B. declared himself ready to accept the invitation, but whether or not he became converted we do not know.

At the Savoy Theatre, the women dancers wore graceful blue dresses designed by Norman Wilkinson and the men were in white flannels with cross-baldricks (the costume of the Headington Morris). Before the formation of the Society the women had worn bogus old-fashioned country dresses complete with sun-bonnets and hair hanging down in two plaits; while the men were arrayed in smocks in order to tone in with their partners. Cecil Sharp did not approve; but when he suggested that the dancers should discard these costumes for something that was less suggestive of 'Merrie England' he was told firmly by the women dancers that plaits and sun-bonnets were necessary as their hair would not stay up with a normal coiffure – this was, of course, before the days of short hair. Cecil Sharp did not want to 'put his head into a hornet's nest' and as the costume was a subsidiary matter and did not affect the style of dancing, he meekly withdrew. In 1913, he gave a series of lectures at the Small Queen's Hall, London and that on the Country Dance was illustrated by men and women wearing ordinary evening dress, in order to stress the present-day social aspect of the dance.

The Society gave several performances abroad: at Paris in 1913 and at Brussels in 1914. The Paris performances were introduced by Julien Tiersot, the great folk-song collector and scholar, and by Yvette Guilbert, the singer; the latter having taken the place of Vincent d'Indy who had been prevented from attending. Cecil Sharp and Julien Tiersot had some conversations, but owing to language difficulties these were not as fruitful as they would otherwise have been. Yvette Guilbert had several times visited Cecil Sharp in his home at Adelaide Road, where he had coached her in the singing of English folk songs. Her greatest difficulty had been to catch the rhythm and pronunciation of jingles such as 'rue dum day fol the diddle dol'; and this seemed to Cecil Sharp to bear out his hypothesis that such meaningless syllables contain, paradoxically, the quintessence of a language.

A less ambitious form of propaganda, but a very enjoyable one for those who took part in it, was what we called the 'quartet show'. The quartet consisted of Cecil Sharp, Douglas Kennedy, my sister Helen and myself. Cecil Sharp lectured, some members of the party sang, three of us danced jigs to Cecil Sharp's accompaniment and we all four danced Country Dances to the accompaniment of a local pianist.

These 'entertainments' – for so they seemed to us – took place mostly in Somerset and Cornwall and Cecil Sharp managed to combine them with a certain amount of collecting. On one of these trips we took part in the Helston Furry Dance. Not being in our best clothes – as is demanded by tradition – we had to tag on at the end of the long procession, but we enjoyed ourselves none the less for that. On other occasions Cecil Sharp introduced us to the Hobby Horse ceremonies at Minehead (Somerset) and Padstow (Cornwall). Amid all the gaiety and festivity of the scene an underlying seriousness of purpose was somehow evoked and one felt as the Minehead Hobby Horse dancer once said: 'It puts new life into you.'

In Cornwall, Cecil Sharp added to his store of carols, of which he had already published some twenty in *English Folk-Carols* (1911). This he dedicated to Vaughan Williams, who said of it:

It is a fine book. I've always loved carols. I remember the time when, if I said 'carol', I could not get a spark out of you. Now as usual you have gone ahead and left me in the lurch.

Vaughan Williams dedicated his *Fantasia on Christmas Carols* to Cecil Sharp.

In the intervals between the Somerset performances Cecil Sharp would hurry off to Watchet, a small port on the Bristol Channel, where lived John Short, a chantey singer. He then held the office of Town Crier, but previously he had spent over fifty years in sailing-ships. Cecil Sharp has remarked on John Short's rich, resonant and powerful voice which is 'yet so flexible that he can execute trills, turns and graces with a delicacy and finish that would excite the envy of many a professional artist'. John Short liked to be near the sea when singing and so he and Cecil Sharp would sit side by side on the quay and John Short would sing happily through the noise of wind and waves while Cecil Sharp smoked his pipe and jotted down the tunes. *English Folk-Chanteys* (1914) is dedicated to George Butterworth. It contains sixty chanteys from a total of one hundred and fifty which had been noted from old sailors living in retirement. Of these sixty chanteys, forty-six were sung by John Short. Cecil Sharp disclaimed all technical and practical knowledge of nautical matters, but the introduction to his collection contains useful information on the relationship of the chantey with the work which it accompanies.

In February 1914, Cecil Sharp arranged the music and dances for Harley Granville Barker's famous production of *A. Midsummer Night's Dream*, with décor by Norman Wilkinson, at the Savoy Theatre, London. The production gained notoriety on account of the 'gold fairies': 'those d—d gilt fairies' as Granville Barker referred to them later when explaining that they were an experiment devised to keep the fairies and mortals distinct upon an unrealistic stage. According to him, 'all the production was really remarkable for was the attempt to get the lyric verse spoken, and this [needed] five years' discipline instead of five weeks, and the pushing of Mendelssohn'.[1]

Cecil Sharp spoke of it as 'the most exciting time of my life'. For the music, he used folk tunes, except for the song, 'Roses their Sharp Spines being gone', which Granville Barker had taken from *The Two Noble Kinsmen* to supply a missing lyric. This Cecil Sharp set to an original composition in the folk idiom. He agreed with Granville Barker that Mendelssohn must be 'pushed' if only

---

[1] In a letter to A. H. Fox Strangways, 7th January 1932.

because his music holds up the action and does not allow the words to come through. With the exception of the Bergomask dance, for which he used the Wyresdale Greensleeves dance, he composed the dances, basing them on folk-dance movements and steps. Particularly lovely was the 'roundel' danced around the sleeping Titania on the 'bank where the wild thyme blows'. As well as arranging the dances, Cecil Sharp taught and rehearsed them and I was privileged to help him. I was even fitted for a pair of gold tights in case of emergency, but, sad to say, I was not called upon to wear them in action.

Cecil Sharp published the songs and incidental music (1914) and in the introduction he discusses the general problem of setting Shakespeare's songs to music. He puts forward three ways in which it might be done: (1) to take contemporary settings, but none are extant for that play; (2) to write in the Elizabethan style, which would be a fake; and (3) to write in the style of today, and to risk going out of fashion. He rejects all these three ways in favour of using folk music, thus 'mating the drama which is for all time with the music which is for all time'.

On 11th May 1914, Granville Barker wrote to Cecil Sharp:

> The Dream is over . . . I cannot say how grateful I am to you for all you did, but then you don't need pretty things said. Workers know each other by instinct and thank each other by what they do, and if you will work with me again I would prefer to thank you that way.

Cecil Sharp did work with him again, in the New York production of *A Midsummer Night's Dream*, as we shall see in the next chapter, and he also undertook the music for his production of Thomas Hardy's *The Dynasts*[1] at the Kingsway Theatre later in the year.

[1] The pianoforte score is in the Vaughan Williams Library at Cecil Sharp House.

XI
Visits to America
1914–18

After all not to create only, or found only,
But to bring perhaps from afar what is already founded,
To give it our own identity, average, limitless, free,
To fill the gross, the torpid bulk with vital religious fire,
Not to repel or destroy so much as to accept, fuse, ehabilitate,
To obey as well as command, to follow more than lead,
These also are the lessons of our New World;
While how little the New after all, how much the Old, Old, World!
                        WALT WHITMAN, *Song of the Exposition*

IN AUGUST 1914 Cecil Sharp was directing the English Folk
Dance Society's Summer School at Stratford-on-Avon. In spite of
a few cancellations the School ran its normal course and the men's
demonstration team remained intact until the end of the month,
when its members dispersed, never to dance together again.

Cecil Sharp quickly realized the catastrophic implications of the
war, and some of his younger friends who found it difficult to
know where their duty lay were grateful to him for his advice. His
son Charles, without any advice, added three months to his age
and, though at first refused on account of short-sight, eventually
got into the Middlesex Regiment as a private. Later on he had a
commission in the Grenadier Guards. Cecil Sharp himself at
fifty-four was too old for active service, and there was no kind of
war-work for which he was suited. Folk-dance and folk-song
activities, except for a few classes, were in abeyance. He found

himself accordingly without any vital occupation and with but little prospect of being able to provide for his family.

At the end of the year Granville Barker asked him to help him with his New York production of *A Midsummer Night's Dream*. He accepted the invitation, hoping that, in addition, he would get some lecture engagements in America which would relieve the financial situation. He sailed in S.S. *Lusitania* and arrived in New York just before Christmas. At that time it was still the fashion to speak with contempt of the 'skyscraper', but Cecil was enchanted by the beauty of New York. He would often, after the day's work, leave his hotel – the Algonquin in West 44th Street – for the pleasure of wandering alone in the Grand Central Station and the neighbouring streets.

He found the new life exciting and stimulating, but on the whole he was not very happy. On Christmas Day, a day or two after his arrival, he writes:

Twenty or thirty years ago, I could have stood this startling change better than I can now. My outlook is so different from that of everyone here that I feel out of everything. At the present moment nothing would please me more than to know that I was returning to England by the next boat. Very likely I shall get used to things by degrees and get on better, but I feel very lonely at the moment.

He was worried too and anxious about his prospects. He writes to Constance:

I only hope I may bring a little money back to pay for the move and to make our new house a bit more decent than Dragonfield. It has been on my mind – as I think you know – that my inability to make money has pressed so hardly on you and the children. I have hated to think that the latter are getting such a bad start in life.

At one time he felt inclined to give up all idea of lecturing and to return home as soon as his work at the theatre was finished, but he resisted the temptation, made up his mind to try his luck and cabled for Mattie Kay to join him in order to illustrate his lectures.

Of his first lecture, at the Colony Club, New York, he writes:

To Maud Karpeles, 18. 1. 1915
I have got through my first lecture – a terrible ordeal. I am afraid I did very badly indeed. I was not nervous, but the audience consisted of a social crowd, 90% of which didn't care a hang for the subject, and I was sensitive enough to realize this and it choked me off after my first

few sentences . . . I am afraid I have ruined my chances here of becoming a popular lecturer – at any rate, of getting private drawing-room
lectures which would pay me best.

And in the same letter:

There is really an enormous lot of work to be done here in populariz-
ing the subject, but it would take ages to do it – in fact, it would be
doing over again all that I have done in England, and this I have neither
the time to do nor the inclination to attempt. It all convinces me that I
am not cut out to make money – I haven't the right temperament for
that sort of thing. So I must be philosophic and resigned to my lot,
and to dying a poor man I After all, the work I have done is far more
important than a mere means of making a living, and I know it has
some permanent value which will last long after I have disappeared
from the scene; so that my own individual comfort is of small moment,

Two public lectures, given at the Plaza Hotel some days later
went better. At the second of these he showed country dances for
two couples, in which he danced himself.

The two lectures went rippingly. Mattie Kay sang a couple of songs, I
lectured, played a lot of Morris tunes, showed slides, played the pipe
and tabor, and finally danced four country dances, or rather five, as
'Merry Conceit' was encored! The people were really most enthusiastic
and everyone remained to the end, i.e. for over two hours.

During the first six weeks most of his time was occupied with
the theatre. Whilst the rehearsing of *A Midsummer Night's Dream*
was still in progress, Granville Barker produced Anatole France's
The Man who Married a Dumb Wife. For this, Cecil Sharp arranged
some songs, street-cries, and dances, introducing the tune of
Dargason, a happy choice, for the Blind Man's Song and Final
Dance. During the rehearsals of *A Midsummer Night's Dream* he
was full of fears. The dancers were unmusical; the musicians and
the conductor were hopeless; and it was 'simply awful to hear
those beautiful tunes spoiled'.

To Maud Karpeles,   29. 1. 1915
    The most annoying part of it all is that Cecil Forsyth, who is over
here, has offered to conduct for me, and of course that would be an ideal
arrangement, but he is not a member of this infernal [Musicians']
Union and if he were to conduct, every member of the band would
promptly walk out of the theatre, followed in all probability by all the
scene-shifters and attendants at the theatre. And he can only become a

member of the Union by paying £25 and then only if he is elected and has previously spent six months in the country. . . . They won't even let *me* conduct my own music except for one performance!

But the first performance belied his fears and after a few weeks he writes:

To Maud Karpeles,   28. 3. 1915
It [the dance in Act II, Sc. ii] went just splendidly, better than I have ever known it go before. It delighted me beyond measure and I know it is beautiful. Indeed it seems to me quite perfect – I don't mind saying this to you – and I am quite certain I shall never do anything half so beautiful again. How I came to do it I really can't imagine. It is the only thing that I can call 'inspired' that I have done. . . .
But I am not really fond of the theatre – still less of theatrical life and theatrical people. I think I must be too serious an artist, but I can't help disliking the slap-dash way in which theatre people work and the way they leave so much to the chance or inspiration of the moment.

So he argues to himself, but he is evidently not quite convinced as is shown by the following letter written to Constance the same day:

There is no doubt that this trip here has opened up all sorts of possibilities. It is a pity that I did not come when I was a bit younger. I feel torn in two ways. The opportunity of trying my hand on theatre music and dancing is very alluring to me, while on the other hand I want to complete my folk-song and dance work in England. Whether it is possible to do both of these things or not I cannot at present say. However, these things have a way of settling themselves if left alone.

As soon as he had finished with rehearsals he worked hard to get lecture and teaching engagements. The dances proved to be more popular than the songs, and so after some weeks Mattie Kay returned to England and Cecil worked single-handed. Besides New York, he visited Boston, Pittsburgh, Chicago, Philadelphia, and Pittsfield. 'I worked terribly hard at Pittsburgh,' he writes, 'taking five or six hours' classes each of the four days I was there and lecturing three times'; but this was surpassed at Chicago, where on his last day he taught for eight and a half hours and finished with a lecture of one and a half hours.
By the beginning of March he can write:

People are really beginning to rise to me and my preaching, and to be attracted by the latter, at any rate, partly because of its novelty and partly because it convinces them.

Three weeks later, as testimony of his belief that the dances had taken root in America, he established a U.S.A. branch of the English Folk Dance Society with Centres in New York, Boston, Chicago, and Pittsburgh. At the same time he agreed to direct a Summer School later in the year.

Cecil's initial motive in seeking engagements had been to earn a living, and he succeeded in making a clear profit of £400 in four months and, no doubt, could have made more had that been his sole, or even his main, interest. On 15th March he wrote to me:

I believe if I had the pluck and I were keen enough – and I am not – I could coin money out here. The way to do it would be to get up a really swagger studio and make a bid for social people and charge enormous fees. But really when it comes to the point I feel I can't do it. Why, I hardly know; but to make money by charging disproportionate fees for the work done goes against the grain . . . The whole question of making money is very much on my mind at the moment and I cannot see through it. The question has never occurred before in my life, because I have never had the chance of making it; and I feel very funny about it. I feel a sneaking satisfaction that I have proved that I could make it after all if I were to get myself to do it! I am afraid you won't make much out of this – nor can I!

And again a week later:

Sometimes I wish I wasn't making money, which is very stupid; at other times I pore over my cheque book and accounts as though I were a miser . . . I believe I am fast becoming a horrid businessman and sordid money-grubber!

He need have had no fear! One had only to accompany him into a second-hand bookshop and hear him discourse with enthusiasm on the great value and rarity of the dance-books which the book-seller was endeavouring to sell him to realize that Cecil Sharp would never be a businessman. He was absorbed in the songs and dances, and his first thought was always to share his interest with others.

Moreover, in spite of his irritation at some aspects of American life, he had come to like the people, and consequently his desire to give rather than to receive became all the greater. This liking afterwards developed into real affection and he numbered many Americans amongst his best friends. On his first visit he became acquainted with Mrs. Dawson Callery of Pittsburgh, and Mrs. James Storrow of Boston, with whom he had previously corresponded. Both became enthusiastic disciples, and 'it was worth while coming to America to make friends with them'. Mrs. Storrow, a name now familiar to folk dancers on both sides of the Atlantic, is described as 'a woman after my own heart, as wise as she is genuine and nice . . . a fine product of this country . . .'[1]

His general impressions after he has been in the country a few months are given in a letter to his daughter Joan (5. 4. 1916):

It is a very exciting life, seeing new people and new scenes almost every day. The people interest me. They are full of vitality, consciously groping for ideals and getting somewhere, but without any clear idea of their objective. They live in a little world of their own knowing little of what the greater world outside is doing, and caring less, but all the time determining to make a great country of the land that belongs to them. I find it very stimulating, and at times, of course, very irritating. It does not make me feel 'superior' at all; indeed, I feel very humble at times in the presence of an enormous population all striving so hard to get somewhere. Some day perhaps you will see it all with me, and perhaps with younger eyes you will see further and deeper than I can.

The aspect of American character that most irritated him was what he termed 'their old maid's delight in exercising moral control over others'. After recovering from an attack of gout, he writes to Mr. Lennox Gilmour (6. 7. 1918):

It was not the result of high living or inordinate drinking! Although if I did take to drink out here it would not be surprising. The superior self-righteousness of the people with regard to that question maddens me sometimes and almost forces me to get drunk by way of protest.

This is an example of the rhetorical tirades with which on occasion he would vent his feelings. They but rarely gave offence, for they were always tinged with good-humour; and no matter how fierce was the onslaught, he usually finished with a laugh against himself. 'Well, I gave them something to think about,' he would say afterwards with the delight of a schoolboy.

On 21st April 1915, Cecil sailed for England in S.S. *Adriatic* having made plans to return to America in June. He was pressed

---

[1] She died in 1944. A room at Cecil Sharp House is dedicated to her memory.

by his friends not to take the risk of the double voyage, or at any rate to delay his journey for a week and sail in S.S. *Lusitania*, which being a faster ship was thought to be safer. But Cecil, who hated a change once his mind was made up, did not 'like the idea of allowing those—Germans' to upset his plans. So perhaps for once his obstinacy saved his life.

After a couple of months in England, he returned to America. I was to have travelled with him but, having contracted scarlet-fever together with other members of the Sharp family, I had to follow a week later. I joined him at Mrs. James Storrow's lovely house at Lincoln, Mass., where he was staying. He had been occupied in directing the dances for a pageant at Wellesley College with the assistance of Lily Roberts who had come out from England for that purpose. Lily afterwards devoted herself to folk-dance teaching in Boston. On 15th December 1917 she was given away in marriage to Richard Conant by Cecil Sharp. She has been and still is one of the leading spirits of the folk-dance movement in America.

After the Wellesley pageant, Cecil Sharp directed a three weeks' Summer School, assisted by three English teachers: Lily Roberts, Nora Jervis, who was residing in America, and myself. The School was held at Eliot, Maine, in a camp delightfully situated on the banks of the Piscataqua River. The students, of whom there were sixty, slept in wooden shacks and the classroom accommodation was provided by a barn and two large marquees with wooden floors, which had been erected especially for the purpose. But the ideal surroundings were marred by abnormally wet weather, and when at the end of two weeks the marquees were blown down and flooded, the whole School moved and took up its quarters at a Hotel and Conference Centre some miles away. It was a happy gathering and the students took to the dancing with great enthusiasm. Among them was Charles Rabold, a musician and teacher, who became one of Cecil's most ardent followers. He gave up his other musical work and devoted himself entirely to the teaching and dissemination of English folk song and dance. He was unhappily killed in an aeroplane accident in 1930.

Another disciple was Miss Susan Gilman who had a fashionable dance studio in New York. So impressed was she by the gospel that Cecil Sharp was preaching that she gave up nearly all her other work in order to devote herself to the teaching of English folk dancing. She and Charles Rabold became two of our most intimate friends.

Cecil Sharp had every reason to be satisfied with the Summer School for it consolidated the interest which he had already aroused and brought in many fresh recruits. But an event which was to have far greater consequences had occurred just before the Summer School. This was a visit from Mrs. Olive Dame Campbell which he received when he was imprisoned in Mrs. Storrow's house at Lincoln with an acute attack of lumbago. Mrs. Campbell was the wife of Mr. John C. Campbell, the Director of the Southern Highland Division of the Russell Sage Foundation, whose work had taken him through the Southern Appalachian Mountains. Mrs. Campbell had on more than one occasion accompanied him and, coming into close touch with the mountain people, had heard them sing. She was impressed with the beauty of the songs, which were unlike anything else she had heard, and noted down some seventy of them. Hearing that Cecil Sharp was in America she decided to seek his help and interest, and made a special journey from the south. Her first meeting with him may be described in her own words:

He was sitting very straight in an imposing high-backed chair . . . a table in front of him. He could not get up, but he greeted me with an easy apology to the effect that he was indulging in a rich man's malady – gout, but that he owed it to his ancestors rather than to any luxuries permitted by his own income. I got a quick impression of his fresh colour, high, clearly cut features and the nervous force of his personality His eye was obviously on my bundle of papers, and I wasted no time in laying it before him.

'How did you take this down?' he asked. I explained meekly that I was not a trained musician. I had had to learn the melodies from the lips of the singer, noting down rough helps. I worked out the whole afterwards, using a piano if I could and going back again to the singer to check myself. A long time after he paid a compliment to my exactness of memory, which I am proud to remember, but at the time: 'Of course, you know that is a very unscientific way of recording', was his uncompromising observation.

The moments fled by. I consulted my watch from time to time, but did not like to interrupt him. Moreover, I certainly could not detect any signs of boredom or exhaustion. When he finally laid the pile of manuscripts on the table and turned to me, it was with a keen but relaxed and almost lenient look. All the charm of his most winning mood was shed upon me as he explained how many people had brought 'ballads' to him before, but that this was the first time that he had come on any really original and valuable material.

I am told he improved from that day.

We returned to England in July in S.S. *St. Paul* and the voyage home was unexpectedly brightened by the discovery of an old chantey singer among the ship's crew. Permission was given him to visit Cecil's cabin when off duty and day by day he appeared punctually at the appointed hour, equipped with a sheet of news-paper which he solicitously spread on the bed before taking his seat on it.

On arrival in England Cecil was met with the distressing news of his wife's serious illness – heart trouble following scarlet-fever. She ultimately recovered sufficiently to be able to get up and about, but she remained a semi-invalid for the rest of her life.

In October 1915, the family moved to 27 Church Row, Hamp-stead, a panelled house of the late seventeenth century, described by Cecil as 'about the time of the sixth edition of Playford'. He spent most of his time preparing for publication *One Hundred English Folk Songs*, which had been commissioned by the Oliver Ditson Company, Boston.[1] Most of the songs had already been published in *Folk-Songs from Somerset* and other collections, but he took this opportunity to revise the texts, reverting more closely to the originals, and of rewriting many of the pianoforte accompani-ments.

After he had finished this work he became very restive. He feared that war conditions had put a stop to his hopes of a per-manent and widespread revival of the dances in England and he was almost at the end of his financial resources. Furthermore, he was itching to get to work in the Appalachian Mountains for, from what he had seen in Mrs. Campbell's manuscript collection, he suspected that there was 'a mine, which if properly and scienti-fically explored would yield results – musical, historical, literary – of the first importance'. He had a faint hope that for this he might get some financial help from the Carnegie Corporation of New York. To Mrs. Storrow he writes (7. 12. 1916):

[1] With some modifications he published the contents later in *English Folk-Songs, Selected Edition*.

I have heard nothing from the Carnegie people so I am almost afraid that nothing will come of that project . . . I think that if they made any sort of offer I should take your advice and come out to America and see if I could continue the work which I started last winter. Apart from ways and means I feel that if the dances are to be firmly rooted anywhere in my lifetime it will be in America rather than in England. The movement is languishing here, of course, and there seems no chance of things becoming normal again for an indefinite time. And I do very much want to see the dances thoroughly well started before I disappear, so that the tradition may not be lost. If therefore, you can see any real prospect of my doing something in this direction in your country, and at the same time something to ease the financial strain from which I am at present suffering, I will come out at once.

Help from the Carnegie Corporation did not come, nor did any definite promise of work, but he decided to take the risk, and in February 1916 he returned to America. He began by organizing classes and lectures in New York. He soon had sufficient engagements to keep him fully occupied until mid-July. In April 1916 he wrote from Kalamazoo to his friend, Paul Oppé:

I have managed somehow or other to get plenty of work since I arrived here about seven weeks ago, and, what is more to the point, I have been able to send something home already to keep the family going. So the anxiety on that score, which was rather acute when I last saw you is, I am glad to say, allayed. I am selling myself for a week at a time to different cities – Asheville, St. Louis, Cincinnati and now here, and after this for a month at Pittsburgh. I charge a pretty high figure – high, that is, to English notions – and then let them get what they can out of me. I usually teach four or five hours a day and give one or sometimes two lectures, so that they get a good deal out of me measured by time and energy! I enjoy it very much, though I feel it rather a strain, especially when the classes are large – they have been as large as seventy or eighty!

After six weeks of highly concentrated work interspersed with long railway journeys the strain told on him rather severely, and on Mrs. Callery's advice he cabled for me to come out from England to help with the teaching. This I did, joining him at Pittsburgh, and I remained with him throughout his subsequent travels in America. I was able to relieve him of some of the burden of teaching and also to help him with his correspondence. The latter was particularly necessary as his neuritis had not completely subsided.

XV(a) Mrs Broughton of
Kentucky

XV(b) Miller Coffey of
Virginia, the singer of
'Arise, Arise'

XV(c) Mrs Donald Shelton (Emma
Hensley) of North Carolina (see p. 170)

XVI(a) Mrs Wheeler and her family (see pp. 167-8)

XVI(b) Cecil Sharp with Aunt Betsy

XVI(c) Cecil Sharp and Maud Karpeles noting a song

XVI APPALACHIAN MOUNTAIN SINGERS

The year 1916 was, as it happened, a particularly auspicious one for Cecil Sharp's work, owing to the numerous Shakespeare Tercentenary celebrations which were being held all over the country. He abhorred most forms of pageantry, but he recognized these celebrations as a useful means of introducing English folk music and dances. Accordingly, when the New York Centre of the English Folk Dance Society was invited to provide an English 'Interlude' in Percy Mackaye's *Masque of Caliban*, to be performed in the New York Stadium, Cecil agreed to compose the scenario and to direct the performance. The Interlude represented the celebration of an Elizabethan May-Day Festival on the outskirts of an English village and consisted of a series of Processional, Country and Morris dances, together with songs, hobby-horse, maypole, and other folk-rituals, all skilfully woven together and set off to advantage by Robert E. Jones's costume designs. The entrance of four or five hundred dancers in the Tideswell Processional accompanied by four clarinets (two Bb and two Eb in unison) with two side-drums, [1] aroused a murmur of delight among the audience of some twenty thousand spectators; and 'This is what I should like to be *doing*' was heard on all sides. Cecil was highly delighted and wrote:

It was like a puff of fresh country air laden with the smell of the hedgerows coming in the midst of artificial, exotic surroundings . . . No country in the world can be gay in the simple, fresh way that England can – it is our contribution to civilization. I felt more proud of being an Englishman than I have ever felt before. And the spirit of the tunes and dances was such that all participants became infected by it and for the moment they became English, every Jew, German, French, Italian, Slav one of them.

To Percy MacKaye he wrote in the same vein, adding: 'Sumer is icumen in' [which was sung as an introduction to the Interlude] is the real motto of the English people.' It was no doubt this quality of 'gay simplicity' which persuaded a judging committee of experts – actors and theatrical producers – to award first prize to this Interlude in preference to those of other European countries. The Interlude was repeated as part of other Shakespeare celebrations at St. Louis and Cincinnati, and these performances occupied Cecil until the date of the Summer School, held in this and the

[1] This combination had been suggested by Cecil Forsyth.

following year at Amherst Agricultural College (Mass.). In expressing his satisfaction at the result of the School he writes:

To Mrs. Storrow   16. 7. 1916
This last School has dissipated the chief fear I have had here, viz. whether the average American student would take the trouble to acquire the complicated technique which our English dances – and indeed all dances worthy of the name – require. I was told so much about the craze for quick results demanded in this country. But so far as this particular subject is concerned I find no difference between the American and the English student, and I find it no more difficult to interest one than the other, nor to inspire one to work as hard as the other.

However, there were many obstacles to overcome. He had to convince his pupils that the English dances as presented by him had more content than the many so-called folk dances of other nations with which the country was overrun; and he had also to overcome the objection that American citizens were not justified in devoting more time to English dances than to those of other countries. He met this by pointing out that culture is determined mainly by language, and that as Americans had adopted the English language it was only logical that English song and dance should likewise play a prominent part as a cultural subject.

Many of his pupils had learned 'aesthetic' dancing, described by Cecil as 'a poisonous, bowdlerized form of the so-called "classical" ballet . . . which produces a peculiarly odious form of obsequious crawl'. This 'crawl' found its way into the country dancing but it soon disappeared together with other faults before his merciless but kindly chaff. He put his pupils at their ease by making their task so absorbing that they had no time to be selfconscious. Combining enthusiasm for his subject with an appreciation of the personalities of his pupils, he could charm academic professors, refined young ladies from a 'millionaire' boarding-school, or crude young men of a physical training class.

Cecil Sharp found nearly everywhere an overweening belief in the power of education coupled with a depreciation of the instinctive faculties. At the end of a week's course of instruction at a large women's college he remarked to the Principal of the Physical Training Department on the fact that not one of the girls had a natural movement in running. Her face fell as she saw the justice of his criticism, and she replied: 'I am afraid it is true, and it is our fault. We have never taught them how to run!'

He got a great deal of satisfaction and amusement from his teaching. To his daughter Joan:

I have been taking a lot of folk-dance classes and am learning how to manage them in the orthodox Karpeles-cum-Kennedy manner!

The other day I was coaching a Morris side made up of University Professors. One of them habitually omitted the hop in the '4/3 step'. So I stood before him and showed him what he was doing and what he ought to do. He said: 'Yes, I know that, but – I am not hopping today.' I heard afterwards that he was going to a tea-party after the rehearsal and didn't want to spoil his collar!

We spent two months in the Appalachian Mountains (see next chapter) from July until September 1916, when we had engagements in Chicago. Towards the end of our journey in the mountains we received the grievous news that three of the English dancers, Perceval Lucas, Reginald Tiddy and George Butterworth had been killed in action and George Wilkinson was missing (afterwards reported killed). Cecil was crushed by the news. It 'put the sun out' for him. It made him realize how much it had meant to him to have the intimate association with the 'choicest spirits of the younger generation' and how he had been depending upon them to carry on his work. He wrote to Peggy Kettlewell: 'Their deaths make me feel very lonely and solitary. Except for Douglas and Vaughan Williams there is no one left among the men.'

On arrival in Chicago he had further bad news. Cables from Constance awaited him informing him that their son Charles had been seriously wounded. For many weeks Charles's condition remained critical and Cecil's anxiety was all the greater because cables were subject to delay. He wanted to throw up his engagements and return home immediately, but he could not afford to do so. So we remained until the end of the year, fulfilling the many teaching and lecturing engagements, including a week's work at Toronto, where at this time of exile he rejoiced to be for a short while under the sway of the Union Jack.

About this time Cecil writes to his wife:

I am in grand dancing form and am making quite a reputation as a dancer! Moreover I have added another accomplishment and now sing my own ballads at my lectures unaccompanied! Maud and I sing some together and I sing some alone! It is really a very effective way of showing them. . . . . The fact that our voices are just ordinary is really the point of the performance.

In fact, we started quite a vogue in unaccompanied singing and in consequence several professional singers felt it necessary to apologize to us when admitting that they sang the songs with pianoforte accompaniment.

From December 1916 to February 1917 we were in England and Cecil walked daily across Hampstead Heath to Highgate Hospital where his son Charles was lying. Charles eventually recovered though his health was impaired. He became a botanist and held various posts in Africa and Malaysia. His widow and two children survive him.

In February 1917 we were back in America and we remained there until December 1918. A few days before our intended departure on a Dutch liner, Germany declared her policy of submarine warfare against neutral shipping and in consequence the sailing of the Dutch ship was cancelled. After some days' delay passages were booked in S.S. *Baltic*, the first available British ship, and New York was finally reached after a fortnight on board ship, including a preliminary four days when we were tied up in the Mersey without any contact with the outside world. During the early part of the voyage Cecil was strained and nervous: as usual, he was alive to physical danger, and, as usual, he did not disguise that fear. In writing to his son he owns to the strain of the voyage and ends his letter with one of his typical jokes:

> There were only five women – including Maud – on board ship, and if they all behaved like Maud and a lady friend . . . their chief anxiety was how to dress for the life-boat. They were not so much concerned with the matter of comfort and warmth as with the look of things. O these women!

After our arrival we fulfilled engagements at the University of Illinois, Pittsburgh, and other towns, and then spent from April to October in the Mountains, except for a break of five weeks to direct Summer Schools in New York and Amherst.

On 23rd November Cecil Sharp gave an invitation-lecture at the Hall of the Russell Sage Foundation on the current year's work in the Appalachian Mountains; and he gave the first performance of the Running Set, the dance we had recently discovered in Kentucky, taking part in it himself. His book[1] containing 323 tunes had been published the preceding day, and with this tangible evidence of the results of his work he had high hopes that some institution would be ready to finance his further efforts. Throughout the year he had made persistent efforts to get support from various public bodies, but had met with no success, and, except for some private assistance from Mrs. Storrow and other friends, had been thrown back on his own resources. Whilst in the mountains he had had a serious breakdown in health and in order to avoid the double strain of earning a living and carrying on his investigations it was important to get some financial backing. An application to the Carnegie Institution of Washington, supported by the highest recommendations, was, however, refused.

In April, after a winter's work in Chicago, we were back in the mountains. From Virginia we made a short trip in May to Washington where Cecil gave a lecture at the house of Mr. Henry White before a distinguished audience which included Monsieur Jusserand, at that time French Ambassador at Washington, and (Sir) Shane Leslie whom Cecil had taught at Ludgrove. The Capitol made a deep impression upon him, and although he found it possible to criticize the details of the decoration, the general effect of the group of buildings produced 'a great emotion'. He felt that the whole conception was an expression of the deep feeling which had been inspired by the ideal of a government of free people, and it gave him a better understanding of American aims and aspirations.

A Summer School at Amherst (Mass.) and classes in New York and Boston occupied July. Cecil had hoped to vary the scene of his researches by going to Newfoundland, thus escaping the intense heat of the south during August, but the expense of the journey ruled out this plan, so we reluctantly gave up the idea and returned to the Appalachian Mountains.

In November 1918 we were hard at work again in Boston, Cleveland and Detroit. We had planned to spend the winter in California and to collect in other parts of the United States and in Newfoundland during the following spring and summer months, but as the end of war came within sight his longing to return home became very great. Already in August he wrote:

[1] *English Folk-Songs from the Southern Appalachians*, collected by Olive Dame Campbell and Cecil Sharp.

I want to get home again. The restless life I am leading begins to tell
. . . I am too old to grow roots in a new country like this.

And on 9th November:

I go nearly wild when I think of a quiet room with my piano and my
books around me.

Armistice Day was passed at Cleveland, Ohio, the streets
'crammed with people, hooting, shouting, rattling and making
every conceivable noise'. In his diary:

11. 11. 1918
A wonderful day, but I do not feel like making a noise . . . I cannot forget
poor Butterworth, Tiddy, Percy [Lucas] and the many others. Here they
have made few sacrifices.

Cecil knew that his work in England would be needed, and so,
throwing up all engagements, we sailed from New York on 10th
December. In mid-Atlantic he wrote:

To Mrs. Storrow   17. 12. 1918
I find it hard to realize the happenings of the last few weeks – those
stupendous events which have influenced the whole world as well as
those which have affected my own little puny plans. What the future has
in store for me I know not, and there is not much use in speculating –
it will all be decided for me. But I believe it is going to be interesting
and full of opportunity. The result of my American experiences should
stand me in good stead and help me to solve some of the problems with
which no doubt I shall soon be confronted. I would that I had visited
America twenty years ago before my character and habits had been so
fixed. Still I have learned something of which I ought to be able to
make good use.

One of the pleasures which Cecil derived from his stay in
America was the meeting and exchanging of views with fellow-
scholars.1 Those he saw most frequently were Professor G. L.
Kittredge, at whose request a copy of the Appalachian collection
was deposited at Harvard University; and Professor C. R. Basker-
vill of the University of Chicago, who in his *The Elizabethan Jig*
(1929) has incorporated some of the theories that he and Cecil

---

[1] It is of interest that during the last fifty years there has been a great increase in
folk-song scholarship in America and also that Cecil Sharp's pioneer work in the
Southern Appalachians has been succeeded by the publication of numerous collections of Anglo-American folk songs which have been gathered from many regions of
the North American continent.

Sharp then discussed. There were also less frequent meetings with Professor H. M. Belden of the University of Missouri, a pioneer in the regional collection and study of folk-song; with Mr. E. Phillips Barry, one of the few who at that time had studied the music of folk song; and with Professor F. H. Gummere (see p. 65) who invited Cecil to lecture at Haverford College.

And thus, with the adventures of the Appalachian Mountains yet to be described, there ends an important chapter in Cecil Sharp's life, for he did not visit America again, although he kept in touch with his many American friends and with the folk-dance organization which he had established. But the chapter has its sequel in the folk-dance activities which have gone on there continuously up to the present time.[1] Cecil Sharp regarded the dissemination of the dances in America as a natural corollary to their revival in England. He held that in spite of superficial differences the two countries had the same ideals and aspirations, and that English folk song and dance belong to both as a common culture. He believed also that the American contribution to the art of folk dancing was genuinely complementary in its vigour, spontaneity and simplicity of expression.

[1] The U.S.A. Branch of the English Folk Dance Society later became The Country Dance Society of America and it is largely due to its Director, Miss May Gadd, that English folk dancing continues to flourish in America.

XII

The Appalachian Mountains I
1916

Great things are done when men and mountains meet;
This is not done by jostling in the street.

WILLIAM BLAKE

CECIL SHARP had often pictured in imagination what it would
have been like to have been born a few centuries earlier, when
English folk song was the common musical expression of old and
young alike. And it seemed almost like a miracle when he discovered that England of his dreams in the United States of
America: in the beautiful country of the Southern Appalachian
Mountains.

The southern portion of the Appalachian Mountain system is
situated in the eastern States, about two hundred to two hundred
and fifty miles from the Atlantic seaboard and running more or
less parallel to it. It comprises several ranges – the Blue Ridge,
Great Smokies, Cumberland Mountains, Black Mountains,
Alleghanies, etc. – and the region, which is an extensive one –
considerably larger than England, Wales and Scotland combined –
covers about one-third of the total area of the States of North and
South Carolina, Tennessee, Kentucky, Virginia, West Virginia,
Georgia, and Alabama. The population is (or was) over five
million, or excluding city-dwellers, about three million.

The history of the settlement of the mountains is to some extent conjectural, but the inhabitants are mainly descended from
colonial stock who had migrated from England, the lowlands of

Scotland, and the north of Ireland (the Scotch-Irish) some time during the eighteenth century. Their motive for doing so was probably to better their fortunes; and where they found coast-lands already occupied, or competition with slave-labour distasteful and unprofitable, they moved westwards. Possibly their aim was to trek through to the fertile Blue Grass region of Kentucky, of which they may have heard from the Indians, but, weary of the struggle of penetrating virgin forests, and finding abundant game, and here and there fertile valleys, they decided to make the best of their immediate surroundings. And there, isolated in the seclusion of the mountains, they and their descendants have been living for many generations, [1] enjoying few of the amenities of modern civilization, but possessing the priceless heritage of their traditional musical culture.

During the years 1916–18 Cecil Sharp and I spent twelve months in the Southern Appalachian Mountains, forty-six weeks being given to actual collecting – nine weeks in 1916, and about twice as long in each of the following years. We travelled over a big area, spending about three and a half months in each of the States of North Carolina, Virginia and Kentucky, a month in Tennessee, and a few days in West Virginia. We visited altogether between seventy and eighty different small towns and settlements.

In the spring of 1916 Cecil had paid a short visit to Mr. and Mrs. John Campbell in order to discuss plans with them and to re-note the tunes that Mrs. Campbell had already collected, between seventy and eighty in number. He writes shortly after his visit:

To me it is quite wonderful that anyone so little in touch with any work of the kind that has been done elsewhere should have set herself such a high standard and, in effect, reached it. She has just the combination of scientific and artistic spirit which work of this kind needs if it is to be of any use to posterity . . . What she has so far accomplished is of great value, but I gather that it is after all only the beginning. The field that has yielded what she has harvested must be a very rich one, and its exploration must be thoroughly done as soon as possible, for I gather from her that present conditions are rapidly undermining and destroying the traditions.

[1] See John C. Campbell's *The Southern Highlander and his Homeland*, Chapter 3, 'Pioneer Routes of Travel and Early Settlements' (Russell Sage Foundation, New York, 1911). This work contains valuable information on the history and life of the mountain people.

Not only did Cecil Sharp appreciate the pioneer work that Mrs. Campbell had done, but he was 'anxious not to do anything discourteous to her nor to queer her pitch in any way', and therefore, before deciding to undertake any investigation, he made certain that he had her complete concurrence. He wrote to her on 15th August 1915:

It would be impossible for me or anyone else to do the work without your good help . . . The simplest scheme would be for us to form a partnership and the results of our work to be published under both our names. You would bring to the pot an intimate knowledge of the district and of the people and a certain amount of material that you have already collected, and I should supply experience in this particular kind of work and a certain amount of musical and scientific knowledge . . . It would be a thousand pities if any personal considerations were to prevent such important work from being done.

Mrs. Campbell's reply left no doubt in his mind. She wrote:

I want the collecting done and done by the person most competent to do it, and if I could have wished for a definite result from my work it would have been to attract to this region just such a person as yourself.

Mrs. Campbell was unable to continue her collecting or to accompany Cecil Sharp on his travels, but she and her husband planned his first expedition and Mr. Campbell acted as guide for a few days.

The first half of 1916 was filled with lecture and teaching engagements and it was not until the last week of July that we were free to start on our travels; and even then it looked as though they might have to be delayed owing to the damage to rail and roads caused by recent floods. Our objective was Asheville in North Carolina, which we had chosen as our first base. Ordinarily it is an easy journey of less than twenty-four hours from New York but the main lines had been washed away in several places and we were told that it would be some days before the trains would be running again. To wait, even for a few days, was more than patience could bear. After repeated visits to railway bureaux and persistent telegraphing it was found that by making a big detour Asheville could be reached by a small branch mountain railway. So on 23rd July Cecil Sharp and I left New York in great heat, and after forty-eight hours in the train and an uncomfortable night in a small and dirty mining-town in Tennessee we arrived at

Asheville and were met by Mr. and Mrs. Campbell who took us to their home.

On their advice we decided to explore first that region of North Carolina which is known as the Laurel Country, so named because of the abundance of rhododendrons (called 'laurel' by the mountain people) which grow on the mountainside. The real laurel is called ivy, the ivy becomes vine, and our vine is distinguished as the grape-vine, 'and after that I suppose they get straight again', Cecil Sharp would add.

The journey from Asheville presented difficulties, for the roads, such as they were, had been greatly damaged by the floods, and the railway which might have served for part of the journey was out of action. The experience is described by Cecil Sharp in a letter to his wife (31. 7.1916):

We breakfasted at 7 a.m., then motored to a place called Weaverville where we transported ourselves and our luggage into a four-wheeled dogcart or buggy [locally known as a Surry] with two seats, one behind the other. Fred, the driver, and Maud sat in front, Campbell and I behind. And then our troubles began. I had never been so frightened in my life! The nerve-strain was really awful. How we went over those roads to Marshall I cannot tell you. They were at times nothing but a morass, at others a dry creek-bed strewn with huge boulders. Of course, we never went faster than a walk, but the road, or the track, was never level, but always precipitous one way or the other. As C. said – and he is thoroughly used to it – it is no use attempting to describe it, for the more nearly you succeed in doing so the less likely it is you will be believed. Of course, our horses – we had a pair – are quite used to the job and the trap was specially built for it. The wheels are very thin, made of hickory with round iron tires about an inch or less in diameter. After Marshall the roads became better, but no less nerve-racking as we went round innumerable hair-pin curves with the mountain on one side and a precipice on the other. Well, we arrived at White Rock about 6 p.m. doing the 40 miles in about 11 hours with an hour off for lunch.

This experience, though mainly due to the effect of the floods, proved to be only one instance of the normal difficulties of travel and was by no means the worst.

The valleys are narrow and the mountains, though they rarely reach a height of more than six thousand feet, rise up sharply, so that a man will boast that he can stand erect to hoe his corn-patch. As there is but little level ground, the people are forced to live in small communities by the side of the mountain rivers, or creeks, which have descriptive names, such as Possum Trot, Owl's Nest, Dish Rag, Kingdom Come, Hell for Sartin (Certain) and Devil's Fork – the last renamed 'Sweet Water' by the missionaries.

The country has undergone many changes during the last fifty years 1 and transport is no longer the difficulty that it was; but at that time there were few railroads beyond the main trunk-lines, which here and there traversed the mountain ranges, and good roads were scarce or non-existent. They were for the most part rough tracks over the mountain passes or along the creeks, or occasionally the creek-bed itself would serve as a roadway for a few miles. The mountain people rode mules, or harnessed them, if a load had to be carried, to a conveyance that was aptly named a jolt-wagon – a cart without springs which could be heard lumbering over the boulders a mile away. Whenever possible we walked, although this was a tiring business when it meant a tramp of fifteen or sixteen miles in great heat over a track so rough that it was necessary to pick every footstep. However, we mistrusted the mules, and to ourselves we excused our timidity on the grounds that as foot-passengers we could more easily pay informal calls, which was probably true enough. If luggage had to be carried we hired a boy and a mule, and hung our two suitcases and my typewriter across the mule's back; or if the distance was too great or the road too much entangled in the river we had resort to a jolt-wagon, and sometimes – though it seemed incredible – to a Ford car. Our particular terror was crossing the foot-logs, that is the trunks of trees which served as bridges over the creeks. In a letter to his wife, Cecil Sharp described one of the many predicaments we found ourselves in:

North Carolina,

August 13th 1916

There was one [a foot-log] we had to cross on the way to Carmen, quite high up over a rushing stream, only about 14 inches wide, but 16 or 17 yards long and very springy – no hand-rail of course! The first time I went across I didn't like it at all, but didn't say anything to Maud for fear of making her nervous too. Coming home I felt it worse than ever, and when she followed me she stuck in the middle and frightened me awfully. However she summoned up her courage and got over

[1] It should be stated that the present social and economic conditions of mountain life are very different from those which we experiencedi n 1916–18 (see pp. 170–1).

all right. Then I told her what a funk I had been in and we decided we couldn't risk it again. You see it meant a bad fall on to the huge boulders – probably a broken leg at the least. So we tried to find a path through the woods, because the road crossed the stream again a few hundred yards further on. But we couldn't get any trail through. So we finally decided that as we *had* to go – the Hensleys [our singers] were on the other side – we would wade at a ford. Everyone said it was too deep, but after a little prospecting we did it, and afterwards repeated it several times. You would have laughed if you had seen me cautiously picking my way across with a tall sort of Alpine stock in one hand and my umbrella in the other. I carry the latter instead of a raincoat as it is easier to walk with and quite as serviceable.

There was certainly nothing of the adventurous, resourceful pioneer about either of us.

The country, though difficult to get about in, was of surpassing loveliness. 'It is a paradise,' wrote Cecil Sharp; 'I don't think I have ever seen such lovely trees, ferns and wild flowers . . . If I had not my own special axe to grind I should be collecting ferns or butterflies or something.'

At White Rock, our first resting-place, where we spent several days, we were entertained by Dr. and Mrs. Packard, and throughout our travels in 1916 we depended for board and lodging very largely on the hospitality of the Presbyterian missionaries, making our headquarters with them and walking sometimes long distances to visit singers in the surrounding country.

At first Cecil Sharp was carefully shepherded and introduced to selected singers, for there was a certain amount of nervousness as to how he and they would 're-act' to each other, but these fears were soon dispelled. After three days at White Rock he writes:

There is no doubt that I am going to add some wonderful stuff to my collection. I have never before got such a wonderful lot in such a short time. The singers are just English peasants in appearance, speech, and manner . . . Indeed it is most refreshing to be once again amongst one's own people.

And a fortnight later:

Although the people are so English they have their American quality [in] . . . that they are freer than the English peasant. They own their own land and have done so for three or four generations, so that there is none of the servility which unhappily is one of the characteristics of the English peasant. With that praise I should say that they are just exactly what the English peasant was one hundred or more years ago.

In other parts of the United States little was known of the mountain people, who were at that time usually referred to as 'mountain whites' or 'poor white trash'. 'White', as a distinction from the 'coloured' Negro, seemed in any case a little unnecessary as there were practically no Negroes in the mountains. We were told by our New York and Boston friends that we should find ourselves among a wild and dangerous community and we were advised to arm ourselves with revolvers. Cecil Sharp paid no heed to the warning; indeed, he said that the handling of a revolver would cause him far greater fear than encountering the wildest savage; and, as a matter of fact, it would have been hard to find any other place where a stranger – and particularly a woman – would be as safe as in the mountains.

The people were mostly unlettered and had no money – serious shortcomings in the eyes of American city-dwellers – but though they had none of the advantages of civilization they had a culture which was as much a tradition as the songs they sang. 'A case of arrested development?' Cecil Sharp replied to a facile critic, 'I should prefer to call it a case of arrested degeneration.' Owing to the difficulty of transport they were to a very great extent shut off from the outside world, and so in the more secluded parts of the mountains they were very nearly self-supporting. Some had built themselves frame-houses, but they lived mostly in log-cabins, usually, but not always, lighted with windows. The following extract from a letter to Mrs. Sharp (3.9.1916) gives a picture of a remote mountain home:

I wish you could have seen us at a home far up Higgins Creek where we spent the greater part of Friday. We arrived about 10.30 (we break-fast here 6.30 week-days and 7 on Sundays) and left about 4, dining with them at 11.30. There were fourteen people in the room at one time, mostly grandchildren and great-grandchildren of the old lady. I don't suppose any of them had any money at all – many of them have never seen any! – they barter a little, but never sell for money. They really live almost entirely upon what they make and grow. All their clothes, blankets, etc., are made by them with the wool their sheep pro-duce. Hardly any of them wear boots. The only meat they ever eat –

and it is very little – is pig, or hog-meat as they call it. For the rest they subsist on vegetables, fruit, and corn-bread, i.e. maize-bread. At the present time they are busy preserving vegetables, fruit, etc., for use in the winter. They make their vinegar out of apples. The only groceries I saw were salt and pepper, and perhaps the latter was grown by themselves.

It may be added that one of the family was a beautiful singer and we noted seventeen songs from him that day – every one a gem of the first water.

Owing to the absence of roads there were no markets, and so there was no inducement for the people to produce more than they needed for their own requirements, and that was extremely little. However, the mountain people seem to thrive on their diet, for physically they are strong, well-grown, and loose-limbed, though spare almost to gauntness. But to us the food was monotonous and unpleasant, mainly owing to its greasiness. The country abounded in little black pigs of the 'razor-back' variety which ran about half wild in the forests, and although little of the flesh of the animal was eaten, its presence was all-pervading. Cooking meant frying, and all things, even apples, were served swimming in fat. Later on, when we lived with the people, we found it hard to keep ourselves properly nourished, for not only was the food not to our liking, but their standard of cleanliness was not ours, and the swarms of flies – the pest of a hot country – did not stimulate our appetites. Many was the time we thanked Providence for having placed eggs inside shells. As far as possible we supplemented the diet with our own provisions, chocolates and raisins being a great standby. In fact, so much so that Cecil Sharp on leaving the mountains said, 'I feel I can never again look a raisin in the eye.'

It was not only in matters of cleanliness that the highlanders showed signs of having remained in the eighteenth century, but also in their patriarchal mode of life. In some homes the women did not eat at table until the men had finished and one of our singers, a hoary-headed gentleman known as 'Frizzly Bill', informed us that he had 'owned three wives'.

Like all primitive people they mature at an early age and they marry young; often at the age of thirteen or fourteen and occasionally even earlier. A young wife and mother is thus described by Cecil Sharp:

Yesterday we called at a cabin and found such a lovely young fair-haired, blue-eyed girl, fifteen years of age with a buxom seven-months-old baby in her arms. I never saw a jollier, stronger, healthier baby or mother in my life; and she must have been married at fourteen, perhaps thirteen! So much for these Eugenic people1

The first marriage is often not a success, and the couple separate, usually without any ill-feeling. A boy when asked where his parents lived replied quite simply: 'My mother and step-father live here and my father and step-mother live at Alleghany' (a neighbouring settlement).

The characteristics of the highlanders have provided good copy for writers of a sentimental and sensational order, who have in particular enlarged upon the custom of blood-feuds and of the illicit distilling of corn-spirit. 'I always thank my stars I am not a literary man having to note characteristics of my friends and acquaintances and turn them into copy,' wrote Cecil Sharp apropos a magazine article on the mountain people.

We heard many stories of the feuds which were sometimes maintained between two families for generations, but we were given to understand that this barbarous custom had been discontinued. Of the whisky-making, or 'moon-shining', as it is called, we saw no signs, but we wisely avoided showing any curiosity in this matter; and doubtless my female presence relieved the people of any suspicion they might otherwise have had that Cecil was a State revenue officer. There is no doubt that the stills were often close at hand though carefully hidden. On one occasion we visited a creek with a bad reputation for moon-shining. It was approached by a steep and narrow mountain pass, and before descending into the valley we called at a log-cabin to make some inquiries. The man answered us courteously enough, but after we had proceeded a few yards he fired his gun into the air – a warning to his neighbours that strangers were abroad. We saw very little drinking – in fact, but two instances. At an evening-party the men retired periodically for refreshment and came back in a merry mood; and a singer, who came to the mission-house where we were staying, unburdened himself of a bottle before entering the house, out of deference to the missionaries, and hid it in a convenient spot in the bushes, where he had recourse to it during the intervals of singing.

Very few could read or write, but they were good talkers, and their talk showed that they had wisdom and knowledge. They used uncommon expressions, many of which were old English. One peculiarity which was universal was the pronunciation of the impersonal pronoun with an initial aspirate – 'hit'.[1] A child who is 'ill' is not sick, but bad-tempered; a woman does not give birth to, but 'finds', a baby; and 'clever' folk are those who are kind and hospitable. They were, too, good listeners as well as good talkers. 'I could go on listening to him for hours,' said one woman, 'he is so – so educating.' And Cecil who never talked down to people, always had something interesting to tell, whether it might be the immediate business of song or dance, or the crops, or some more remote subject: the Pyramids, for instance, or the locks in the Panama Canal or the Dardanelles campaign – three subjects on which one singer sought information. Generally speaking, the people had not much knowledge of the outside world. They had all heard of the war, but they were not always certain whether England was fighting with or against Germany; and fact and fiction were sometimes strangely confused, as with the woman who wanted to know whether mermaids were real people.

Though unlettered and isolated from the affairs of the world, the social instincts of the people were highly developed, and their charm of manner was a constant source of delight. Cecil Sharp says of them:[2]

They have an easy, unaffected bearing and the unselfconscious manners of the well-bred. I have received salutations upon introduction or on bidding farewell, such as a courtier might make to his sovereign . . . Strangers that we met in the course of our long walks would usually bow, doff the hat, and extend the hand, saying 'My name is — ; what is yours?'.

And the children would greet us with 'Howdy', accompanied by a little bow or curtsy.

Strangers were, of course, rare in the mountains, but our presence never aroused the slightest sign either of curiosity or of surprise. We would call, more often than not without any intro-duction, at a log-cabin, first shouting 'Hullo' from a little distance, as is the custom in a country where a gun is always within reach, and we were invariably received with the utmost friendliness. We were as a matter of course invited to 'partake' with the family; and

[1] The latest quotation in the *O.E.D.* for *hit* is 'To truste my life in anothers hand and send hit out my owne' (Queen Elizabeth, 1586).
[2] *English Folk-Songs from the Southern Appalachians*, vol. i. p. xxiii.

when we rose to say good-bye the frequent request was, 'But surely you will tarry with us for the night.'

Cecil Sharp had high hopes of what he might discover in the mountains, but the actual result surpassed his fondest dreams, and after a fortnight's collecting, when he had noted ninety tunes, he wrote:

It is the greatest discovery I have made since the original one in England sixteen years ago.

There was not as in England the tiresome business of having first to listen to popular music-hall or drawing-room songs of fifty years ago before extracting the genuine traditional music, because the people knew little else but folk music; and everyone was acquainted with the songs, although, as in any other community, not everyone was a singer. We endeavoured therefore to find out who were the best singers in the district and to get all we could from them. A certain amount of chance, or hard work, or both, was needed to discover them, for singing was not an accomplishment which was used for public entertainment. There was no such thing as a concert, or even community-singing, but song was just part of everyday life. 'There now,' said a woman who had momentarily forgotten a song that Cecil wished to hear, 'if only I were driving the cows home I should remember it at once.' The whole time we were in the mountains we never heard a poor tune (except sometimes at the missionary settlements, or on the rare occasions when we stayed at a summer resort hotel) and nearly all were of surpassing beauty.

We had not as a rule any difficulty in getting the people to sing to us; in fact, their readiness was sometimes an embarrassment, as in the case of the Kentucky woman and her three married daughters, all of whom insisted on singing their favourite songs at the same time at the top of their voices. When by chance the interest flagged we stimulated it by singing ourselves, promising an English song in exchange for every song that we received. It was in this way that Cecil Sharp first discovered the delight of singing to others, and his voice, or lack of it, did not, as we have seen (p. 135), in the least embarrass him. It was the songs he was asking people to listen to and not his singing.

One obstacle we had to contend with was that of religious scruples, particularly with the 'Holiness' sect, or 'Holy Rollers' as they were commonly called, who thought it wicked to sing 'love-songs'. Cecil Sharp respected their scruples and never tried to overcome them, but sometimes they would of their own accord relent, saying they were sure that Mr. Sharp would do no harm with the songs. The religious-minded did not invariably frown upon the songs, however, as the following extract from a letter to his daughter Joan shows:

> Kentucky
> June 4th, 1917
> We had one curious experience the other day. We called on a Mrs. Talitha P ——, who was living with her sister and a brother. Mrs. P. sang us several good songs, whereupon we rose to go, when the sister, a very grim, flat-chested, gaunt sort of person got up and said, 'You have made my house a house of songs, but it is also a house of prayer', and immediately dumped down on her knees. I with my recollection – rather dim – of family prayers turned round and put my head in the seat of my chair while she fired off an intimate talk with the Deity . . . When she had exhausted her inspiration, her brother who was between me and her took up the strain and 'offered up' another prayer and did it very well indeed, in excellent language and ease of expression. In the middle of his conversation with the Almighty he mentioned the two strangers at his house and asked for a blessing on our work 'which I deem most profitable'. It was very funny, of course, but very sweet of him to pay us this compliment in a way which precluded any acknowledgement on our part. When he had done I was perspiring with fear lest I should be called upon to take up the strain, so I rose noisily to my feet immediately.

The majority of those with whom we came into contact were Baptists, whose preachers won fame for themselves in proportion to the carrying power of their voices in the open air; there were also Methodists, Presbyterians, and Episcopalians. We found an austere Calvinistic doctrine was prevalent in which the devil was regarded as an object of fear and respect.

Some of the best songs were sung to us by children. One small boy edged his way into a cabin where Cecil Sharp was noting songs from an old man, a singer of some repute. 'Hullo, what do you want?' said Cecil on seeing him, and the boy answered, 'Please, sir, let me stay. I love to be where there is sweet music' Of course, Cecil let him stay, and later on when the singer professed ignorance of a certain song, the small boy piped up, 'Please, sir, I know it.' And without any persuasion he sang the long ballad of 'Young Hunting' [1] in a way, as Cecil said, 'which would have shamed many a professional singer'.

Another of our singers in whom Cecil took a great interest was Emma Hensley, a girl of thirteen, of beautiful, Madonna-like appearance, who lived with her mother and father in a remote mountain valley. Cecil Sharp writes:

13. 8. 1916

I spent three days at the Hensleys, walking over each morning after breakfast about 8.30 (we breakfast at 7.30), getting there about 10 and leaving again about 5. We sat on the verandah of their little home amongst the mountains, surrounded by huge trees and small clearings covered chiefly with corn (maize) and tobacco. All three sang and he played the fiddle. I got about 30 tunes from them and had an awfully jolly time. I got very interested in Emma, the child, who is crazy to go to school . . . Her mother is anxious for her to go for two reasons: (I) because she does not want her to marry as young as her sister (who married at fifteen), and (2) because she chews tobacco, which very un-ladylike habit she learned from an aunt; and her mother feels that school discipline is the only thing that will break her of the habit!

Her father, too, wanted her to go so that she might learn to play, having promised that if she did he would sell the cow and buy an 'organ' (harmonium). Cecil was doubtful whether the school was the best place for Emma and whether she would be able to resign herself to the loss of liberty; but we interviewed the headmistress, paid for the outfit, and helped with the fees. The day Emma arrived at the school we happened to be staying in the same small town, which is on the railway and has quite a large and not un-fashionable summer resort hotel, and so we invited Emma to dine with us. She arrived at the hotel looking very neat and demure in her grey school uniform – she had been barefoot when we last saw her – and although she had never left home before, she comported herself as though dining out were an everyday occurrence. She showed no sign of embarrassment or even surprise at her unaccus-tomed surroundings. She watched to see what I did with my napkin and the many knives and forks, and without comment did the same with hers, conversing the while in an easy, friendly way. Early next morning we were standing on the bank of the French Broad river, waiting for a ferry to take us across – the floods had

[1] *See English Folk-Songs from the Southern Appalachians,* vol. i, p. 102.

washed away the bridge – when whom should we see but Emma and a schoolfellow, both carrying suitcases. Emma looked slightly flushed, but otherwise her usual dignified and composed self. 'Good morning,' she said sweetly, 'we have just run away'; and before we could find a suitable reply they had jumped into a boat. We shouted to them to wait for us on the other side, which they did. Cecil, though secretly rejoicing, felt it his duty to try to persuade Emma to go back; but Emma was quite decided. 'No,' she said, 'I am going to my mother. Perhaps later on I may return – I don't know: I haven't yet made up my mind.' And then, just a little crestfallen: 'I'm sorry, because you have been so good to me.' But the next moment she had brightened up and asked if we would not go back with her. We declined the invitation, and the last we saw of Emma was as she started off on her twenty-mile walk across the mountain. She did not return to the school, and no doubt our gifts of clothes formed an attractive trousseau. 'I am filled with admiration for her,' Cecil wrote to his wife. 'She is just unique; and it seems awful, nothing less than barbaric, to spoil her and turn her into an ordinary respectable half-educated American girl.'[1]

Cecil Sharp acknowledged the hospitality and friendliness of the missionaries towards himself, but he thought that much of their work amongst the mountain people was misguided and harmful particularly their educational methods. He writes of it:

To Mrs. Storrow.   13. 9. 1916
Some of the women [missionaries] I have met are very nice and broadminded. But I don't think any of them realize that the people they are here to improve are in many respects far more cultivated than their would-be instructors, even if they cannot read or write. Take music, for example. Their own is pure and lovely. The hymns that these missionaries teach them are musical and literary garbage . . . The problem, I know, is a very difficult one. For my part, I would leave them as they are and not meddle. They are happy, contented, and live simply and healthily, and I am not at all sure that any of us can introduce them to anything better than this. Something might be done in teaching them better methods of farming, so as to lighten the burden of earning a living from their holdings; and they should certainly be taught to read and write – at any rate, those who want to, ought to be able to. Beyond that I should not go.

[1] Emma was saved from this fate (see p. 170).

The singers took the greatest interest and delight in our noting of the songs. Cecil Sharp used the phonograph for a short time when collecting in England, but the transport of phonographic apparatus would have presented insuperable difficulties in this mountain country; so he noted the tunes in ordinary musical notation, whilst I took down the words in shorthand. The singers regarded this process almost as a conjuring trick, especially when by looking at our books we could sing the songs back to them. An old man, who could neither read nor write, was shown the musical notation of the song he had just been singing. 'Look, there's your song,' said Cecil, handing him his little notebook. The old man looked thoughtfully at the page of manuscript for a few moments, then, shaking his head, said: 'Well, I can hardly recognize it.' Another singer, the father of nineteen children (not all by the same wife), commended our efforts in these words: 'Singing is a great power in the world and you are doing a noble work.'

The first eight weeks were spent mostly in Madison County, North Carolina, and Unicoi County, Tennessee. Then, having only a week to spare before we were due to leave for Chicago, we decided to spend it in the university town of Charlottesville, Virginia, partly in order to sample the Blue Ridge section and partly to get into touch with Professor Alphonso Smith, the founder of the Virginia Folk-Lore Society, who, as Professor of English at the University of Virginia, had aroused an interest in balladry amongst his students and had encouraged them to collect.

Inspired by the monumental work of Professor Child of Harvard, the universities of America have taken great interest in the English and Scottish popular ballad; but at that time the subject had been treated almost entirely from the literary standpoint and such collections of mountain ballads as had hitherto been made by the State folk-lore societies, the universities and other individual effort were with a few exceptions restricted to the texts, and the tunes had been ignored. It is, however of interest that shortly before Cecil Sharp went to North Carolina a similar expedition had been made, unbeknown to him, by Miss Loraine Wyman and Mr. Howard Brockway, who had spent April, May and June collecting in Kentucky.[1] Miss Josephine McGill had also noted

---

[1] See *Lonesome Tunes* (25 songs) (New York 1916) and *Twenty Kentucky Mountain Songs* (Boston 1925). The songs in both volumes are arranged with pianoforte accompaniment by Howard Brockway.

some songs and ballads[1] in Knott and Leech counties, Kentucky, in the autumn of 1914.

Cecil Sharp, as we have seen, was unwilling to poach on other people's preserves, and so before venturing into Virginia he wrote to Professor Smith:

I have an idea, though it may be a wrong one, that in the majority of cases it is the text only and not the tune that has been noted. If I am right, it seems to me very important that the investigation, initiated by your students, should be followed up by someone, like myself, who can take down the tunes; for I am sure you will agree with me that the tune is every whit as essential a part of the ballad as the text. So it occurred to me that it might be . . . profitable for me to spend my last fortnight in your neighbourhood . . . But I should not wish to do this without your approval, or unless I felt assured of your co-operation . . . Apart altogether from the question of collection it would be a great pleasure to me to visit Charlottesville, show you the tunes and ballads that I have already taken down and discuss them with you.

Professor Smith extended a cordial welcome and the last week was profitably spent in exploring the country around Charlottesville.

The quality of the tunes – nearly four hundred – which Cecil Sharp noted during that first expedition of nine weeks far exceeded his most cherished ambition and we also noted many fine texts, both of ballads and lyrics. We had our disappointments, of course, and there were some long weary trudges with poor results; but sooner or later the luck turned, sometimes quite unexpectedly, as at the end of a tiring and fruitless twelve-hour day in Tennessee when without hope we paid yet another call and were instantly rewarded by hearing 'The False Knight upon the Road'.[2]

[1] Twenty, arranged with pianoforte accompaniment, are published in *Folk-Songs of the Kentucky Mountains* (New York and London 1917).
[2] See *English Folk Songs from the Southern Appalachians*, No. 2A.

XIII
The Appalachian Mountains II
1917–18

When I travelled, I took a particular Delight in hearing the Songs and
Fables that are come from Father to Son, and are most in vogue among
the common People of the Countries through which I passed; for it is
impossible that anything that should be universally tasted and approved
by a Multitude, though they are only the Rabble of a Nation, which hath
not in it some peculiar Aptness to please and gratifie the Mind of Man.

ADDISON, *Spectator*

IN 1917 we were in the mountains during April and May and
again during August, September and the first half of October. The
first three weeks were spent in Tennessee and the rest of the time
mostly in Kentucky.

This was our first experience of the mountain country in
spring and it appeared a real fairyland. Cecil Sharp wrote to his
wife:

6. 5. 1917

I wish you could see this country in its fresh spring green. The trees
are almost fully out now, and there is plenty of shade and the country
looks wonderful. I miss the singing-birds of England, and the woods
sound very quiet for the time of year, but the flowers and flowering
trees are just wonderful. The dogwood tree is very lovely, a pure
white Christmas-rose kind of flower, which covers the tree before its
leaves come out like the blackthorn. Then there is the magnolia, which
they call the wild cucumber, because of the scarlet, cucumber-shaped
seed it bears in autumn. It grows very freely from twenty to forty feet

156

in height and is thick with blossom. Then there is a small purple iris which grows pretty well everywhere. Lots of violets, but no primroses; and a lot of flowers I have not yet named.

Our travels throughout the year were fraught with anxiety owing to Cecil's poor state of health. He managed to do a fortnight's collecting, and then, while staying at the Lincoln Memorial University, at Harrogate, Tennessee – a school for mountain boys and girls – he had a severe attack of fever with delirium which kept him in bed for three days. Even then he could not put the collecting aside, but took down twenty-four tunes from students, whom I first tested and then brought to his bedside.

While he was still painfully weak we moved on to Pineville, a railroad town of some three thousand inhabitants in Kentucky, where there was a comparatively comfortable hotel, and singers were to be found in the neighbourhood; but after a week he felt he had for the present exhausted the district, and so, leaving creature comforts behind, we moved on to Barbourville, a small town, also on the railway, where oil had recently been discovered. Although the prospects did not at first seem very good, we soon struck a 'nest of singing-birds'; but our satisfaction was short-lived, for after a few days Cecil had an alarming return of the fever, which the local doctor diagnosed as 'probably typhoid'. As soon as they heard of his illness Mr. John Campbell and Dr. Packard came to his assistance, making a two-days' journey over the mountains. When they arrived at Barbourville the fever had subsided and Cecil, though barely strong enough to sit up in bed, was taking down songs from a woman-singer, whom I had brought to his bedside in the hope of dispelling the acute mental depression from which he was suffering.

The journeys into the 'wilds' which he had planned were now quite out of the question, but, as he could not be persuaded to give up the collecting completely, we compromised and, with the assistance of Dr. Packard and Mr. Campbell made the journey to Berea, in the foothills of Kentucky, where there is a College for mountain students and a comfortable hostelry run by the College. We remained there a fortnight and during that time Cecil Sharp added another hundred tunes to his collection, but the field was not a very good one, for the people had become sophisticated, and the singing of traditional songs was apt to be despised as belonging to a past and discarded mode of existence. We were told that the singing of love-songs was only practised by the rough, common people, and an earnest young College student was reluctant to sing a version of 'The Swapping Song', as he cared only for songs which contained 'great thoughts'. On another occasion, though not in this district, Cecil Sharp was told by a woman that she and her husband made it a rule never to sing love-songs nor to swear before the children. 'What the connexion between the two was, I don't know,' Cecil wrote to his daughter Joan; 'I do both to *my* children, as you know!'

In the meantime his state of health continued to be precarious. He suffered from extreme weakness and exhaustion and seemed on the verge of a nervous collapse. So after a few days at Pineville he gave up the collecting, and at the beginning of June took a ten-days' rest at Asheville, in order to fit himself for the work of his Folk-Dance Summer School.

At the end of July we were back in the mountains. We first spent a few fruitless days in North Carolina, on the Asheville-Murphy line (which had been our first approach to Asheville in the preceding year), trying in vain to combine song-collecting and physical comfort.

30. 7. 1917

To Mrs. Storrow,

The fact is we are too close to Waynesville, a large industrial centre, and the inhabitants have been partly spoiled, that is from my point of view. The log-cabins are primitive enough, but their owners are clean, neat, and tidy, looking rather like maid-servants in respectable suburban families! It is sad that cleanliness and good music, or good taste in music, rarely go together. Dirt and good music are the usual bed-fellows, or cleanliness and rag-time! So we move farther on tomorrow and in a day or two shall be roughing it pretty badly, I expect.

– an expectation that was fulfilled.

We decided to continue our researches in Kentucky, which had been cut short two months earlier by Cecil's illness. The train journey from Asheville was a trying one. 'I have never felt the heat so much since my last trip through the Red Sea,' he wrote in his diary.

A terrible experience waiting for the train, herded – about 150 of us – like pigs in a sty, not even with the information that we were in the right sty! After nearly half an hour of this purgatory the train drew up and we were let out one by one through a narrow opening. The windows so dirty in the train that we could not see the mountain scenery. Heat almost unbelievable – no air. There we remained till 9 p.m. when we reached Knoxville and decamped to the hotel. How we lived through that night I shall never know. I am feeling very seedy – headache, asthma, and general lassitude.

Some such comment on his health is, unhappily, an all too frequent entry in his diary.

From Knoxville we proceeded by train to Barbourville, and after a few days there we made our way to Manchester (Clay Co.), a small county town in the heart of the mountains, by an insecure branch railroad. 'And such a railroad!' writes Cecil,

The cars swayed to and fro and creaked and wheezed like an old sailing-ship riding out a severe storm. They say it is safe because they travel so slowly – about nine miles an hour – but I don't look forward to the return journey.

Manchester (pronounced Manchéster) was enjoying a newborn prosperity due to the opening of coal-mines and the running of the light railway.

To Mrs. Storrow,   26.8.1917
Manchester, though the County seat, has no made roads nor water (except very doubtful wells – shallow at that) and no system of sanitation. The hotel faces a vacant square with a dry creek running across it covered with large boulders. Residents just throw the contents of their dustbins out upon the streets where the hogs which are numerous eat of it what they can! . . .

And to Mr. John Glenn, the Director of the Russell Sage Foundation, a kind and much valued friend, he writes (2. 9. 1917):

This trip is causing me to modify the opinion that I first formed that the singing of folk-songs was universal in the mountains . . . Primitiveness in custom and outlook is not, I am finding, so much the result of remoteness as bad economic conditions. When there is coal and good wages to be earned, the families soon drop their old-fashioned ways and begin to ape town manners, etc. And where the land is rich and the valleys broad and it is easy to accumulate surplus wealth the same thing follows. I found, for instance, that Clay County despite its remoteness was quite sophisticated. Frame-houses were the rule along many of the creeks, rather than the cabins; and here the inhabitants received my remarks about the old songs with a superiority of air that was almost contemptuous. Still even in country of this sort it is possible to extract songs, and often very good ones, but only with difficulty, and then mainly from the older inhabitants . . . Here is a curious instance of superficial sophistication. A young girl was staying at Manchester . . . who had come from a very remote part twenty-five miles back. She was so ignorant that she imagined that England was a province of Germany and that America was at war with both. Yet she apologized one morning at breakfast because she had omitted to use her face powder.

This sophisticated air of superiority was well described by a singer, one of the 'really nice people' with whom we made friends. 'Those people have got rich before they have any money,' she said. We spent many long hours with her and a friend who lived with her, delighting in her racy talk and enjoying the songs that the two women gave us. They both smoked pipes, although when we visited them they had only one between them. She told us she had married three times: the first husband had killed a man and was serving a long sentence in a penitentiary; the next one drank, so she kicked him out; and the third wouldn't work and so had to depart in the same summary fashion. She had a three-roomed house and each room contained an enlarged framed photograph of one of the husbands which she showed us with great pride. She had always been the same to everybody: 'I've just got one face and I've worn it out – that's why it's so ugly,' she said. Two months after our visits she wrote to thank Cecil for some snap-shots and books he had sent her, for she could read and write. Her letter is given as she wrote it, except for the correction of a few spelling errors and the addition of punctuation:

I received your letter yesterday and all our pictures. And I have no words to express how well pleased I was to hear from you and dear little Maud, for I know there is something in your lives as well as mine that brings grief instead of pleasure. Well, I received the novels you sent me and you can guess whether I was pleased or not. Bet your life I was more than pleased. Well, you spoke of the pipes, it is impossible to get them and I had rather have a pair of spectacles, as a pipe I can smoke in most any kind of pipe and I can not see through any kind of glasses. Well, I truly hope you and Maud will get back to Manchester some day and that before long, for it would do my heart good to see you. Excuse paper and pen and hand.

The pipes referred to were meerschaum pipes. When Cecil had asked her what she would like as a present from New York, she had replied: 'A pipe made of the foam of the sea.'

At the end of August we visited the Pine Mountain Settlement School in Harlan County. There was then no road to the school and it was reached by a steep, rough trail over Pine Mountain. Cecil was enthusiastic.

To Mrs. John C. Campbell   2. 9. 1917
There is a mountain-school – if you can call it a school – after my own heart! It is just a lovely place, fine buildings, beautiful situation, and wisely administered. Miss Pettit and Miss de Long are cultivated gentlefolk, who fully realize the fine innate qualities of the mountain children and handle them accordingly. And the children, many of them little more than babies, are just fascinating, clean, bright, well-behaved little things, who come up, put their hands in yours, and be-have like the children of gentle-folk – which is, of course, just what they are. This settlement is a model of what the mountain-schools should be. Everything is beautiful . . . Flowers are grown everywhere and large bowls of them in every room. They do not emphasize the school side of things, nor, I am glad to say, the church side. They sing ballads after dinner and grace before it.

The visit was a memorable one, not only to Cecil Sharp, but to the members of the school staff. One of them, Miss Evelyn Wells, writes (1931):

I remember what a hot August day it was when Mr. Sharp and Miss Karpeles came walking in across Pine Mountain. Most visitors from the outside world were heralded by the guide, who came ahead to open gates for his mule passengers – not so these two, who were quietly at our doorstep before we knew it . . . There are many highlights on that visit of five days . . . There was the hour after supper in our big dining-room, where after the day of farm-work and canning and other vaca-tion occupations, we settled back in our chairs while those two sang to us – 'The Knight in the Road', 'All along in the Ludeney', 'Edward', 'The Gypsy Laddie', and many nursery songs. I can remember the twi-light creeping in on us, the youngest children falling to sleep, dropping on their crossed arms at the table, as if they were being sung to by their own firesides, the voices of the singers getting more and more im-personal in the dusk as song after song was finished.

There were the two noon hours when eight workers from the staff learned 'Rufty Tufty', 'The Black Nag' and 'Gathering Peascods' on the porch of Laurel House to Mr. Sharp's teaching and Miss Karpeles's singing of the tune. I always think of that when I watch a Pine Mountain May Day now with its four or five sword teams, its varied country dances, its early morning Morris . . . All the work of the day stopped during those lessons – children stopped weeding the vegetable gardens, girls stopped washing the clothes, even the workmen stopped building the school-house. And this was in the days when we worked incessantly to put roofs over our heads and to can food against the winter, and every minute counted.

I remember the first morning when Mr. Sharp came to our six o'clock breakfast late, having lost his way to the dining-room in the thick mountain mist that filled the valley – suffering terribly from an attack of asthma, which to my inexperienced eyes seemed highly alarming – and then going off down the valley within the next hour, walking miles to get songs from Singing Willie Nolan. I remember tea under the apple-trees, where again we let the Pine Mountain world stop, while he talked of his mountain experiences, and of collecting in England and the dancing there . . .

Mr. Sharp summed up for Pine Mountain much that till then had been implicitly taken for granted. That he found there the right soil in which to plant again the native crop of songs and dances made us realize our responsibility as never before and we have never since let the heritage of the children die out.

Another mountain school that Cecil Sharp thought well of was at Hindman (Knott Co.). We spent a happy week there and Cecil Sharp noted sixty tunes, which included some first-rate songs. Although only twenty miles from the railway, the journey by mail-hack took about ten hours. The return journey is described by Cecil Sharp in a letter to an American friend.

To Miss Peggy Scovill   26. 9.1917
   Travelling here is an arduous affair . . . There aren't any real roads, merely dirt-tracks strewn with boulders and plentifully besprinkled with large cavities. We had seven people in the mail-hack, the driver and his cook on the front seat, Maud, self, and another female jammed tight like sardines on the back seat, and two stalwart men standing on the mail-bags behind us. The cook was of 'cookly' proportions or I should have shared the front seat with the driver, but for Maud's sake I sacrificed myself and placed my thinner body on the back seat – but all the thanks I got was an acid remark to the effect that, though larger, the cook would have probably made a softer companion! There is no pleasing some people.

This letter was written at Hazard, where we stayed a few days in order to rest after our journeys, and Cecil, finding that he could have the use of a piano which was not too badly out of tune, spent his time in harmonizing, making the first draft of arrangements for all the songs in his *American-English Folk-Songs*.[1]

Our next journey was from Hazard to Hyden, the county town of Leslie. Again the distance was about twenty miles and it took the whole day to do. 'The journey,' writes Cecil Sharp, 'was the worst we have yet experienced.'

The waggon was without springs or cushions on the seat – a tumble-down affair which rocked and creaked and bumped most ominously all the way. Indeed, so impossible was it to sit in that we walked all the way except for the five miles or so when the road went down the middle of the creek. We crossed five mountains on the way and were just dead when we arrived.

Hyden he described as 'the most primitive county town I have struck'.

We hadn't been there more than a day or so before everyone in the place knew us and knew our business and everything about us. It was like entering a family party.

They all spoke of him affectionately as the 'old gentleman', and they followed our movements in search of songs with the greatest interest. It was an excellent centre for collecting, and the songs in our notebooks were rapidly increasing, but after a week Cecil was again stricken without any warning with a sharp attack of fever, which was alarming, as we were two days' journey from a big town. Happily, it did not last long, and after five days we decided to risk the journey and move to a more accessible place.

A few days before he was taken ill, we saw and noted the Running Set, an unsophisticated form of the now popular American Square Dance. We had seen the dance first at Pine Mountain, and the scene is thus described by him:

It was danced one evening after dark on the porch of one of the largest houses of the Pine Mountain School with only one dim lantern to light up the scene. But the moon streamed fitfully in lighting up the mountain peaks in the background and, casting its mysterious light over

[1] Published by Schirmer, New York, 1918, and reprinted as *Folk-Songs of English Origin*, vol. i, by Novello, 1919.

the proceedings, seemed to exaggerate the wildness and the break-neck speed of the dancers as they whirled through the mazes of the dance. There was no music, only the stamping and clapping of the onlookers, but when one of the emotional crises of the dance was reached . . . the air seemed literally to pulsate with the rhythm of the 'patters' and the tramp of the dancers' feet, while, over and above it all, penetrating through the din, floated the even, falsetto tones of the Caller, calmly and unexcitedly reciting his directions.[1]

The dance had on that occasion been sprung upon us unawares, and we were unable to make more than a few casual notes. We saw it again at Hindman at a party which had been arranged for our benefit, but the dancing was not good, and it would in any case have been difficult to note the dance owing to the crowded state of the room. There is no such thing as a private party in the mountains; all come who wish, whether invited or not. At Hyden we were fortunate enough to see undisturbed a good set of dancers and, a few days later, after Cecil Sharp had been taken ill, I went to a 'bean-stringing' in the neighbourhood, where I witnessed and took part in the dance. It was performed in a small, unventilated room about twelve feet square into which thirty or forty people besides the dancers managed to squeeze themselves. Set-running has a bad name in the mountains, possibly because of Puritan prejudices, but more probably because it leads often to drinking and sometimes to shooting. Whatever the cause, all but the most sternly religious-minded continue to dance, only they speak of it as 'playing' and not dancing.

After leaving Hyden we remained in Kentucky for a few days and then proceeded to Asheville. An entry on 17th October in Cecil's diary reads:

So now this tour is finished. I am feeling rather sad but greatly relieved to know that I have reached a haven of rest without mishap where I can eat, sleep, write music, and, I hope, get flesh and strength again . . . And there are the 600 tunes in my trunk collected this year – not without some expenditure of physical vitality.

In 1918 we again had two periods of collecting in the mountains: the first from April to June, and the second from July to October. The whole of the first period was spent in Virginia, except for a few days in West Virginia; and we returned to Virginia for the

[1] Introduction to *The Country Dance Book*, Part 5.

first five weeks of the second period, spending the remainder of the time – about six weeks – in North Carolina. Living conditions were at times very primitive and there was some rough, hard travelling, but Cecil had no return of the fever, and although he often felt ill and exhausted he got through without any serious collapse.

The mountains of Virginia – or at any rate those parts that we visited – were free from the industrial towns of mushroom-growth which were an objectionable feature of Kentucky, and on that account our travels were pleasanter, but we found that the songs were not so widely diffused as we would have expected. Cecil Sharp sums up the situation in a letter to Professor Alphonso Smith (1.9.1918):

The tradition [in Virginia] is steadily approaching extinction owing to the establishment of schools and the contaminating influence of what is usually called modern progress. In North Carolina everyone sings and the folk-song is still vital.[1] In Kentucky the tradition was, I imagine, in full blast up to a few years ago, and still is in some of the most remote districts, but is now being rapidly killed in its prime by industrialism. In Kentucky it is a case of sudden death; in Virginia of euthanasia.

In the same letter he states:

I have found the tunes in Virginia extraordinarily beautiful; I think of greater musical value than those that I have taken down anywhere else in America.

Sometimes we were able to stay at a hotel or a school, but generally there was no alternative but to live with the people themselves, and however poor might be the accommodation they were always ready to 'take care' of us and to give us of their best. One of the pleasantest times was that which we spent in the Tye River Valley with a family consisting of our host, his wife Salina, and three children. It was there that we first heard the rumour that we were German spies, a suspicion which we afterwards had to contend with in other places. We were told that after an evening prayer meeting the whole congregation stayed and discussed us. It was generally agreed that we were highly suspicious characters

[1] This applied particularly to the region we explored on our first journey, i.e. the mountain range between North Carolina and Tennessee: 'The Great Divide' as it is called.

and that noting tunes was merely a blind to hide our nefarious actions which included the poisoning of springs among other things. All this we heard from our host and hostess, who enjoyed the joke, and from other friends. These included the postmaster, who was convinced that we were not Germans, for he had once seen one, and neither of us bore any resemblance to that specimen of the race. Whether or not they believed us to be spies, everyone seemed glad to see us. Some neighbours, an old man of the name of Philander, who gave us many good songs, and his blind wife, did their best to persuade us to come and live with them in their tiny log-cabin, and every time we visited them the old blind lady would anxiously inquire: 'And is Salina still familiar?' hoping that if we fell out with Salina we might be willing to change our lodging.

The tunes came in apace, but there were some disappointing periods, as for instance a short stay in the Shenandoah Valley, where the population proved to be very largely of German extraction, and a tiresome journey into West Virginia, where we found that the continuity of rural life had been disturbed by the coal industry. On 1st September 1918 Cecil Sharp wrote to Mrs. Storrow:

This is to let you know that we are both alive, though somewhat chastened by the heat and the bufferings of a rather unkind fate! For the last month we have struck a rather unproductive patch, but in this work it is necessary to explore all the ground and every now and again we must expect to meet with failure. It was rather disappointing in this case because we had expected the last two counties in Virginia – Franklin and Patrick – to be especially productive as the railways are very few and the mountain districts more than ordinarily isolated. We had built many hopes upon a place with a thoroughly bad reputation for illicit stills, shootings, etc., but when we got there (it was twenty-five miles from the station) there was a Missionary revival going on and in the evening the residents crowded to the 'preaching', dressed in fashionable garments, low-necked dresses, high-heels, and well-powdered faces . . . The fact is the price of whisky has so gone up that 'moon-shining' has been exceedingly profitable and they are rolling in money. Songs were, of course, out of the question and we retired next day somewhat crestfallen . . . Then again, we had set our expectations on the Meadows of Dan, partly because of its delightful name, but mainly because of its extreme isolation and altitude of 3, 500 feet. And it was certainly one of the most arduous and dangerous journeys we have ever undertaken. We motored to the county town, Stuart, and then, after many refusals, prevailed on a driver to take us up to the Meadows in his motor, a matter of seventeen miles. The road which is ordinarily a very steep, narrow, and dangerous one was far worse than usual on account of some recent thunderstorms, which had washed it clean right down to the native rock. In some places the inclination of the car was so great in turning a corner, with a sheer fall of five or six hundred feet over the side, that the driver himself suggested that we should get out while he negotiated it – which we did with alacrity! How a car could have driven up at all I can't imagine. I am sure nothing but a Ford could have done it. And then we got up to the top of the ridge we found a large plateau of rolling meadows and fertile land occupied by a thoroughly respectable, church-going, school-attending population, making money at a great rate owing to the advance in food prices and many of them housed in comfortable frame-dwellings and sporting their own motor-cars . . . Still we did get some songs and a few rather good ones, but nothing like the bag we had expected to make.

Then there were the day-to-day difficulties and disappointments. On two separate occasions we toiled up a steep mountain in tropical weather to call on an old lady of eighty-nine who had a great reputation as a singer, only to find on the first occasion that she had gone out visiting, and on the second that she was preparing to receive the preacher for dinner and was in such a fluster that she would scarcely talk to us. It was on one of these occasions that we proved with bitter experience the fallacy of the 'nigh-way'. The directions were clear: we had only to walk up to the top of the mountain and then drop down to our destination on the other side – a matter of six or seven miles; but the mountain was densely wooded, and after having walked for several hours we made inquiries at the first log-cabin and discovered that we were only a mile from where we had started. We had walked up the mountain and down again on the same side.

However, such difficulties and hardships only served to throw into relief the pleasant experiences of our journeys – the beautiful country, the charm of the people and the prevailing musical atmosphere.

An incident that lives in the memory was that which occurred in a poor home in Virginia. We were noting songs from a woman who was surrounded by her family of thirteen children – seven of her own and six step-children. Eagerly but quietly they watched the strange proceedings, and then as their mother began to sing a

beautiful modal tune[1] they joined in, softly and almost uncon-
sciously, enhancing the beauty of the tune by the haunting loveliness of their young voices.

The last six weeks which were spent in North Carolina were
very productive. During the last month we were more or less
comfortably housed in a little summer hotel at Burnsville, Yancey
County, and the field was so rich – we noted two hundred songs in
the district – that there was no need to move elsewhere.

It was with mingled feelings of relief, satisfaction and sadness
that we ended our mountain travels: relief that we had survived
our arduous experiences without serious mishap, satisfaction that
we were carrying away such rich treasure, and sadness at having
to say good-bye to the many friends we had made. When we called
upon one of our singers to say our last farewell, she said: 'My
husband and I are sorry you are going. We like you both – you are
so nice and common.' Cecil considered that the greatest compliment he had ever been paid.

From the Grove Park Inn, Asheville, our haven of rest, Cecil
writes to Mrs. Storrow (13. 10. 1918):

Here we are at last. We arrived yesterday, safe and sound, I am glad to
say . . . I am dreadfully tired and worn, but a week's rest here and good
feeding will, I am sure, make me quite fit again . . . I am sorry to have
said good-bye to the mountain people, but I suspect I have seen the last
of them. There is enough work left, which might be well worth doing,
that would take perhaps another year, but I am satisfied with what I
have done, and the rest can be left to others. Without your active assistance the work would never have been done, and I am deeply grateful
to you.

It would seem that Cecil Sharp had every reason to be satisfied. He
had collected from 281 singers a total of 1,612 tunes, including
variants, representing about 500 different songs and ballads. Of the
artistic and scientific value of his work he had no doubt. He
regarded it as the coping-stone to what he had done in England.

Practically all the songs and ballads can be traced to English or
Lowland-Scottish sources. Some of the tunes have an affinity with
those collected in Aberdeenshire,[2] but on the whole they have a

[1] 'The Green Bed', *English Folk Songs from the Southern Appalachians*, No. 58D (see
Plate XVIa).
[2] See Gavin Greig's *Last Leaves of Traditional Ballads and Ballad Airs* (Aberdeen
1925).

distinctive quality. Whether they have suffered a sea-change, or whether they represent English folk music of an earlier period is open to argument. A large proportion are cast in the pentatonic scale. On the whole, they are more austere than the tunes collected in England, possibly less mellow, but no less beautiful, although their beauty may not be so obvious. Many of the tunes have a primordial intensity of expression, which strikes at the very roots of our being and the best of them can surely be accounted among the most lovely in the world.

From the scientific standpoint the value of the collection lies in the fact that it is an expression of the innate musical culture of a homogeneous community. To Cecil Sharp the mountain community was an outstanding example of 'the supreme cultural value of an inherited tradition'.

Their language, wisdom, manners, and the many graces of life that are theirs are merely racial attributes which have been acquired and accumulated in past centuries and handed down generation by generation, each generation adding its quota to that which it received.

It must be remembered also that in their everyday lives they are immune from that continuous, grinding, mental pressure due to the attempt to make a living, from which nearly all of us in this modern world suffer . . . In this respect, at any rate, they have the advantage over those who habitually spend the greater part of every day in preparing to live, in acquiring the technique of life, rather than its enjoyment.[1]

His experiences in the Appalachian Mountains strengthened his belief that 'the hope for the future of art is that the leisured class may become the whole community and not one small part of it'.

When Cecil Sharp lectured about the mountain people and stressed their charm of manner and their innate musical culture there were usually some sceptics in his audiences. 'Surely,' they said, 'he is looking at these people through rose-coloured spectacles.' Yet he was only describing human beings in their natural state; but in our ordinary lives the real person gets so covered over with the veneer of civilization that when he appears to us naked and unadorned we do not always recognize him.

With the eye of the artist Cecil Sharp saw beneath the surface, and where some might have seen only poverty, dirt and ignorance,

[1] Introduction to *English Folk-Songs from the Southern Appalachian Mountains*.

he saw humanity, beauty and art. To Cecil Sharp it was axiomatic that any natural and sincere human expression must be beautiful, because human nature is beautiful. Or, as a woman in Kentucky put it, on hearing that the ballad of 'The Death of Queen Jane', which she had just been singing, had some historical foundation: 'There now, I always said that song must be true because it is so beautiful.'

In the early autumn of 1950 and again in the summer of 1955 I made return visits to the Southern Appalachian Mountains. On the first visit, which was sponsored by the Washington Library of Congress, I was accompanied by Mrs. Sidney Robertson Cowell and on the second by Miss Evelyn Wells. On both occasions we were equipped with a recording machine. I went over a good deal of the ground that I had covered with Cecil Sharp on those memorable journeys in 1916, 1917 and 1918. I found, as was perhaps to be expected, that life in the mountains had undergone something like a revolution in the intervening years. Roads and electricity have brought 'civilization' to the mountains. The country has been opened up and to some extent industrialized. The log-cabins have nearly all disappeared. People no longer ride mule-back, but they go spinning along the roads in motor-cars; and journeys that used to take several days can now be done in a matter of hours. It is all very much more comfortable, but not entirely a change for the better. Roads have made markets accessible and people are now so busy making money in order to buy electric washing-machines and other labour-saving devices that, ironically, they no longer have leisure; and some of the graces of life have had to be sacrificed.

The region is no longer the folk-song collector's paradise, for the serpent, in the form of the radio, has crept in, bearing its insidious hill-billy and other 'pop' songs.

I went to the mountains in the hope of finding some of our former singers, but alas, the majority had died or could not be traced. I did, however, manage to visit some forty or fifty: either the singers themselves or their children, including Emma (see p. 152), to my great delight. She had married and was living in one of the few remaining log-cabins on top of a mountain. She had retained her love of the songs and we spent many happy hours together while she sang and we chatted of old times.

Emma is one of the few who is carrying on the song tradition. In most cases, our former singers and their children had allowed the songs to recede into the background of their memories, replacing them by those they hear on the radio. They feel they have got to keep up with the times, yet they all agreed that the old songs are better than the new ones and it needed but little encouragement for them to start searching their memories for them.

On many occasions I was able to bring back the remembrance of songs that they or their parents had sung to Cecil Sharp by producing the book [1] in which they were printed; and their joy at finding them there was very moving. Indeed, the history of such songs is a romantic one. They originate in England; are carried to America where they live for a couple of hundred years by oral tradition; they are then written down by Cecil Sharp who brings them back to England; some thirty years later they are carried back in printed form to America, the country of their adoption, where they again take on a new lease of life.

[1] *English Folk-Songs from the Southern Appalachians.*

XIV
Post-War England
1918–23

John Barleycorn sprang up again
And that surprised them all.

Folk Song

AFTER AN ABSENCE of nearly two years Cecil Sharp and I returned in 1918 to 'a new England but a very nice one all the same'.
We joined his family in their new home at 4 Maresfield Gardens,
Hampstead, and there Cecil spent the rest of his days. After
'perhaps the happiest and most peaceful Christmas' within his
memory he plunged straight into work, the immediate business
being the direction of the Stratford-on-Avon Christmas Vacation
School which was attended by seventy students. The majority had
learned their dancing before the war, and the coming together of
these fellow-dancers, after the upheaval of the last four years,
established a sense of continuity which was not without its
poignancy.

Cecil found the change of climate – 'the dull sunless cold winter
after the exhilarating air of America' – very trying. He felt 'more
or less collapsed, as a man would feel who had lived on stimulants
for some years and then had suddenly given them up'. But to
those attending the Vacation School he seemed rather to be
charged with dynamic energy. His teaching experiences in
America had given him a deeper understanding of the art and
technique of the dances and as usual he was longing to impart it to
others. Then there was the exciting Running Set dance to be

172

taught, experiences of the Appalachian Mountains to be told and ballads and songs to be sung. But perhaps the most stirring occasion of all was one in which Cecil Sharp took no active part but listened, together with the rest of the 'School', to four members of the staff describing how they had taught folk dancing to the troops in France.

Folk dancing was introduced into the army in May 1917 by Lena Ashwell's concert-parties and the Y.M.C.A. The moving spirit was Miss D. C. Daking. It was, she said, extraordinarily difficult to know how to begin. No one would learn till he had seen the dance, and there were not numbers enough to show it him. Then the halls were wanted in the evenings for entertainments, and the men had work in the mornings. Miss Daking began in the Convalescent Depot, where the morning was free, with a Northumbrian Sword Dance, 'because a man likes the feel of a tool in his hand'. Everyone crowded round; no one laughed; someone said, 'That's the stuff to give 'em.' No. 5 danced it through with an amputated toe in a new boot; No. 3 sat down looking pale and shiny (a heart-case). From that small beginning the interest spread to isolated groups of men. Then 'The Granary' was found, with puddles in the floor and holes in the ceiling, but at any rate a central meeting-place with dancing-room. Men with whole limbs came in slowly; a paper and comb provided music, then a fiddle, then a piano. The dancing made fame; neighbouring commands heard of it and indented upon the teachers for an evening or a week of evenings. The English Folk Dance Society sent out more teachers. The dance was put on parade with squads of men and the band playing. By Christmas there were twelve teachers with every minute occupied in promoting the most popular sideshow in France. The work was continued in convalescent camps in England and with the army on the Rhine after the war was over. [1]

Not many of the men actually joined the Society after they had been demobilized, but the introduction of folk dancing into the army contributed to its general acceptance as, a normal activity by helping to dispel the idea that it was merely a pastime for cranks. This was evidenced at the Peace Day celebrations in 1919, when a thousand performers, accompanied by the band of the Fourth Royal Fusiliers, joined in the folk dancing which was organized by

[1] Cecil's daughter, Joan, was one of the teachers.

the Society in Hyde Park. This was the first of many open-air gatherings in the London parks and elsewhere.

At the beginning of 1919 the Right Hon. H. A. L. Fisher, President of the Board of Education (1916–22), decided to emphasize the musical side of teaching.1 He asked Cecil Sharp to call on him and discuss the best way of instilling into the minds of children 'a sense of rhythm and love of our old English national songs and dances'. He saw that Cecil was 'marked out by his great knowledge and single-minded enthusiasm for the task, and that the place where his peculiar gifts would tell most, and soonest, was the training colleges'. It may be mentioned that two other Presidents of the board thought highly of Cecil's work. In 1923, when a special performance of folk songs and folk dances was shown to members of the Imperial Education Conference, Lord Halifax (then the Rt. Hon. Edward Wood), speaking for the Government in the House of Commons, mentioned Mr. Cecil Sharp as one 'to whose work in this field British education owes an almost irredeemable debt of gratitude'. And Sir Charles Trevelyan has called him 'one of the greatest educational influences of the time'.

In April 1919, Cecil Sharp was offered the appointment of Occasional Inspector of Training Colleges in Folk Song and Dancing. The first proposal had been that his work should come under the Medical Department as a branch of Physical Training. To this he demurred holding fast to the view that folk dancing must be presented as an art and that to appoint a physical-training expert to inspect the dancing would be as ridiculous as to appoint a throat doctor to inspect the singing. Ultimately he gained his point and he held the appointment from 1919 to 1923.[2] During that time he visited sixty training colleges, practically all of them twice and many three or four times. It was a wonderful opportunity and, as he wrote to Mrs. Storrow (7. 6. 1919): 'It is nice to find oneself no longer wasting energy and beating on the doors from the outside, but now entering in as a welcome visitor.'

In his report to the Board of Education, Cecil Sharp thus described his aims:

---

[1] It is probable that Mr. Fisher's interest was to some extent aroused by Vaughan Williams, who was his brother-in-law.

[2] Cecil Sharp was the only inspector of folk dancing appointed by the Board with the exception of Mrs. Douglas Kennedy who held the position of Occasional Inspector of Folk Dancing in the elementary schools during the year 1920.

To present the dance to the students of the Training Colleges as a Fine Art; to demonstrate its technical principles and to foreshadow its artistic possibilities; and to prevail upon the college authorities to make it one of the regular subjects of study.

The interest of the students was soon secured and the college authorities were not unwilling to make room for the folk dance in a crowded curriculum. Cecil Sharp advised that it be made a voluntary subject and associated wherever possible with the social activities of the college.

Cecil Sharp also had direct contact with the schoolchildren themselves through his adjudication at competitions and, when invited, by visits to the schools. He visited on more than one occasion an elementary school for boys in a poor district of Exeter and he presented them with a set of swords. He received this charming letter of thanks from the pupils:

We wish to thank you for the swords you promised to send us when you visited us in July last, and which we received safely on Wednesday morning. As you told us you were coming to see us in January, we are going to prepare a new Sword Dance to convince you that we can dance just as well as senior dancers. When you come we mean to give you a hearty welcome and show you we have improved our dancing since the last time you saw us. Now we have the swords we shall be able to show people at our exhibitions that we can use them in the proper manner. We shall be proud to dance with the swords presented to the school by the organizer of all the folk-dances. Again we thank you for your gift which we accept with the greatest of pleasure, and wish you success in your work.

When we visited the school some months later Cecil confided to me that he felt a greater satisfaction in having aroused the interest of those boys than in having introduced the dancing to the undergraduates at Oxford and Cambridge.

He had, too, particular affection for the boys and girls of a school for mentally retarded children at Bristol who danced very beautifully and usually came out first in the competitions they entered. After Cecil's death, their headmistress wrote to me that the children were so glad to think they had pleased him the last time he saw them and they were determined to try harder than ever to dance well 'so as to show people what Mr. Sharp liked'.

The Board of Education appointment came just when the English Folk Dance Society needed much time and attention.

To Mrs. Storrow   10. 3. 1919
   The way in which the E.F.D.S. is prancing along is quite miracu-
lous . . . I feel very happy about it all. I knew from the beginning that
things would turn out this way sooner or later but I never dared allow
myself to hope that I should live to see it all.

The sudden and rapid increase in the numbers who wanted to
dance made it imperative to strengthen and extend the organization and in particular to secure more teachers.

   In January 1919, a public meeting at the Wigmore Hall,
organized by Winifred Shuldham Shaw was called by Lady Mary
Trefusis to consider means of obtaining a headquarters for the
Society. Sir Henry Hadow, who was in the Chair, expressed his
belief in the principles of nationalism in music and said it was the
duty of all who cared about the development of music in this
country to propagate our heritage of folk song and folk dance.
Other speakers were Cecil Sharp, Arthur Somervell, Plunket
Greene and Granville Barker.

   The meeting did not produce any concrete results and the
Society continued to operate from a small one-room or two-room
office. And there was the added difficulty of finding suitable halls
for the Society's social functions and the rapidly increasing
number of classes. During 1920 the average weekly attendance in
London rose to nearly seven hundred and by 1924 it was a
thousand.

   The organization of the dancing in London was the least part of
Cecil Sharp's work, for all the time he was keeping in touch, by
correspondence and by constant visits, with the local branches
which were scattered all over the country. At the end of the war
there were twenty-three provincial branches which now had to be
reconstructed; by 1924 there were forty-three. Their organization
was not rigid; each branch was responsible to the parent society
for the artistic standard of the dancing, but otherwise managed
its own affairs. The branches were started in towns and their
areas were extended as occasion demanded. In 1923, partly
in consequence of a grant from the Carnegie United Kingdom Trust, Cecil Sharp devised an organization on a county
basis.

   The Vacation Schools were among the activities that Cecil most
enjoyed, for through them he was able to evoke an immediate
response to the gospel he was preaching and it was gratifying to

him to see the dances and songs taking root and waxing strong under his very eyes. Certainly, they were among the most effective ways of inculcating the art of folk music. They attracted students in ever-increasing numbers; and Easter Schools were added to the existing Summer and Christmas Schools. Stratford-on-Avon was unable to accommodate the enlarged attendance and the Summer School of 1919 was the last that Cecil Sharp held there. The Christmas Schools from 1919 onward were held in London at the Chelsea Polytechnic. Of one of these Cecil writes (27. 12. 1922):

We open tomorrow with 578 students, 21 teachers, and 21 accompan-ists, a motor-bus service between the outlying rooms and the central building, and a rotten Director doubled up with lumbago, coughing and spluttering with bronchitis, and otherwise displaying symptoms of galloping senility.

For three years, from 1920 to 1922, the Summer School was held at Cheltenham with headquarters at the College. Among the 'students' at the School in 1922 was Sir Arthur Somervell, who from being an interested spectator became an enthusiastic dancer. In 1923 a move was made to Aldeburgh (now famous for its music festival) where the Belstead House School was placed at the disposal of the Society by its head, Mrs. Dudley Hervey. This was Cecil Sharp's last Summer School.[1] It lives in the memory as one of the happiest and most productive of all the Schools that Cecil directed. It was attended by several hundred people and there could not have been one among them that did not feel a quicken-ing of spirit as under Cecil Sharp's direction they each played a part in bringing the dances and songs to life. At this School his lectures were particularly inspiring. They may, in a sense, be said to constitute his 'Apologia'.

His main tenets were: that beauty is not the aim of art but the proof of it; that all forms of artistic utterance are natural and inborn and that every human being is a potential artist, or, in other words, that art is what everyone can practise in a small way, but only experts or the especially gifted can do in a great way. Further-more, he believed that technique and artistry – body and soul, matter and spirit – are two aspects of the same thing and that

[1] See 'Our Folk Dances' by A. H. Fox Strangways in *Music and Letters*, October 1933, for an account of the School.

nearly all the troubles in the world come from trying to divorce the one from the other;[1] that technique is valueless in itself but invaluable in the hands of an artist; and that technique is not the enemy of enjoyment but the condition precedent of it, or, more precisely, that self-forgetfulness (when technique has been acquired) is the measure of the higher forms of enjoyment.

The following is a shortened form of a memorable address that Cecil Sharp gave on the peasant (whom nowadays we should normally call the 'folk') and his attitude towards his art:

The peasant is the sole survivor of a homogeneous society with few class distinctions. Looking back on twenty years' contact with him, I should name as his chief characteristics reserve, personal detachment and dignity. He is gentle, unobtrusive, unassertive, both to his fellows and to a cockney like myself. He illustrates what Steven Guazzo (1594) has said, 'that it is no lesse admirable to know how to hold one's peace than to know how to speake. For as wordes well uttered shewe eloquence and learning, so silence well kept showeth prudence and gravitie'. This habit of reserve and reticence has often been misinterpreted as proceeding from a low intelligence, a restricted vocabulary, or churlish manners. This is not so: his mind moves more slowly than ours but just as effectively if you give him time. He is considerate to a fault and has a quiet natural courtesy of his own.

This attitude of restraint is illustrated in the songs and dances he invented and performs. His song has no superfluous words; it repeats stock phrases such as 'gay gold ring', 'pretty fair maid', 'skin as soft as silk', 'milk-white steed'; and the tune has few ornamental notes. In his dance he cuts out the unnecessary and eschews all personal display. He learned both song and dance, as he learned his speech, from his parents. He regards his songs not as something to be brought out on special occasions, but to be performed whenever he feels so inclined. He enjoys his songs and dances for what he gets out of them, not for anything he might put into them; and in this respect he contrasts with the professional who is all for an 'original' reading. Such exhibition of personality may be necessary with poor music; it is to be deprecated with music such as Bach – or with the Bible. It is because the peasant has always regarded art not as an ornamental addition to life, but as a vital, integral part of it, that the songs and dances he has created are such real, sincere, genuine utterances – pure gold without dross.

It was only when I began to understand the characteristics of those

[1] Putting this theory into practice, he disapproved of dissociated technical exercises and held that technical difficulties should be tackled, as and when they arose, during the execution of a particular dance, song, or piece of music.

who sang and danced to me and more particularly their attitude towards art that I perceived the full difficulty of my task and the great
responsibility with which circumstances had saddled me. I realized that
while the recording of the actual words and tunes of the songs and the
figures, steps and movements of the dances were comparatively easy
and straightforward matters – a question of industry, care and accuracy
– the real difficulty would be to transmit to others the style, character
and artistry of the songs and dances. I felt then – and I feel more
strongly now – that the spirit of the age was against me, that the tendency of the twentieth century was in the direction of licence rather
than liberty, of indiscipline, and of impatience with authority in any
form.

Nevertheless, I found myself charged with the responsibility of
transmitting two elaborate forms of artistic expression from one small
class of the nation to the rest of the community; arts which although
surviving among only a small section of the community belonged to and
expressed the ideals and aspirations of the entire nation.

There was ever before me the fear that the dances and songs might
become a cult, appropriated and patronized by a few choice spirits and
protected from the common herd. Whereas it was the common herd
from which they had proceeded and it was the common herd to which
they belonged; and to whom it was my intention to restore their lost
heritage.

After recounting some of the dangers with which the movement had been beset and against which he had at some time or
other had to fight, he concludes:

So far we have won, but the dangers still threaten us – sometimes
even now they crop up insidiously among our own people – and it will
not be safe to relax our efforts until the songs and dances are more
deeply rooted than they are at present.

Cecil probably gave as many lectures during the last few years of
his life as at any other period. The story of collecting in the
Appalachian Mountains was a favourite topic. As Mattie Kay was
abroad, Cecil and I provided the illustrations ourselves as we
had in America. This added greatly to his enjoyment and one
hopes to that of his audience. After an interval of twelve years,
Sir Michael Sadler described the lecture he had heard as 'a romantic
tale and a great adventure – so told that it left a deep mark in my
memory and became a landmark in my mind'. At his first public,
lecture on the subject in London at the Aeolian Hall, May 1919,
the songs were illustrated by Owen Colyer; and in the second part

of the programme, Cecil, having changed into flannels, danced the Running Set with seven other members of the Society.

Cecil Sharp was a convincing speaker. Plunket Greene has said of him that he was one of the most illuminating and enthralling lecturers he had ever heard and one of the very few people who completely hypnotized him when he spoke.

After two and a half years of steady but more or less unobtrusive work, Cecil Sharp thought it desirable for the Society to make a more public appearance; and so, in July 1921, the King's Theatre, Hammersmith (now demolished) was taken for a week's Festival, and performances were given every evening and on two afternoons, with four separate programmes. The Hammersmith Festival was repeated in the summer of 1922 and 1923. Cecil Sharp orchestrated most of the tunes and conducted the theatre orchestra with Elsie Avril leading. Interludes at the Festivals were provided by the Oriana Madrigal Society, the English Singers, Violet Gordon Woodhouse, Clive Carey and others. Douglas Kennedy was the only member of the pre-War men's team to take part, but a new generation of dancers had grown up, mainly undergraduates from Oxford and Cambridge. In fact, Oxford had already had its own Festival in New College Gardens, where young men and women, trained by Miss Marjorie Barnett (Mrs. Arthur Heffer), danced to the accompaniment of an orchestra conducted by the Heather Professor of Music, Sir Hugh Allen.

No attempt was made to stylize the dances. The whole company was on the stage throughout the performance and there was a minimum of stage management. Even to one like myself who had been familiar with the dances and songs for the last twelve years, their beauty and variety came almost as a revelation. Cecil Sharp had been warned by Gordon Craig that the theatre would tarnish the dances and rob them of their freshness and spontaneity. Referring to this warning at a later date, Cecil pronounced it as 'no mean triumph that we have given three Festivals in a London theatre and have come out – both dances and dancers – unscathed.'

The press notices were laudatory.

I found myself [wrote Ernest Newman] growing more and more interested in the dances as an art . . . astonished at the variety, and enchanted with the perfect harmony between the steps and the music . . .

However cosmopolitan a man's culture may make him, there always remains deep down in him a love for the ancestral things of his own race.

The appreciation of this distinguished music critic was all the more welcome in view of his previous attitude to folk music (see p. 67).

At the 1922 Festival, the Society was honoured on the opening night by the presence of Her Majesty Queen Mary. The following year, at the request of the Board of Education, a special performance with an address by Cecil Sharp was given for the delegates of the Imperial Education Conference and Members of Parliament.

Cecil Sharp very seldom showed the traditional performers at a public performance – the exceptions, as far as I remember, being the Morris dancer, William Kimber, the Handsworth Sword Dance team and a group of Country dancers from Warwickshire. The majority of the traditional dancers were getting on in years and, although people who had eyes to see and ears to hear might be able to discern the art that lay beneath the externals, the nature of the performance was such, in Cecil Sharp's opinion, that it could not normally be effectively uprooted from its habitual surroundings.

Cecil Sharp's position as Director of the English Folk Dance Society had been an honorary one until the end of 1919 when he accepted a salary of £400 a year from the Society. This addition to his income, though it did not make him a wealthy man, did at least relieve him from acute financial anxiety, and three years later – at the end of 1922 – he relinquished his Civil List Pension on the grounds that his books were beginning to provide a fairly adequate income. To his friend, Paul Oppé, he confided (24. 11. 1922) that the consideration which had prompted him to take this action was

the fact that W. H. Hudson resigned his pension in similar circumstances and for the same reason . . . The matter has been on my mind, as you know, and I found it perpetually troubling me because my instinct told me I had no longer a right to it.

And in reply he was congratulated on a relinquishment which did him even more honour than the original award.

Though the last few years brought relief from poverty, there were other troubles. In 1920, his wife had to undergo a major

operation and, although she recovered, she remained an invalid
for the rest of her life. And Cecil's own condition was that of a
sick man fighting against time. The dilemma in which he finds
himself is described in a letter to Mrs. John Campbell (20. 5.
1920):

I really hardly know how I have got through this last winter. I have
worked – slaved – like a pack-horse, fighting all the while against indifferent health. How I am going to survive another winter I really
don't know! This country is the most beautiful in the world but its
climate is the most detestable. I have coughed incessantly for nearly six
months and shall continue to do so till the weather gets warmer . . .
And all the time the drafts on my time and energy have been and are
steadily increasing, and I do not see any way in which I can lighten my
work. The men who would by now have shouldered the responsibili-
ties I am bearing were, as you know, killed in the war and as yet no one
has come forward to take their place. I am just longing to retire from
active work and get back to my books and writing, but I do not see
how it is to be done in the circumstances. It is really a very dreary
look-out for me and I am getting very depressed. Perhaps I shall buck
up again when the weather gets warmer. If I could only get away for a
month's holiday I might get better, but I do not see any chance of
being able to do so. The vacation schools occupy my time in the
regular holidays, and they have grown enormously.

It was not only asthma and bronchitis with which Cecil Sharp
had to contend, but recurring spells of fever similar to those he
had had in the mountains. The fever would attack him suddenly
and sharply, producing a short period of high temperature, often
accompanied by delirium, and a subsequent condition of extreme
exhaustion which lasted for several weeks. He consulted doctors
and submitted to a course of inoculation; but the fevers persisted,
and the convalescence after each attack became more and more
laborious.

From the winter of 1921 onwards he tried to regain strength by
making occasional short stays in the country, first at Malvern
and later on at Sidmouth. 'The enforced and unaccustomed leisure'
which he had on these occasions and during periods of convalescence at home was not spent in idleness. He kept up his voluminous
correspondence and took the opportunity of working at the songs
and dances. During these times of comparative inaction he had
some comfort in the thought of what had been achieved during

the last few years. To Mrs. James Storrow he writes (16. 3. 1922);

It is nothing less than amazing to see the way in which the dances and songs have taken root in every part of England. The educational people have all been won over and it is very rare to meet with anyone who does not bless me. And this is not by any means because of the super-excellence of our organization, but because of the vitality and beauty of the songs and dances themselves.

Despite his poor health and an overcharged programme of work, Cecil managed to do a little collecting each summer.

To Miss Priscilla Wyatt-Edgell.   30. 9. 1922.

I am just back – with the faithful Maud, of course – from a strenuous collecting expedition in the Midlands – Bucks, Northants, Oxon., Warwickshire, Berks, etc. – chiefly after survivals of morris, but getting songs incidentally. We instituted definite enquiries in 45 villages. I got a few more dances and several songs. I enjoyed it very much and am feeling very downhearted at having to return and take up routine work again. I am better at collecting than anything else; it suits my health as well as my temperament – for one thing the only people who seem really to understand and enjoy my jokes are the old peasants. I suppose my sense of fun is not very subtle – at least that is what my daughters and others seem to insinuate!

The last tune he collected – a version of 'Three Maids a-milking' – was sung to him on 13 th September 1923, by an old woman of eighty-three in the Headington Union, only a few hundred yards from the spot where he had noted his first folk tune on 27th December 1899.

On 25 th February 1923, Sharp was offered the honorary degree of Master of Music by the Vice-Chancellor of Cambridge. On 8th June this was conferred on him, and the following speech was made by the Public Orator:

Haec credo invenietis si generis humani velitis annales investigare: primum gentes omnes suis artibus vigere, mox dum vitae cupidi dig-nioris alienas sectantur homines suas fastidire, omissas tandem frustra revocare. Vixisse quidem ante Agamemnona fortes, auctorem habemus Horatium, sed omnes una nocte obscuratos esse. Nemo Homero, nemo Vergilio vitio verterit quod civium animos sibi devinxerint; dolebunt omnes carmina simpliciora temporis antiquioris et apud Graecos et apud Italos omnino periisse. Hoc apud Anglos quam paene vidimus accidere! Hic tamen, quem vobis praesento, ubique in villis et in vicis rusticos seniores ita amicitia et concordia permovit ut carmina antiqua recitarent; immo inter montes Appalachicos, inter montanas illos moris aviti et linguae tenacissimos, carmina patriae conquisivit invenit ser vavit. Descripta in ora virum redeunt, et quae incuria rusticorum et oblivione paene deleta erant, jam tandem florent omnium amore. Unus homo nobis, dicemus, cantando restituit rem. Ergo gratis animis hono- ramus Cecilium Sharp.

Duco ad vos Cecilium Jacobum Sharp. [1]

[1] You will find, I think, if you care to examine the earliest records of mankind, three stages. People first made much of their own arts and crafts; then they began to worry about the 'ideal', and to adopt those of their neighbours; lastly, they despised their own, and were sorry for it afterwards. For, if we may trust Horace,

> many a man was brave
> Long before Agamemnon's day,
> But one and all have gone their way
> To silence deeper than the grave.

Without wishing to blame Homer and Virgil for binding their compatriots with a spell, we may regret the total disappearance of the old Greek and Roman folk- songs. A little more, and that would have happened in England too. That it did not, we owe to the man I am presenting to you. He went round the farms and villages, and by his friendliness and sympathy induced the elder generation to sing him their songs. And it was the same in the Appalachian mountains; he sought, found, and preserved the songs of a countryside where they had never forgotten the language and customs of their forefathers. These live again in his description and on our lips, and now everybody loves singing what by the indifference and forget- fulness of the peasants was all but lost. We shall say with the poet:

> One man with a song at pleasure
> Shall go forth and conquer a crown.

And so with grateful hearts we honour Cecil Sharp.
   I present to you Cecil JAMES SHARP.

(*Translation by A. H. Fox Strangways.*)

XV
Last Days
1923-4

Thyme, thyme, it is a precious, precious thing;
  It's a root that the sun shines on;
And Time it will bring everything unto an end
  And so our time goes on.

Folk Song

DURING 1923 Cecil's health became worse; the fevers increased
and he had thirteen severe attacks in that year. In October he
reluctantly decided to take a rest. We went to Montreux together,
where my eldest sister was living, and remained there for two
months. Cecil consulted a doctor who diagnosed his attacks of
fever as malaria and treated him accordingly. The treatment was
effective and he had no further attacks, but his doctor warned him
that if he wanted to prolong his life he would have to live mostly
out of England. 'But is it worth doing?' Cecil wrote to his friend
Paul Oppé. 'A difficult problem to decide – probably it will be
decided for me.'

During his stay in Montreux his general health improved and he
enjoyed the rest and quiet, although he was far from idle. He kept
in touch with the affairs of the English Folk Dance Society by
correspondence. Also he tried to improve his 'public school'
French by taking lessons with a French lady, but this was not
altogether successful. He had never been a good linguist and after
two months' instruction his French conversational powers were

still very limited. However, he could read French (even old French) and we employed our leisure in translating Thoinot Arbeau's *Orchésographie* (1588).

It is curious that hitherto no English translation of so important a book as the *Orchésographie* had been published, and it is even more curious that in the year 1923 two men should, unbeknown to each other, have been engaged in making one. On his return to London Cecil had occasion to visit Cyril W. Beaumont (till then a stranger to him) in his bookshop in the Charing Cross Road, and during the course of conversation it was casually revealed that they had both just completed a translation. Whatever complications might have arisen when it came to publication, [1] the immediate result was the delight of discussing a common interest. Cecil invited Mr. Beaumont to dinner and met his inquiries about the interpretation of certain obscure passages by placing his manuscript in Mr. Beaumont's hands, an act of generosity which Mr. Beaumont accepted with the remark that he felt as though he had his hands in another man's till.

Cecil's translation of Arbeau was evidence of a widening of interest in the dance. He had approached the study of folk music with a previous comprehensive knowledge of the art and history of music in general, but with the dance the process was reversed; it was his interest in the folk-form which led him to study and acquire a knowledge of the general history of dancing. This was undertaken with a folk bias, that is to say, his chief interest was in the correlation of the folkdance with other dance forms.

Early in 1924, Paul Oppé proposed to Cecil that they should together produce a short illustrated history of the dance. Cecil agreed to the proposal. This he did partly that he might unburden himself of the mass of knowledge that he had accumulated (and so prepare the way for a book on the folkdance, which unhappily he did not live to write) and partly from a sense of obligation and a pride in making, as a folk-dance expert, a contribution to the general subject.

The Dance: an Historical Survey of Dancing in Europe was published in 1924 after Cecil Sharp's death and without his final revisions. In fact, throughout the writing of it he was worried for fear that he would not be able to finish it by the appointed time.

[1] Beaumont's translation was published in 1924; Cecil Sharp's manuscript has remained unpublished.

The abundant and beautifully executed illustrations selected by Paul Oppé are taken from contemporary sources which also form the basis of Cecil Sharp's text. Given more time for consultation, a closer integration of text and illustrations might have been effected. The text does not attempt to give a full and connected history of the dance but is rather in the nature of an essay. It is, however, an ingenious marshalling of sparse and sporadic data and every opportunity is taken of tracing development. As Cecil Sharp points out, the task of the dance historian is not an easy one, for, unlike the art of music, dance has not in the past been favoured with a satisfactory system of notation and consequently there is a scarcity of records. He also suggests that the lack of an adequate notation has been a hindrance to the development of the dance.

The subject is treated under three headings: the Folk Dance, the Social Dance and the Spectacular Dance. He considers that the basis of the folk dance is unconscious and racial, while its superstructure is conscious and individual. He shows that the social dance was in its early days closely associated with the folk dance. The spectacular dance he traces through its various uses as an element in composite forms of entertainment known as mummings, disguisings, masquerades, etc., many of which are partly derived from folk customs, until it culminates in what we term the Classical Ballet.

In his Preface, Paul Oppé admits that one of his reasons for urging Cecil Sharp to write this survey was the hope that it might lead him to substitute writing for lecturing, thereby giving permanent and authoritative expression to the ideas which underlay his efforts to revive the English traditional dances. He is aware that the importance to history of the English Country Dance has been stressed at the expense of balance in the book as a whole. In other circumstances he would have suggested a curtailment, believing that Cecil would have returned to this theme more fully and amply in a separate book. 'But,' he writes, 'with no hope now of postponement everyone will be glad that . . . he devoted so much space to the subject which was nearest to his heart.' One may add that it is particularly gratifying to have Cecil Sharp's clear exposition (pp. 24–7) of the origin of the Country Dance and his reasons for refuting the theory that either the name or the dance itself are derived from the French contredanse.[1]

In the concluding paragraphs Cecil Sharp deplores the fact that technical development has been achieved at the expense of expressive quality. He refers to the Russian dancers who, under the direction of Diaghilev, have tried to bring about a reformation, and he quotes Fokine (*The Times*, 6. 7. 1914) who says that the conventions of the older ballet with its artificial form of dancing on the point of the toe, with the feet turned out, has been rejected. How far the Russian dancers have been successful in translating their ideals into practice, Cecil Sharp is doubtful. In fact, he questions whether reform can come from within and believes that the better way is – as the Florentine reformers of music did three centuries ago – to revert to first principles and to endeavour to create a ballet which shall be formed on the folk-dance technique.

For the last ten years, in fact since his experiences in 1914 of arranging dances for the theatre, Cecil Sharp had had in mind the possibilities of the development of English folk dance. In September 1919 he, together with twelve members of his staff, had spent a week at Burford where he had rehearsed daily a ballet he had written to a sonata of Corelli. At the end of the week he reported to Mrs. Storrow:

> The ballet as I have written it won't do, but with the experience gained I shall be able to improve it and perhaps eventually achieve something. . . . Now that we have established a distinct dance technique we must launch out and build upon the folk-dance something that will be distinctively English. I do not suppose I have the necessary creative ability to do this but I think I may be able to show the way to others.

In a lecture given at the Aldeburgh Summer School in 1923 he

---

[1] The facts are thus summarized: (1) 'since 1650 the word Country Dance has been used in England as the generic title of our national dance in its various formations, Rounds, Square-eights, Longways, etc.; (2) before the eighteenth century the word contredanse occurs but once in French literature, when it was used as the French equivalent of the English Country Dance; (3) the word did not come into general use in France until 1706 when Feuillet published his collection of Longways dances under that designation; (4) during the first 30 or 40 years of the eighteenth century the word was used in France exclusively to denote our Country Dance and its Longways formation; and (5) subsequently it came to be applied in France to a Square-dance founded upon the Cotillion or some other French folk-dance, which in the latter years of the century came to be called the Quadrille.'

expounded his views on the subject. [1] One of his contentions was that an English ballet founded on folk dance would dispense with miming; for he was convinced 'that the normal development of the dance should be along its own specific lines, unaided by alliance with any art other than music'. Furthermore he believed that the English folk dance could 'provide all the necessary physical movements necessary to enable the composer, by combination and expansion, to build up his English ballet. He should not find it necessary to rely on miming'. And this, he pointed out, would be more in accordance with the spirit of the Englishman, who is naturally sparing in his use of gesture.

Reviewing what had already been done, Cecil referred to his own tentative effort with *A Midsummer Night's Dream* (1914); to Mrs. Shuldham Shaw's far more successful and ambitious attempt in 1920; to *Old King Cole* by members of the Cambridge Branch of the E.F.D.S.; to music by Vaughan Williams (1923), which marked a great advance; and, finally, to Douglas Kennedy's skilful attempt to create a ballet of 'absolute' dance to Haydn's quartet in G (Op. 64, No. 4), which opened up 'immense possibilities'. In his opinion these experiments showed what can be done when people have acquired a fully developed technique. He adds:

The E.F.D.S., as a Society, cannot itself do anything, because dance development is not within its province. But its individual members can and have already done much, while the Society can indirectly assist – and will do so.

Cecil and I returned from Montreux in time for the Christmas School at Chelsea which he directed as usual. During the first winter weeks of 1924 he managed to keep fairly well by seldom leaving the house. In fact, he felt better than he had for the last few years; and he was full of plans for the future. He wanted above all a time of quiet and leisure in which he hoped, among other things, to write a comprehensive book on the English folk dance and to publish the remainder of his Appalachian collection. 'For twenty years,' he writes, 'I have been accumulating facts first-hand, and have had no time properly to digest them.' And six months before his death:

[1] See 'The Development of Folk Dancing' in *E.F.D.S. News*, November 1924.

I seem to have spent my life in making a largish heap of raw material, and now have but a short time to sift it and display its value.

Whether he would ever have been content to give up his active work, and particularly collecting, is doubtful. For, as he said of himself: 'There is that little devil within me which makes me tax my strength always up to its limits.' He was considering another visit to America in order to strengthen the organization of that branch of the English Folk Dance Society; and he was constantly thinking of Newfoundland. Percy Grainger, who had on many occasions expressed his admiration for Cecil Sharp's work, had for years been trying in vain to persuade Cecil to accept a share of the royalties in his arrangement of the Morris Dance tune, 'Country Gardens'. He made a final attempt in April 1924, and Cecil, feeling it would be churlish to continue to refuse this generous offer had accepted and had written (8. 5. 1924):

There are two things I should like to do before I disappear from the scene: (1) publish the rest of the material I collected in the Appalachians ; (2) make a dive into Newfoundland and prospect for songs and ballads. It is a beastly climate, but I think I might manage the three or four summer months with the help of Miss Karpeles. [1]

None of these plans was fulfilled.

The weeks preceding his final illness were spent in full activity as is shown by the following entries in his diary:

April 20–4. Harrogate – directing the E. F. D. S. Vacation School
    24–6. Exeter Vacation School.
May   2–3. Torquay – judging competitions.
     6. General Meeting of E.F.D.S.
     7. E. F. D. S. Committee meeting and conference of E.F.D.S. Branches.
    9–10. Sheffield – folk-dance examinations.
    14. Cardiff – lecture.
    15. Newport – lecture.

---

[1] Percy Grainger's reply to this letter came too late for Cecil to receive it. When Percy Grainger received the news of Cecil's death, he asked me to accept the money and to use it in whatever way I thought would accord with Cecil's wishes. I used this generous gift to subsidize the publication of *English Folk Songs from the Southern Appalachians*. In 1929 and 1930 I went alone to Newfoundland and noted nearly two hundred tunes (including variants). A selection was published in 1934 by the Oxford University Press.

16–17. Bath – folk-dance competitions.
20. Birmingham – E.F.D.S. meeting.
21. Lincoln – Inaugural Meeting of E.F.D.S. Branch.
23–4. Norwich – folk-dance competitions.
25. Visit to a Watford School.
26–8. Ilkley – folk-dance competitions.

On 25th May he wrote:

I am flying all over the country, and all my literary work is at a standstill. I go away again tomorrow till 3rd June; then, a slight respite, I hope!

Whilst at Ilkley, he was taken ill with what seemed to be a very severe cold. He managed to get through his work and came on to Retford, where he had arranged to stay the night with Mr. Hercy Denman, his intention having been to investigate a hobby-horse ceremony in the neighbourhood. He and I were due to go to Newcastle the next day to adjudicate a three-day competition, but he was unable to leave his bed; and I went to Newcastle alone. On 3rd June I rejoined him and we travelled back to London together. On the journey he felt mortally ill and he arrived home in a state of collapse.

From the beginning there was little hope of recovery, for an X-ray photograph showed that he was suffering from a fatal illness. At first he managed to get up for a few hours every day, but as he got gradually weaker this became impossible, although within quite a short time of his death he was still working at his history of the Dance and dealing with his correspondence. He was strangely incurious about the nature of his illness. He knew that he could not get well and his only fear was a long illness. He did not mind dying, although there were things and people that he was sorry to leave; but he felt his work was unfinished and that worried him. As soon as he realized that the end might be very near, he began to make plans for the future organization of the English Folk Dance Society and expressed the wish that Douglas Kennedy should direct it.

During the last few days he was semi-conscious for most of the time, and lucid intervals became fewer. He was restless and troubled. 'So many questions,' he murmured; and then after a while, 'But there is no need to ask them – they answer themselves', and with that he became calmer. He died peacefully in the early morning Midsummer Eve, 23 rd June 1924.

His body was cremated at Golder's Green on 25 th June and a Memorial Service was held at St. Martin-in-the-Fields on 27th June. By his wish no memorial tablet was set up. He left his manuscript collection of songs, tunes and dance-notes to Clare College, Cambridge, and his library to the English Folk Dance Society.

With the exception of the cancelling of the Festival at the King's Theatre, Hammersmith, and an open-air country dance party in Hyde Park, the work of the English Folk Dance Society continued without interruption. A board of Artistic Control was appointed, consisting of Vaughan Williams, Douglas Kennedy and Maud Karpeles; and the following year, after he had been able to relinquish his post at the Imperial College of Science, Douglas Kennedy was appointed Director.

In 1932 the English Folk Dance Society which Cecil Sharp founded and the Folk-Song Society, of which he was for many years a member of committee, were amalgamated under the title of the English Folk Dance and Song Society. This is not the place to recount its history, but mention must be made of the building that bears Cecil Sharp's name.

A month after Cecil Sharp's death a special meeting of the English Folk Dance Society was called by its President, Lady Mary Trefusis. At this meeting it was resolved that a memorial should be raised to Cecil Sharp to take the form of a central building in London to serve as the headquarters of the Society. A committee under the chairmanship of the Rt. Hon. H. A. L Fisher was formed for the establishment of the memorial: that it achieved its object after six years was due in no small measure to the work of its Honorary Secretary, Mrs. Shuldham Shaw.[1]

[1] A. H. Fox Strangways has paid this tribute to her: 'Honorary secretaries may be defined as people who work all day and every day and receive *ex-officio* thanks on state occasions. For Winifred Shuldham Shaw that occasion never came; indeed, she never even saw the completed work for which she had toiled during six years, as she was too ill to come on 7th June, and on 14th August she died; but all her life she had run away from thanks. She had a quick mind and a merry soul. With her full share of actual suffering, she never complained; she was too busy thinking about others. She put heart and soul into the building of this house out of a deep seated admiration for Cecil Sharp's character and work; she divined in these the high quality that some others have discovered only by reflection on their results.'

(*Cecil Sharp,* 1st edition).

On 24th June 1929, I had the privilege of laying the foundation stone with William Kimber assisting. It bears the inscription:

This building is erected in memory of Cecil Sharp who restored to the English people the songs and dances of their country.

Midsummer Day 1929.

The building which stands in Regent's Park Road was declared open by Mr. Fisher on 7th June 1930 and called 'Cecil Sharp House'. As Granville Barker said, 'In so far as a building can be like a human being, it is like Cecil Sharp himself. It is as his taste was – classical without being severe and pervaded with an extraordinary sense of gaiety.'

In 1940, Cecil Sharp House was hit by a bomb and partly destroyed, but it was rebuilt after the war by the members of the Society which, on its amalgamation with the Folk-Song Society in 1932, had become the English Folk Dance and Song Society. On 5th June 1951, Cecil Sharp House was formally reopened by Her Royal Highness Princess Margaret who since 1948 had been first Patron and then President of the Society. In her speech she referred to the personal link she had with Cecil Sharp through her father, King George VI, who as a boy had learned music from him; and she paid tribute to his work in the following terms:

The origins of our native songs and dances lie far back beyond the reach of history, and their spirit has thrived throughout countless generations of a people whose whole heart was in the land. With the rapid growth of industry, the towns were soon to rob our countryside of its prosperity and even of its people; and their age-old customs, once so fondly cherished in song and dance, began to die out. Happily, and before it was too late, it was given to Cecil Sharp to see in them an element in our national life which should be treasured for ever, and with a genius and vision for which Englishmen must be thankful he sought to restore them to us once more.

XVI
Epilogue

I have strayed into no field in which I have not found a flower that was not worth the finding, I have gone into no public place in which I have not found sovereigns lying about on the ground which people would not notice and be at the trouble of picking up.

The Notebooks of Samuel Butler

IN HIS SUMMARY (p. 208) Fox Strangways has pulled together the threads that make up the pattern of Cecil Sharp's life. Now, over thirty years since that chapter was written and over forty years since Cecil Sharp's death, it seems desirable to attempt some re-appraisal of his work. In order to see it in perspective we must first reconstruct the scene as it was when he entered it and then turn to the present day.

It would be true to say that the practice of folk song in England was at its lowest ebb at the turn of the century, for the intro-duction of primary education, the spread of industrialism, the disruption of village life and the consequent weakening of the community sense had all played their part in breaking the con-tinuity of tradition. The folk singers who had acquired their songs by oral transmission were growing old and, for lack of appreciation by the younger generation, they had in most cases allowed the songs to fade into the background of their memories. The life of the folk-dance tradition was even more tenuous. Nor had folk music been transplanted from its traditional environment to any great extent; for although other collectors, among them Lucy Broadwood, Frank Kidson and the Reverend S. Baring-Gould, had preceded Cecil Sharp in the field and had laid the foundations of our folk-song literature, the knowledge of their work had reached only a small proportion of the population.

Now, primarily owing to the work of Cecil Sharp, our English folk songs are familiar to people in all walks of life. The folk dances, too, have spread far beyond the village communities in which they were formerly practised.

In all countries and at all times collectors have called attention to the dangers that beset the folk-song tradition. 'The folk-music tradition is dying' is an almost universal cry and one that has been heard many times in England. Yet it never has died. In fact, in some ways the traditional practice of folk song in the present day is more vital than it was in Cecil Sharp's life time. For tradition is sensitive to public opinion and the present popular revival of folk music has led to the restoration in the minds of country people of songs that had been lying fallow for many years.

In the past, the creation and practice of folk song were insepar-able, but that is no longer the case. Folk song today is not de-pendent on the old traditional methods for its continued existence. It can be acquired through printed collections, gramophone records and radio programmes; and, paradoxically, the very agencies that have in the past been the enemies of folk song are now ministering to its perpetuation. Even the bearers of the tradition, the folk singers themselves, have been affected by the changed circumstances. They feel that the songs and dances which formerly they alone treasured have been given an added signifi-cance and security. Practically all Cecil Sharp's English singers are now dead, but in the Appalachian Mountains of America there are several who have had the joy of re-learning the words of a for-gotten song from Cecil Sharp's printed collection. A daughter of one of his best singers said: 'I do not keep mother's songs in mind as I used to, but I know I have only to look at them in Mr. Cecil Sharp's book and they will come back to me just exactly right.'

In reviving English folk song and dance Cecil Sharp was not, as some have suggested, endeavouring to re-create an outworn expression of the past. He believed that folk music – the song and the dance – was capable of dissociation from the circumstances in which it was created and that, like other musical creations, it would be upon its intrinsic artistic merits that it would stand or fall. He himself had no misgivings for the future of the songs and dances provided that they were treated with reverence and humility. His controversy with the Esperance Club over the presentation of the Morris Dance, which has filled many pages of this book, may read like ancient history, but the danger of the lowering of standards which he feared has not passed; and one recalls his words spoken at Aldeburgh in 1923 that 'it will not be safe to relax our efforts until the songs and dances are more deeply rooted than they are at present'. Both the dances and the songs are now far more widespread than they were during his lifetime, but how deep-rooted they are posterity alone can tell.

The problem of safeguarding the dances is more difficult than that of the songs. For whereas the essence of the song can be transmitted from the printed page, the description or notation of a dance needs to be supplemented by visual demonstration. A tradition of performance has to be built up and maintained by living practice. The tradition which was built up by Cecil Sharp with such loving care is not, unhappily, widely adhered to at the present time. It has even been said that he made the dances 'too artistic'. Were this true it would be a denial of his whole philosophy and teaching: that man is by nature an artist.

That is not to say that every 'natural man' is necessarily able to give expression to the art that lies within him. There are good and bad performers in traditional circles as there are in other milieus. But Cecil Sharp had a rare gift for discerning the intention that lay behind the physical movements of a dancer and for distinguishing between the essentials and the accidental accretions which might be due to old age, infirmity or other causes. This gift of discernment is not given to everyone; and those who like to get their dances direct from the source are handicapped in that, apart from the Sword dancers, there are not many traditional dancers at the present time who can be taken as models.

Happily there are still a number of men and women who were associated with the dance revival when there was a more general acceptance of standards of performance than there is now; and one hopes that their teaching will gradually permeate the great mass of present-day folk dancing. Failing this, there is danger that the image of the English folk dance in its full glory will become tarnished, or even that it may fade from the scene to await re-discovery by a future generation.

The folk song, unlike the dance, can at any time be lifted from the printed page and brought to life. But its image has been blurred in recent years owing to its confusion in the public mind with popular, or would-be popular, songs. Commercial agencies, in particular, have been quick to exploit the appeal of folk song and have used the term to promote songs of a very different – and often indifferent – genre. Again, though the circumstances are not the same, we are reminded of Cecil Sharp's controversy with the Board of Education and his insistence on terminology. [1]

Many of the so-called folk songs that are being composed today are based on genuine folk songs and some have real merit; but that does not make them folk songs, any more than the Drover's song in Vaughan Williams's opera *Hugh the Drover* is a folk song. [2]

Cecil Sharp held the view that the evolution of folk song through oral transmission was mainly an unconscious process which operated primarily in the pre-literate stage of a community and that the conditions for the making, as opposed to the practice, of folk song no longer obtained in England. [3] The creative process will continue: new songs will be composed, but they will not be folk songs. Meanwhile, we can take comfort from the thought that the classical folk song is unlikely to be cast aside for something of an ephemeral nature; and we can be gratified that folk song has stimulated the creative efforts of young people and has provided them with models of such excellence on which to base their compositions.

The ever-growing popularity of folk song has brought to the fore the question of its interpretation. Cecil Sharp has stressed that there is a distinctive quality in the traditional style of singing which is determined in part by its content – as is true of all types of song – and more particularly by the circumstance that style and

[1] As a reminder we may take the definition of folk music which was adopted by the International Folk Music Council at a meeting of its General Assembly held at São Paulo on 1954: 'Folk music is the product of a musical tradition which has been evolved through the process of oral transmission. The factors that shape the tradition are: (i) continuity which links the present with the past; (ii) variation which springs from the creative impulse of the individual or the group; and (iii) selection by the community which determines the form or forms in which the music survives.'

[2] When asked if it was a folk song, Vaughan Williams replied with a mischievous twinkle in his eye: 'Well, it hasn't yet been collected.'

[3] This is even more true in the present age of communication by mass media.

content have grown up side by side. He did not believe that folk song lay outside the professional concert singer's competence, though he recognized that there were but few who were sufficiently familiar with the genre to do it justice. He believed that such is the vitality of folk song that it can lend itself to the interpretation of singers of widely varying musical background without suffering injury, provided that it is approached with sincerity and artistic sensibility.

We are fortunate in having a certain number of gramophone records of good traditional singers – though not as many as one would wish – and these offer a fine opportunity for study as well as enjoyment. Unfortunately, there are but few recordings of the traditional singers who sang to Cecil Sharp. Yet there are, perhaps, some compensations in having come to know the songs first through the printed page where they are free from individual interpretation and there is consequently no temptation slavishly to imitate the singer's personal idiosyncrasies.

Turning to other developments since Cecil Sharp's death, one must regret that he did not see the rise of international co-operation in the study of folk music, to which an impetus was given by the formation of the International Folk Music Council in 1947, for he would undoubtedly have played an active part in it. Though his work was confined to England and America he was held in high esteem in other countries. To give but one illustration, we would quote Dr. František Pospíšil, the renowned Czechoslovak expert on the Sword Dance, who thus expressed his displeasure at something that has been written about Cecil Sharp:

[He] was not a person cultivating some odd 'hoppsasology', but he was a serious scholar and the very soul of the modern revival of the scientific treatment of folk dance and folk song, whose merits reached to the skies.

This reminds one of Cecil's dictum that 'enthusiasm that is uninformed' is capable of doing much harm. On the other hand, he had but little sympathy with the attitude which regards folk music primarily as a subject for scientific research without reference to its artistic import; and he would deprecate the ever-increasing gulf between the study of folk music and its practice.

Cecil Sharp valued folk music first and foremost for its own sake. He saw it as a thing of beauty, complete in itself, 'an objective expression of the mystical and spiritual imaginings of man's inner nature'. Yet he did not ignore the many purposes it might serve and in particular he believed in its power to influence the art of music in England. He had an unwavering belief in the creative musical genius of the English people. He argued that a country that could produce Byrd and Purcell could not be devoid of musical expression even though it might languish for a while; and in folk music he found the confirmation of his faith. And now, England's musical genius, which had shown only flickering signs of life during the past two hundred years or so, has once again burst into flame. May we not believe that this renaissance of English music is in part due to the discovery of a national musical language which has not only served as an inspiration to our composers but has enabled them to speak in such a way that they can be 'understanded of the people'? 'When the time comes for the history of English music of the twentieth century to be written, Cecil Sharp's name will stand out above all others.' This was the opinion voiced by Gustav Holst in the 1920s. [1]

Reviewing Cecil Sharp's work in retrospect, one cannot but marvel at what he achieved in a comparatively short space of time – a period of twenty-one years between the noting of 'The Seeds of Love' in 1903 and his death in 1924 – particularly when one takes into account the frustrations and hindrances due to ill-health and the need to earn a living. Collecting, writing, teaching and organizing: had he been engaged in only one or two of these activities it would still have been a full life. His work was not finished and that he well knew. It is in its very nature that it can never reach finality; but we may believe that the seed he sowed will continue to bear fruit.

And what of the man himself? Many have remembered him as a delightful companion with interests ranging far beyond his particular subjects; others have been attracted by the gaiety which permeated his being, despite – or perhaps because of – his intense seriousness of purpose; while others were drawn to him because of the fundamental serenity of his nature which, born of conviction and single-mindedness, remained unruffled by surface waves of irritability. But it was above all his love for and his understanding of his fellow-creatures which endeared him both to those who knew him in person and to those who knew him only through his

---

[1] *Gustav Holst* by Imogen Holst (1938).

work. 'We did not know Cecil Sharp, but we feel he was a friend of ours.' This comes from the letter of a small boy, enclosing the pennies that he and his schoolfellows had collected for the Cecil Sharp Memorial fund. One thinks, too, of the Winster Morris dancer who recalled that when Cecil Sharp first came to their village they all hid from him because they did not want him to have their dance. 'But then,' he said, 'we discovered that he was a good man and so we helped him all we could.' 'A good man': that was the expression that so many of his singers and dancers have used when speaking of him. What did they mean by it? I believe they had an instinctive awareness of the great love that he bore to his fellows and of his utter selflessness.

Cecil Sharp understood the human significance of the songs and dances he had gathered and through them he gave us the means of realizing more fully the possibilities of our own natures. And that perhaps is the greatest thing that friendship can do. He saw it all so clearly. Folk Music: the Star in the East that points to the meaning and purpose of artistic endeavour. And in the story of his life we see the complete integration of his faith and his works.

Cecil Sharp's Publications[1]

FOLK-SONG ARRANGEMENTS

With pianoforte accompaniment:

Folk Songs from Somerset. 5 pts. Pts. 1–3 (1904–6) with Charles L. Marson. 133 songs. (Wessex Press, Simpkin, Schott.) — 1904–9

Songs of the West by S. Baring-Gould, H. Fleetwood Sheppard and F. W. Bussell, under the musical editorship of Cecil J. Sharp. 121 songs of which 83 are arr. by Cecil Sharp. — 1905

    The original edition, entitled *Songs and Ballads of the West*, was published in 1889. (Methuen.)

English Folk Songs for Schools with S. Baring-Gould. Arr. by Cecil Sharp. 5 3 songs of which 26 were previously published in *Songs of the West, Garland of Country Song and Folk Songs from Somerset*. (Curwen.) — 1905

English Folk-Songs: (1) 'Lord Rendal; (2) 'O No John'; (3) 'The Keys of Canterbury'; (4) 'My Bonny Bonny Boy'. (Schott.) — 1908

'The Sheep Shearing' arr. for S.A.T.B. — 1908

Novello's School Songs: Bks. 201–2, 212–13, 222, 245, 261–3,2 68,274,[*] 116 songs. Also Bk. 269 (coll. H.E.D. Hammond arr. Cecil Sharp (1922). 9 songs. — 1908–22 (1925)[*]

    The majority of the songs in this series are also included in other publications.

[1] Published by Novello, London, unless otherwise stated.
[*] Published posthumously.

Folk-Songs from Dorset [1] coll. H. E. D. Hammond, arr. by Cecil Sharp. 16 songs.	1908
Children's Singing-Games with Alice Gomme. 5 sets. 36 games.	1909–12
English Folk-Carols. 21 carols. (Novello, Wessex Press).	1911
Folk-Songs from Various Counties[1] 11 songs.	1912
English Folk-Chanteys. 60 chanteys. (Schott, Wessex Press.)	1914
One Hundred English Folk-Songs. (Oliver Ditson, Boston). Most of these songs are also published in *English Folk-Songs*, Selected Edition (1920).	1916
American-English Folk-Songs. 12 songs. (Schirmer, New York.) Also published under the title, *Folk-Songs of English Origin*, 1st series (see next entry).	1918
Folk-Songs of English Origin collected in the Appalachian Mountains. 2 series. 26 songs. See also English *Folk-Songs from the Southern Appalachian Mountains* (1912).	1919, 1921
English Folk-Songs, Selected Edition. 2 vols. 100 songs. Published in one volume (1959) as The Centenary Edition.	1920
Nursery Songs from the Appalachian Mountains. 2 series. 3 5 songs. Illustrated by Esther B. Mackinnon. See also *English Folk Songs from the Southern Appalachian Mountains.*	1921, 1923

Without accompaniment:

Journal of the Folk-Song Society.

Vol 2. No. 6. 69 songs.	1905
Vol. 5. No. 18. 79 songs.	1914
Vol. 5. No. 20. 35 songs.	1916
Vol. 8. No. 31.* 40 songs.	1927*

The number of songs given includes variants.
(The English Folk Dance and Song Society.)

[1] *Folk-Songs from Dorset* (1908) and *Folk-Songs from Various Counties* (1912) constitute Bks. 1 and 4, respectively, of the *Folk-Songs of England* series, ed. by Cecil Sharp. The other volumes are collections by R. Vaughan Williams, G. B. Gardiner, (arr. G. Holst) and W. Percy Merrick (arr. R. Vaughan Williams). The series has been published in one volume under the title *English County Folk Songs* (1961).

English Folk-Songs from the Southern Appalachians with
Olive Dame Campbell. Contains 323 tunes noted by
Cecil Sharp in 1916 and by Olive Dame Campbell
at an earlier date. Practically all are included in the
1932 edition. (Putnam, New York.)

1917

*English Folk, Songs from the Southern Appalachians.**
2 vols. 274 songs and ballads with 968 tunes including 39 tunes contributed by Olive Dame Campbell.
Ed. Maud Karpeles. 2nd impression 1952. In one
volume 1960. (Oxford University Press.)

1932*

FOLK-DANCE COLLECTIONS
MORRIS DANCES
Notations:
The Morris Book. 5 pts. Pts. 1–3 with Herbert C. Mac-
Ilwaine; pt. 5 with George Butterworth.

1907–14

Pt. 1

1st ed. 1907. 11 dances: 8 from Headington
(Oxon.); 3 from Bidford (Warwickshire). 2nd ed.
1912 Revised and rewritten. 14dances: 8from
Headington (included in 1st ed.); 5 from Ilmington
(Warwickshire); Processional from Tideswell
(Derbyshire). The 3 Bidford dances from the 1st
ed. are omitted.

Pt. 2.

1st ed. 1909. 14 additional dances from Headington.
2nd ed. 1919 Revised and rewritten. 16dances: 11
from Headington (2 from the11st ed. have been
omitted and 2 others have been substituted5
from Addcrbury (Oxon.).

Pt. 3.

1st ed. 1910. 21 dances: 10 from Bampton (Oxon.);
1 from Eynsham (Oxon.); 3 from Bledington
(Glos.); 2 from Brackley (Northants); 2 from
Winster (Derbyshire). 3 Headington dances from
Pt. 2 are repeated. The Bledington and Brackley
dances were later revised.

2nd ed. 1924. Revised. 25 dances: 12 from Bampton; 3 from Winster; 7 from Brackley; one each

from Eynsham, Wheatley and Abingdon (all in Oxon.). The Headington and Bledington dances are omitted. The latter appear in revised form in Pt. 5.

Pt. 4 1911. 22 dances: 7 from Sherborne (Glos.); 6 from Longborough (Glos.); 9 from Field Town (Oxon.).

Pt. 5 1913. 21 dances: 3 from Badby (Northants); 5 from Bucknell (Oxon.); 7 from Bledington (Glos.); 3 additional dances from Longborough and Field Town; Processional from Helston (Cornwall); Castleton Garland dance and Greensleeves dance from Derbyshire.

Accompanying tunes arr. for pianoforte:

Morris Dance Times. 10 sets. Sets 9 and 10 with George Butterworth.   1907–24

COUNTRY DANCES

Dance notations:

The Country Dance Book. 6 Pts. Pts. 3 and 4 with   1909–22
George Butterworth, Pt. 5 with Maud Karpeles.

Pt. 1.
  1st ed. 1909. 18 dances from Warwickshire, Derby-shire, Devonshire, Somerset and Surrey.
  2nd ed. 1934[*] rev. and ed. by Maud Karpeles with 2 additional dances.

Pt. 2. 30 dances from Playford's *The Dancing Master*.
  1st ed. 1911. 2nd ed. 1913. 3rd ed. 1927.[*]

Pt. 3. 35 dances from Playford.
  1st ed. 1912. 2nded. 1927.[*]

Pt. 4. 43 dances from Playford.
  1st ed. 1916. 2nd ed. 1918. 3rd ed. 1927.[*]

Pt. 5. 1918. The Running Set from Kentucky.

Pt. 6 5 2 dances from Playford.
  1st ed. 1922. 2nd ed. 1918. 3rd ed. 1927.[*]

Accompanying tunes arr. for pianoforte:

Country Dance Tunes. 11 Sets.   1909–22

An Introduction to the Country Dance containing the description together with the tunes of 12 dances. (All the dances are published in The Country Dance Book.)   1909–22

The English Country Dance. Graded Series.* Ed. Maud Karpeles. 9 vols. 54 dances, with notations and tunes. (All the dances are published in *The Country Dance Book.*)   1926–34*

SWORD DANCES

Dance notations:

The Sword Dances of Northern England. 3 Pts.   1911–13

Pt. 1. Long-Sword: Kirby Malzeard, Grenoside. Short-Sword: Swalwell, Earsdon, Abbots Bromley Horn Dance.

     1st ed. 1911. 2nd ed. 1950. Ed. by Maud Karpeles

Pt. 2. Long Sword: Sleights, Flamborough. Short Sword: Beadnell.

     1st ed. 1913. 2nd ed. 1951.* Ed. by Maud Karpeles.

Pt. 3. Long Sword: Escrick, Handsworth, Ample-forth, Askham Richard, Haxby. Short Sword: Winlaton, North Walbottle.

     1st ed. 1913. 2nd ed. 1951.* Ed. by Maud Karpeles.

Accompanying tunes arr. for pianoforte:

The Sword Dances of Northern England. Song and Dance Airs. 3 Pts.   1911–13

PIANOFORTE ARRANGEMENTS OF FOLK TUNES

Folk-Song Airs. 3 Pts. 28 tunes.   1908–11
Folk-Dance Airs. 15 tunes.   1909

ARRANGEMENTS FOR VIOLIN AND PIANOFORTE

Four Folk-Airs.   1914

BOOK ON FOLK-SONG

English Folk-Song: Some Conclusions. (Wessex Press,   1907
Simpkin, Novello).
Subsequent editions* ed. by Maud Karpeles:
2nd ed. 1936; 3rd ed. 1954 (Methuen): 4th ed. 1965
(Heinemann Mercury Books), xxv +199 pp. The
3rd and 4th editions have an Appreciation by Ralph
Vaughan Williams.

PAMPHLETS ON FOLK SONG AND FOLK DANCE

Folk-Singing in Schools. 20 pp. (English Folk Dance   1912
Society.)
Folk-Dancing in Elementary and Secondary Schools. 16 pp.   1912
(English Folk Dance Society.)

VARIOUS

A Book of British Song for Home and School. (John   1902
Murray.)
The Songs and Incidental Music arranged and composed for   1914
*Granville Baker's production of A Midsummer Night's
Dream.* (Wessex Press, Simpkin, Novello.)
The Dance. An Historical Survey of Dancing in Europe   1924*
with A. P. Oppé.* (Halton and Truscott Smith.)
A Midsummer Night's Dream – Songs, Incidental Music   1930*
*and Dances.** Ed. by Maud Karpeles. Dance nota-
tions have been added. (Oxford University Press.)

ARTICLES IN PERIODICALS, ETC.

'The Folk Song Fallacy. A Reply.' *English Review*, July 1912. See
also articles by Earnest Newman, May and August 1912.
'Some Notes on the Morris Dance.' *E.F.D.S. Journal*, 1914.
'English Folk Dance: the Country Dance.' *Musical Times*, Novem-
ber 1915. See also correspondence. December 1915 and January
1916.
'Folk-Song Collecting in America.' *The Vineyard*, Easter 1919.
'The English Folk Dance Revival.' *Music Student*, August 1919.

'Folk Dancing and the Ballet.' *The Dancing Times*, October 1919.
'Folk Song.' *Harmsworth's Universal Encyclopedia*. Amalgamated Press, 1920–2.
'Dances, Sword, Morris and Country.' *Encyclopaedia and Dictionary of Education*. Pitman, 1921, 1922.
'The Development of Folk Dancing.' *E.F.D.S. News*, November 1923. A précis of two lectures given at the Aldeburgh Summer School, 1923.

ORIGINAL COMPOSITIONS

'Nursery Ditties . . . for 4 voices.' 3 pts. (Metzler, 1891–3 Cramer.)
　'Menuet　.　.　.　pour　piano.'　(Laudy.)　1895
　'La　Fileuse　.　.　.　pour　piano.'　(Laudy.)　1896
Two Songs: 'Cradle Song.' 'The Banks of the Doon.' 1898 (Laudy.)

APPENDIX

SUMMARY BY A. H. FOX STRANGWAYS[1]

Like a New Moon's exquisite Incarnation
  In the Ebb and Flow of a Surging Sea,
Wave-breasted Beauty, the whole Creation
  Wanes, and waxes, and rocks on thee!
For we rise and fall on thy Bosom's Billow
  Whose heaving Swell is our Home Divine,
Our Chalice at Dawn, and our hot Noon's Pillow,
  Our Evening's Shrine.

F. W. BAIN

OF THE LIVERS of all who have devoted themselves to music in this country, Cecil Sharp's life was the least to be prophesied by others or foreseen by himself. What he regarded as the turning point of his life happened on his forty-first Boxing Day, and his true vocation was not clear to him till he was forty-four. His whole work was, therefore, packed into the relatively small space of twenty-one years. One's first thought is to regret that so much time was wasted before he got to his real work; one's second is to reflect that the time was by no means wasted, but was, though he did not know it, a very good preparation for what he was going to do and be.

After four years at the University in which, as we have seen, he took hold of life with both hands, and, without any exceptional powers of mind or body, yet made himself felt by his companions as a man of character, goodwill and open intelligence, he spent ten in seeing the world in a colony, far removed from the accepted standards and set conventions of home. He took things as they came. He was a hand in a mews, a clerk in a bank (wielding the

[1] Reprinted from the 1st. edition.

208

then new typewriter), articled to a lawyer, and secretary to a Governor; and he made such music as he could, unpaid or paid, on pianoforte or organ, establishing a choir, writing an operetta, and directing a music school – more or less, but rather more than less, as an amateur. The last twelve years of this preparation he gave to strictly professional duties. He taught, with fixed hours, in a school and in a conservatory, he conducted a choir, and gave a series of lectures on musical subjects.

He married for love, and love stood the strain of poverty and ill-health. His honest work made him many friends. His determined character brought him some testing opposition. His constant asthma depressed him and made him irritable, but it never finally damped his spirit, which, as Mr. Fisher said, had the qualities of a good folk-song – gaiety and lightheartedness.

Some men become early immersed in their profession and never see life. Some swing through life's ups and downs without the steadying influence of a profession. Cecil was happy in having both the outlook of an amateur and the discipline of a profession. He emerged from them a scholar, who knew when he knew a thing, and a man, who could be all things to all men; and those are precisely the qualities that were needed for his life's work.

Two things in particular were noticed about Cecil as a boy. He was always able to turn his hand to the thing that happened to be wanted. Besides the pianoforte, his lifelong friend, and the violin and organ with which he did not go far, he taught himself the cornet and banjo (when he was ill in bed), made a xylophone, and used whittle and dub for his lectures (until his daughter Joan eclipsed him). He could act a bit, sing in a musically unmusical voice, dance enough to illustrate his point, put you wise on cathedrals, and beat you at chess. He wrote a good letter because he had a great deal of practice in answering them at once and at length; but he was not a writer of prose. He read and knew his books, not merely collected them. His mathematics had made him a logical thinker, and that prevented his art from running away with him.

The fact is, he had an overwhelming curiosity about the world he lived in and was, therefore, good company, conversing easily and well. And his lectures, of which no one has spoken ill, and which many have praised, were this conversation mounted on a platform with a glass of water in front of it. He was genuinely interested in other people because he was not thinking particularly about himself. He liked to know how they lived their lives, how they came to be what they were, and what they hoped to make of it all. He did not want to analyse anyone or to search for motives; he was not introspective, and he hated anything beginning with 'psych'. He tried various plans of life – spiritualism, Fabianism, Christian Science – as settings for the gay world of fact and idea. He was opposed for a long time to Women's Suffrage by prejudice, and was a vegetarian by conviction. In politics he called himself a Conservative Socialist.

Another thing that is spoken of by those who knew Cecil as a boy is his generosity. After all these years there are certain bunches of fruit and boxes of chocolate bought with his pocket-money that are not forgotten. He took the trouble to think what people would like – an ounce of tobacco, a photograph, a Christmas dinner, a visit if sick, an outing if well – and to give it to them. And it was true giving, because he had to go without something himself sooner or later. That was, no doubt, one of the points that drew him to Marson, who took the precept of his Master literally, and when he possessed two coats gave one of them away. But he did not learn it at Hambridge. Later on, also, when his traffic was rather in the less obviously good things of life, in ideas rather than in facts, he could leave an attractive field untilled because someone else had a better right there, or when he had carried his harvest, could empty his voice of any note of triumph.

He always thought, and with good reason, that what he had to give was especially fine. One great gift – or rather, two at different times, folk-song and folk-dance – he set before himself as worth making. He intended, at whatever cost to himself, to give these back to the rightful owners, the English people. There have been, there are – besides the utilitarians who will admit no non-self-regarding act, the Gallios who care neither for these nor any other form of art, and the cosmopolitans who have got rid of the family now look askance at the nation – those who doubt both the value of the possession and the magnitude of the cost. Cecil had no doubt; and it is his mind we are trying to understand. E. V. Lucas calls this gift 'a piece of the most exquisite patriotism'.

Exquisite patriotism: not the half-baked conception of 'England for the English', which underrates the benefits of a true *commercium mentis et rerum;* nor the hasty misconception of 'Homes for Heroes', which tries in a phrase of the moment to balance a century of neglect. It was finer things than those that Cecil saw and loved and remembered at his homecoming after ten years' absence. He did not idealize their homes; he did not exaggerate their virtues nor excuse their defects. He could have taken on his lips these words, if he ever saw them, written thirty years ago:

> Put things at their lowest, it was worth while for me to belong to a country like ours. No other country could have given me such a portrait to paint, so full of contrasts and opposing moods. I could have painted them all – the vulgarity, the snobbery, the hypocrisy, and the greed. But anyone can see all that, and, you know, it is only the difficult that counts in art . . . In our country I saw hidden things very difficult to discover – a flicker of generosity in spite of greed, a gleam of honour in the midst of vulgarity, and somewhere in the very depths of hypocrisy some little grain of faith. These were the things I painted in her portrait, being her lover, and caring only to paint what is so difficult to see, and my reward would have been to see her grow more and more like the picture I had drawn. For the meanest begins to straighten up when you call him the soul of chivalry, a girl will grow in beauty directly you call her beautiful, and certainly it would be the same with one's country.

H. W. NEVINSON

The picture that Cecil drew, 'being her lover', was this corpus of folk-song and dance that he collected and promulgated. He was not the first by any means to collect the songs, nor the first to promulgate the dance; but he was the first to do both for both of them, because he saw that both were emanations from the same spirit, and that until they became vocal and articulate neither could properly be said to exist. He knew them as a man knows the voice and gait and gesture of his friend, and he loved them with a passion that few have ever felt, and none have expressed but Shakespeare:

> I saw, but thou couldst not,
> Flying between the cold moon and the earth
> Cupid all arm'd; a certain aim he took
> At a fair vestal throned by the west;
> And loos'd his love-shaft smartly from his bow,
> As it should pierce a hundred thousand hearts;
> But I might see young Cupid's fiery shaft

Quench'd in the chaste beams of the watery moon;
And the imperial votaress passed on,
In maiden meditation, fancy-free.
Yet mark'd I where the bolt of Cupid fell:
It fell upon a little western flower,
Before milkwhite, now purple with love's wound,
And maidens call it, Love-in-idleness.
Fetch me that flower.

It is easy to see the prose of everyday lives, hard to read the poetry behind them. Though he would have winced at being called a poet, which implies a gift he did not possess, his faith and insight were of that quality.

In the Introduction to the third series of the *Folk-Songs from Somerset* occurs this passage:

> No one man, even if he were a Beethoven, could compose tunes of such good general level, and at times of such surpassing excellence, as those which have been evolved or composed communally by many generations of men in the long period of the racial life. If any one questions this, let him compare the folk melodies of England, not with the harmonic compositions and the orchestral pieces, symphonies, and sonatas of great writers, but with the melodies, the sheer melodies, of any one man he chooses to name.

This is signed by Marson, but presumably endorsed by Sharp, in 1906. It conveys possibly to the average reader some false ideas – that the general level of folk-song is higher than that reached by any individual composer, that some specimens are better than any that even the greatest composers wrote, and that comparison between harmonic and non-harmonic melodies is possible.

What I believe Sharp meant was this: that the qualities which make communal song good are precisely those that make individual song good. In the broadest sense there is their obedience to instinct, which Robert Bridges raised to a high plane when he bade us listen to 'those small folk-songs' of the 'thoughtless' birds, and

> see then how deeply seated is the urgence whereto
> Bach and Mozart obey'd, or those other minstrels
> who pioneer'd for us on the marches of heav'n.

And in a narrower sense there is their conformity with certain basic tendencies, such as the maintenance of an established point, the alertness to modifying circumstance, the avoidance of anti-climax, and the like; all of which are the principal marks of any good music whatsoever.

But the training which produces the result is different. Training proceeds by imitation and criticism. Of imitation, as far as folk-song is concerned, we can say nothing, because not only do we not know the date of the songs, but we do not know where they come from. (From Somerset, for instance, you will say: yes, but where did Somerset get them from? Some of the phrases are found in old Dutch songs, some in the songs on the Bayeux tapestry, and so on.) Of criticism we can say more. The individual composer is his own critic, and if he listens to his critical self, may modify his work accordingly: after that, he fixes it, by writing, from further modification. But with communal song the criticism comes after the maker of the song is buried, and is delivered not in words but in the act of singing, and without appeal, because nothing is in writing. So, when Sharp says that even a Beethoven does no more than this, he means that we have in this simple instance the principles on which all the great men have worked. And he means probably a little more: that though great works are complex, we apprehend them only as elaborations of the simple; and, if they are new to us, we look in them for the simple in order to clarify and bring home to ourselves the complex. How often has one noticed this in talking to 'the folk'! They are surprised at the number of words we seem to think necessary to explain an everyday matter. To them it seems to be all summed up in an aphorism, or a trite quotation from some piece of poetry or the Bible; to us it seems that in so doing they miss half the 'points'. Similarly, a folk tune has in it something aphoristic, and we turn to it as being not wiser, but simpler and deeper, than our more highly organized music.

Some confusion has been introduced by thinking of folk-song as 'archaic', or as a process of 'unlettered' minds. The point is neither the age of the song, which, though implied by the modal texture, we are not in a position to affirm or deny, nor the musical or literary status of the singer, who is no more than the mouth-piece of the race; but its rejection of the elaborate. The whole communal doctrine supposes an eloquence which has discarded the purple patch and ornament of any kind, and is content with no more than everybody may hope to understand. And what drew

Sharp to it, and may draw others, was his rooted belief that 'in the long run the mob is generally right'.

A folk-song, then, is more alive than printed music; as much more alive as an heirloom is (which has passed through many hands, has been put to many uses, and has acquired many associations), than a will, which may be interpreted but not altered. A will gives us pleasure or displeasure; we can judge it: but we are usually too fond of an heirloom to be able to say whether it is beautiful or ugly; we accept it, and leave the judging to others. That was what Sharp felt about these heirloom-songs – that they were alive, and that they were objects of deep affection. He knew, of course, as we all do, that some were more beautiful than others; otherwise he would not, out of a collection of five thousand, have published only five hundred. But he felt, as every collector does, that their beauty lay in their genuineness, though the conviction of this genuineness cannot easily be conveyed to other ears.

The accompaniments he wrote were partly an attempt to convey this; but they had also the practical object of getting the songs quickly and widely known. For this purpose of bringing the tunes to the cognizance of everybody, they have not often been surpassed. The accompaniment never interferes with the tune. The tune is not overlaid with bits of imitation or pianistic devices or compelling harmonies. It is not ornamented or corrected or sophisticated. The 'mode' was strictly followed in the accompaniment, after the first few experiments, not as a piece of purism, but so that nothing should obscure the tune. The technique in the best of them is that of Schubert – the invention of a flowing figure, capable of adapting itself to environment, and consonant with the general style of tune and words. When Sharp failed, which was not often, it came of his being afraid of the education authorities, who might not wish to put forth the unconventional as the norm, or of the harmony professor, who might not like to see his rules broken, or of the limitations of executants, who might defeat his ends by putting the song aside as too difficult. He told me once what a comfort it was to him when Vaughan Williams said to him one day, 'Take any chord you want.' He loved harmonizing these songs, and taught himself much in the process.

It was a revelation to hear him play them himself. He made everyone want to sing them, from Mattie Kay downwards. And the same with the dances: his fingers seemed to pull it all together.

This is generally called rhythm; but so many things are called rhythm that a word or two more seems necessary. The only positive direction he seems to have given is 'Play them as if they were music'; and the worst of that is that, though those who would have played them so in any case will be fortified by the prescription, those who would not will be left in the dark. He played definitely: definitely loud or soft, definitely fast or slow; no 'subintents and saving clauses'; nothing tepid; no wily rubatos, no gushing crescendos. He never thumped. You felt the beat, rather than heard it. He seldom drew attention to single points, least of all when they were his own. He did not, like an executant, beautify ornament, nor, like a composer, exhibit structure. It was all simple, unobtrusive, right.

Absorbed in the songs and ballads, Sharp, when one friend drew his attention to carols and another to the dance, rather put these aside as not being his job. What he valued most in the dances, like many who see them for the first time, was their simple invigorating tunes. He changed his mind when he saw the instantaneous effect the Morris had on Miss Neal's girls. But to get hold of these dances was a much more difficult matter. The dance is and must be concerted, and the few complete 'sides' left in the country were hard to find; and there was no available notation. The dance he pieced together often from fragmentary indications; the notation he invented with a friend's help. He would rush off to any part of England to get a new dance, or merely to verify a detail of an old one. The practical knowledge thus acquired enabled him to interpret with some certainty the brief indications in Playford's *Dancing Master*, a. riddle no one had yet solved.

On the strength of this knowledge he became the only authority on the subject, and when he saw the dance being used as a handmaid to philanthropic, antiquarian, or dramatic, or even sartorial projects, he was driven to protest. This position was difficult to maintain, since he had as yet no visible credentials. He saw that unless the river was to run underground and be lost in the sands an authoritative course must be made for it, and that, in point of fact, he must make that course. So after half a dozen years he created the English Folk Dance Society. He set himself to the task of organizing this society with its members scattered over England, no light matter for one who suffered from two tiresome ailments – asthma and penury. As the Society was getting into its stride, the war came. During that time the Society was in abeyance, there was nothing for it to do, though it took its part, later on, with other agents of recuperation at the rest-camps. For himself, in poor health, at fifty-four, there was also nothing. He decided to work on at his job, but that being impossible in England, he carried the gospel to America, and he spent three summers (1916–18) in the Appalachians collecting, with Maud Karpeles, many songs and the only dance they had. He loved the adventure of it, but felt the expatriation, endured some illness and much discomfort, and suffered the several pangs of the death of his dancers and close friends at the front. His expeditions added a new chapter to the history of folk-song, and the friendships he made there did something to foster the friendly feelings between the two countries.

After the war the Society went ahead again. Its numbers grew year by year, helped greatly by the Vacation Schools held two or three times a year at some likely centre. At these Sharp was a kind of self-effacing tyrant. He got his way without ever seeming to lay down the law: everyone knew he knew, and there was no more to be said. Besides, dancing is so amazingly good for body and soul that querulousness cannot exist with it.

A man of such distinct flavour could not fail to make some enemies. If we look for a moment with their eyes, we find that they saw in him one who claimed more limelight than they liked to concede to him, and who maintained his artistic principles, which were not theirs, with a tiresome obstinacy. The limelight he secured was not for himself but for his subject. He never disparaged the work of others in the same field; he helped them where he could. But obstinate: yes. It was annoying; but obstinacy can usually be forgiven in people who do in the end get their own way. In fact, if they believe in what they profess, it is a little difficult to see what they are to do in an imperfect world but fight for it. The obstinacy which is difficult to forgive is that which makes a fuss without making its point, and no one accused him of that. With this obstinacy went something of irritability, bless him. One has seen him rate a porter when the train had missed its connexion as if the poor man bore through the wilderness of that particular junction the sins of the whole railway company. A man must have some safety valve. Others again thought him arrogant in the way he monopolized the conversation; and even his best friend called him 'confoundedly dogmatic'.

Appendix: Summary by A. H. Fox Strangways

Of these objections the only one that matters is the question of artistic ideal. Were they right in holding that the dance was a social amenity, to be pursued only for the pleasure of doing it, and not to be made into a task or a toil? Or was he right in holding that the standard set by tradition must be upheld and that the pleasure is only to be got by a dancing which combines, in a single sweep, both accuracy and imagination. This question is vital: it is still the question for the Society he left behind. Each must settle it for himself. All that this book has tried to do is to detail the history of the question as impartially as might be.

This was the rough and tumble of life. But a man is to be judged less by his average performance than by the heights he can reach. His love for folk-art, whether it was 'told', or sung, or danced, has been spoken of; it proceeded from a love of the 'folk' and a respect for their attitude towards life. But it was always a real enjoyment of utterances that are in themselves beautiful, and what was rare about it was his power of finding uncommon beauty in common things. To find that is to be in spirit an artist – to know that it is on beauty that 'the whole Creation wanes and waxes and rocks'. With that knowledge in his heart, the troubles he was called upon to endure seemed light.

He approached this task of getting to understand simple human nature, which turned out to be his life work, through music; he was indeed, primarily, a musician. Although the editor of *Grove* was not alert enough to recognize him as one in 1911, his University conferred on him a year before his death the degree of Master of Music. It is possible that the music of this country owes him more than it yet knows. It is not a small thing to have set the elementary schools and the factories singing songs that no one doubts to be true music, that are their own songs, and that they take kindly to; and to have made from twenty to thirty thousand people happy and contented with dances that are their own, and that combine two virtues by which they set much store – an absence of swagger, and the skill of playing not for themselves but for the side. The song is melody; the dance is rhythm; all that there is else in music is, however desirable, an adjunct. If then some future historian writes of our period as a time when music took a step forward, he will have to put in a high place the name of Cecil Sharp, who, more than anyone, prepared the soil in which the seed should grow. This is not in the least to belittle the labours of others, but it is indisputable that he alone, without any lowering of the standard – a thing which the Folk-Song Society feared and the Guild of Morris Dancers desired – made folk-song and folk-dance available to all.

He did all this as looking beyond the present to the future. He was convinced, not, as has sometimes been supposed, that a native music would eventually be made out of folk-song, but that if a large part of England, especially the young, had the songs and sang them, it would not be long before the true composer would come from among them. He believed that all men have something of the artist in them, and that to 'lead that out' is an 'education' worthy the name. He believed that when we say all souls are equal in the sight of God, it is not a mere theory for Sundays but a truth to be lived; and he held therefore that this song and dance whose beauty goes straight to the soul, short-circuiting, as it were, the mind, would be the simplest and best means of bringing about that equality. He was more, then, than a musician. He was an artist in humanity and a patriot. Just as the great doctor used his medical experience to reclaim poor little waifs and start them in life with a new hope, or the great soldier seized upon the imagination of boys and girls with his 'today's good deed' to remind them that unselfishness, too, is a power, so Cecil Sharp, the musician, found and used with the young the words and melodies and rhythms which all can grasp, to help them to simple sincerity. What can we call these three men but artists in English humanity?

Index

Abbots Bromley Horn Dance, 103
Accompaniments, *see* musical
  accompaniments and piano
  playing
Adelaide College of Music, 9, 10
Adelaide Philharmonic Choir, 9
Adelaide Road, Hampstead, move to,
  22
Adelaide, South Australia, 7–11
Albert, Prince (H.M. King George
  VI), 56–7
Allen, Sir Hugh, 180
America: first visit (Dec. 1914–
  April 1915), 124 ff.; second visit
  (June-July 1915), 129 ff.; third
  visit (Feb.–Dec. 1916), 132 ff.;
  fourth visit (Feb. 1917–Dec. 1918),
  136 ff.; impressions of New York
  and of the people and life in
  America, 124, *et passim*; lectures,
  124, 125, 136, *et passim*; *A
  Midsummer Night's Dream*, (New
  York 1915), 124 ff.; teaching, 126,
  132, 134–5, *et passim*; formation
  of U.S.A. branch of the E.F.D.S.,
  127; vacation schools, 129, 133–4,
  136, 137; Shakespeare Tercentenary celebrations, 133; his
  appreciation of American dancers,
  134, 139; Toronto, 135;
  Washington, 137; meeting with
  fellow-scholars, 138–9; (*and see*
  Appalachian Mountains
American-English Folk-Songs, 163

Ampleforth Sword Dance and Play,
  101–2
Ampthill, Lady, 114
Angell, Elizabeth (Mrs. Joseph
  Bloyd) (grandmother), 2
Appalachian Mountains;
  geographical situation and
  settlement of, 140–1; difficulties of
  travel, 143, *et passim*; missionaries,
  145, 153; characteristics and
  culture of the people, 145, *et
  passim*; notation of songs, 154;
  other collectors, 154–5; quality of
  tunes, 155; sophistication of
  Kentucky mountaineers, 157–60;
  summing-up, 168–70; return
  visits by Maud Karpeles, 170–1;
  and see Campbell, Olive Dame
Arbeau, *Orchésographie*, 107;
  translation of, 186
Armscote country dancers, 85, 181
Army, folk dancing in the, 173
Association for the Revival and
  Practice of Folk Music, 74, 79
Australia, *see* Adelaide
Avril, Miss Elsie, 116, 180

Bagnall, Fred, 5, 6
Ballet founded on folk-dance
  technique, 188–9
Bampton Morris, 92, 96
Baring-Gould, Rev. Sabine, 27, 51–2,
  61
Barker, Dr. E. Phillips, 85, 107, 111–12

Index

Barry, E. Phillips, 139
Bartók Béla, 67
Barton, Dr. James Kingston, 7
Baskerville, Prof, C. R., 138
Batchelor, Arthur, 113
Baughan, E. A., 119
Beaumont, Cyril W., 186 and n.
Belden, Prof. H. M., 139
Benfield, Charlie (fiddler), 97–8
Benson, Sir Frank, 81–2, 87, 110
Berea College, Ky., 157–8
Bibliographies of folk song, 27 n.
Bidford Morris, 70
Bigge, Sir Amherst Selby, 87
Birch, Constance, see Sharp, Mrs. Cecil
Bispham, David, 13
Black wood, Arthur, 21–2
Bloyd, Jane, see Sharp, Mrs. James
Bloyd, Joseph (grandfather), 2
Böhme, Franz, *Altdeutsches Liederbuch*, 64
Book of British Song, A, 4 n., 26
Boothby, Guy, 9, 10, 11
Borwick, Leonard, 13
Boult, Arthur, 9
Bradbury, Laurence, 73 n., 74
Broadwood, Rev. John, *Sussex Songs*, 27
Broadwood, Miss Lucy, 26, 27, 48, 49, 61, 62, 63
Brockway, Howard, 55 and n., 56, 154 and n.
Brompton Oratory schoolchildren, 83
Bronson, Bertrand Harris, *The Traditional Tunes of the Child Ballads*, 28 n., 89; appreciation of *English Folk-Song: some Conclusions*, 66
Bruce, J. Collingwood, 27
Burrows, E., 73 n., 74, 75
'Bushes and Briars', 49
Bussell, Dr. F. W., 51
Butterworth, George, 49, 85, 86 n., 100, 116, 121, 135, 138; on C. Sharp's genius for compromise, 83, 84; collection of Morris

Dances and arrangement of tunes, 108; appreciation by Fox-Strangways, 117–18

Callery, Mrs. Dawson, 128, 132
Cambridge: his life at, 5–7; rowing, 5 and n.; received Hon. Degree, 183–4
Campbell, John C., 130, 141 and n.; 142–3, 157
Campbell, Olive Dame (Mrs. John C. Campbell), 130–1, 141–2
Canning Town children's club, see Mansfield House
Carey, Clive, 69 n., 80, 180
Carnegie Corporation of New York, 131, 132
Carnegie Institution of Washington, 137
Carnegie United Kingdom Trust, 176
Carols, 120
Carter, Lucy (folk singer), 34–5
Cathedral Choral Society, Adelaide, 9
Cecil Sharp House, 193
Chambers, Sir Edmund K., 94, 102 n.
Chanteys, 121, 131
Chappell, William, *Popular Music of the Olden Time*, 26, 27–8
Chelsea Physical Training College, 75–6, 79, 83
Child, Francis J., *English and Scottish Popular Ballads*, 28, 154
Church Row, Hampstead, 131
Civil List Pension, 82, 181
Clare College, Cambridge: C. Sharp's life at, 5–7; manuscript collections deposited at, 53, 192
Coffin, Charles Hayden, 7
Collinson, Francis, *The Traditional and National Music of Scotland*, 27 n.
Colyer, Owen, 179
Conant, Mrs. Richard (Lily Roberts), 129
Copyright in folk song, 56

Index